Copyright © 2015 – 2021 by Alex E Kheyson. All Rights Reserved

Published by Alex E Kheyson

No part of this book may be reproduced or used in any manner without express written permission of the author

About the Author

My name is Alex E Kheyson. Personal and Professional Development is my life's passion, and my goal is to share this passion with others through verbal and written authentic communication that comes from my heart and mind. Every day I strive to motivate and inspire other people to become better and stronger leaders, overcome their fear of change and of the unknown, to keep moving forward every single day, week, month, and year in pursuit of their personal and professional goals and lifetime dreams. My work is based on many years of trial-and-error personal experiences in the field of personal and professional development, overcoming many obstacles, dealing with challenges, failures and, of course, celebrating wins and accomplishments along the way. If you ask me what do I know about experiencing and overcoming challenges in life, I will tell you that immigrating to the United States at the age of 14, without speaking or understanding a single word of English language when rest of your family depends on you, while attending school with requirement to learn the language and to graduate in 3 years without knowing where to begin or whom to ask for help, that's what my life was like about 20 years ago.

Table of Contents

Chapter 1 – Facing Fears and Learning from Failures 4

Chapter 2 - Finding Happiness – Tips & techniques to deal with life's challenges 23

Chapter 3 - Get Up and Grind – Hard Work & Persistence as a Way to Achieve Desired Results in Life..54

Chapter 4 - Designing and Living the Life that You Want - Challenging the Status Quo.............65

Chapter 5 - Self-Reflection and Discovery – Stop Worrying and Start Doing 86

Chapter 6 - Life-Long Student Never Stops Learning – How To's of Personal Development and Leadership..115

Chapter 7 – Creating Strong Foundation and Inviting Opportunities into Our Lives 134

Chapter 8 – Starting and Running a Part-Time Online Business While Working Full Time 147

Chapter 9 – Leadership, Empowerment, and People Development 159

Chapter 10 – Team Development and Leadership 177

Chapter 11 - Interview Tips & Resources for Beginners and Experts Alike................................195

Chapter 12 – Useful Tips for Business Professionals..200

Chapter 1 – Facing Fears and Learning from Failures

Overcoming Fear of Failure

What is fear of failure and why we are so often being controlled by it?

We all have fears and that is completely normal, however, how we choose to react in face of fear can determine if the outcome of a particular situation will be positive and successful or negative and result in failure. The choice that you are going to make is always yours. We often miss great opportunities in life simply because we are afraid to fail, but how do you know if you are going to fail or succeed if you never try? You do not know the answer to such question until you give it a try and see the type of outcome it would result in. Sometimes you will fail and sometimes you will succeed, however, if you never take the next step and try you will continue to wonder what would have happened and remain in the same place that you were. I am not referring to any specific situation or business decision here, yet simply referring to a daily situations and decisions that we face in our business and at home. We often allow fear rule how we act, what we say and what decisions we make. Is that how we suppose to act, or is that how we choose to act?

I have had many situations in the past where my decisions or lack thereof, were controlled by my fear of failure. Many opportunities were missed because of my inactivity. The questions I had in my mind were: "what if this does not work?" or "what if I fail?" and because of those questions I was afraid to take a chance on various ideas that I had at that time. Well, guess what, I still do not know if those ideas were successful or not, because my fear of failure prevented me from testing them.

One day, approximately 1 year ago, I was reflecting on my goals that I have set for myself, I realized that I will never reach my goals and my lifetime dreams if I continue to allow fear of failure to dictate my actions. Therefore, I have decided to not only listen to what my mind and what it was telling me, but also listen to my heart – my "gut feel." As a result of my decision, I have opened my first online business without having any experience of running a business online. I have decided to follow my true passion in life, and that is leadership and personal development. I wanted to share my passion for leadership with other people and, in turn, help them to become better leaders, as well as develop personally and professionally. The outcome of my decision was a launch of www.heartandmindofaleader.com. I did not have any technical knowledge about website building and hosting, did not know how I will be sharing my knowledge and experiences with other people online, I did not have the money to launch my business either. However, what I did have was strong desire to follow my passion in life and help others who share the same passion.

Today I know more about running an online business, marketing, podcasting, blogging, and many other online platforms and services than I ever did before. Since I have decided not allowing fear of failure to determine my actions, I am able to share my passion about leadership and personal development with others through www.heartandmindofaleader.com today.

What are takeaways from my story?

Do not allow fear of failure to run your life. Listen to your heart, your "gut feel", and your mind when you are faced with a decision to make. Of course, whenever you are making any important financial or investment decisions, you should consult your financial adviser or consultant. Do not let your goals and lifetime dreams slip away and remember that your actions determine your future. Fear of failure begins and ends in your mind. Now, let us review some mind-re-conditioning questions that you can ask yourself, followed by 10-step Failure Analysis method that I use to help me refocus and reset.

Failure Analysis Method – Mind Re-Conditioning Questions & 10-Step Failure Analysis Method

What to do if you had failed at something that you had attempted to start?

We all at some point in our lives had failed at something that we had attempted to start. This does not have to be a major project or business idea, but even something as small making a paper airplane. I know that I have attempted many projects in the past, big, and small, in which I had failed shortly after starting them. Was that a disappointing experience? Of course, it was, however, that did not stop me from continuing and trying again.

What often happens when someone fails at a particular task or project, they stop trying, because they are afraid to fail again and experience the same dissatisfactory feeling. Additionally, after experiencing failure, some people will tend to blame either the situation, day, time, another person, or anything else they can find to blame for their own failure, versus analyzing their own mistakes and learning from them.

People that tend to point blame on situation, product, service, or someone else, tend to have a fixed mindset. They usually are not looking for ways to learn from their own mistakes or failures and improve, instead they strongly believe that it was not them who made a mistake, but another person or that a specific situation was the cause of failure. As a result, people with fixed mindset tent to give up on trying again after failing the first time. Therefore, they may leave many great opportunities behind and shift their attention and focus on something else instead.

And then, there are people who learn from their mistakes, have open and growth-focused mindset, and seek every possible opportunity in learning how to re-create previously failed attempts with focus on improvement and ultimate success. To learn from and overcome mistakes and failures, one needs to have an open and growth-focused mind. If you give up on something that initially you were passionate about but failed in, you may be leaving something special to you behind, something that you did not have a chance to see or experience, simply because you decided to stop trying.

Whether you are someone who tend to have a fixed mindset or someone with growth-focused mindset, you can always recondition yourself to focus on continuous improvement and growth by simply asking yourself the following questions:

Why is this important to me (whether it is a particular project, task, new book, or your own business)?

What will I gain from stopping now?

What could be the best outcome if I keep trying and succeed? What does success look like?

What can I learn from my original mistake, attempt, or failure, to ensure that it does not happen again?

How will I feel when I finally succeed?

How will I feel knowing that I have stopped, being potentially a step away from succeeding?

What do I need to change or adjust to ensure that I am successful next time?

These are the questions that I ask myself when I face a failure. By doing so I re-condition my mind to focus on finding an opportunity in every failure, learn from my mistakes and try harder, until I finally reach success. Last thing that I want is to look back 5-10 years and regret that I could have done something to reach my goal or dream, but because I had stopped trying, the life-time dream was placed on pause or even worse forgotten.

If your dream is to start your own business and pursue your passion in life, do not stop trying simply because you may be facing some small or even large obstacles or limitations, regardless of what they may be. You may be working an 8-5 job and putting in 40-50+ hours weekly and do not see a way of starting something of your own, something that you love, while continuing working your day job. You may be thinking that I only have 2-4 hours every evening or less that I can spend at home with my family and children before it is time to eat dinner and go to sleep. You may also be facing financial challenges right this moment in your life and not seeing any way possible in finding resources to start your business after paying all your bills and putting food your family's table.

Well, guess what, I have been there and had faced every single obstacle mentioned earlier. If I had stopped trying and gave up, I would never start my own business online to pursue my passion in life, which is helping other people to become better, stronger, and more confident leaders, as well as helping them to develop personally and professionally by sharing my personal leadership experiences and knowledge.

So, please, do not stop trying of reaching your lifetime dream simply because you had failed once or several times before. Just know that you may be one step or one attempt away from success of reaching your life-time dream. Keep going, keep making mistakes, learning from them, and trying again and again until you succeed

10 – Step Failure Analysis:

1. Failure acceptance – understand and accept the failure
2. On paper list all potential reasons which could have contributed to the failed outcome
3. Review each reason separately and begin brainstorming potential solutions or alternative steps to try
4. Ask for feedback from the people whom you know and trust
5. If you are facing a financial roadblock and simply do not have required financial capital to start, look for alternative free ways to get going. It may not be exactly how you envisioned at the beginning stages, but at least it is a start. You can always revisit non-free options once you are in the position to do so
6. If you are facing motivational roadblock, find and watch or listen several great motivational videos on YouTube or podcasts. There are many great motivational and inspirational videos available online. If you need some suggestions, just let me know.
7. Do not procrastinate. Do not put your dream on backburner, act quickly. The longer you wait, the harder it will be to start again.
8. Find a good mentor to encourage and support you along the way. If you think that this was your last roadblock, you are wrong. That is why a mentor, someone who will keep you accountable and support you is a good idea.
9. Stay focused on your goal every day, regardless how difficult it may be at times

10. Ask yourself mind-refocusing questions, mentioned earlier in this e-book, to re-condition and re-focus your mind.

Do not be afraid to make mistakes

There are so many people in this world who have so much potential to be successful, but what is holding them back is fear, fear of making mistakes.

We have been conditioned that failure or making a mistake is bad and looked at as a negative. Many of us grow up hearing that we should always be the best, make only the highest grades in school, be the best in any extracurricular activities we participate in, and so on. Even as adults we are conditioned to be the best employees in the companies we work in and have no room to make any mistakes, because we are expected to be perfect.

Such conditioning is so engrained in us that we view a mistake, regardless of its size, as a failure, and usually hesitant to keep trying because we do not want to be in the same position again, the position of failure. Instead of trying again and learn from our failures, many people choose simpler and easier to attain tasks and goals. So, how do we expect to accomplish something great when all we settle for is simplicity and goals that can be accomplished by almost anyone? The expectation of achieving something great should be aligned to the appropriate level of effort required to achieve greatness. The question we should ask ourselves is when were great victories ever achieved without mistakes and failures? As far as I know, the answer is never. We usually would never know if something is working as designed until we test our ideas in real life.

Origins of safety or mistake-free zone and expectation of greatness

So, what are the origins or sources of our mistake-free conditioning, and where does expectation of perfection come from?

In most cases, it originates with our parents who, of course, want only the best for their children, and therefore, expect for us to be the best wherever we may be and regardless of our age. Our parents expect us to do very well in school, be at the top of our class, receive full ride scholarships, and go to the best and most prestigious universities to receive education necessary to pursue our dream career. I say our dream career, but is this really the case, or are we often pursuing our parents' dreams that they expect for us to pursue? In many situations, our parents had to work extremely hard and overcome many obstacles to give us the life that they want us to have – safe, and rewarding lifestyle, where we encounter only minor risks, and usually our parents are there to resolve them for us.

This is comfortable and safe environment, but how much are we actually growing and developing personally and professionally in such protected environment? We are afraid to make mistakes; therefore, we are not trying to start something new that may have a chance of failure or risk. We do not want to disappoint ourselves and, of course, our parents who only expect the best from us. When we make mistakes or try something new and different, something that we want, and then fail, we beat ourselves up for trying, risking, wishing to change something, and potentially disappoint our parents as a result. We want and expect to be perfect because that is all we know and what is expected of us. Our lack of persistence, bravery, and belief in ourselves, despite the popular belief, limits our opportunities that we would otherwise pursue and eventually succeed, finding what we really want for ourselves.

Other origins or sources of mistake-free conditioning

The other sources or origins where mistakes may be discouraged and only perfection expected are our own peer groups with whom we interact and environment in which we grew up in.

Peer-Group Effect

If people with whom we interact everyday view failure, risk, and mistakes as negative and something to avoid, vs. as an opportunity to learn from, we begin to think and act as people around us, even though somewhere deep inside we may feel differently. However, because we want to fit in, we tend to keep our ideas to ourselves, potentially missing great opportunities to keep moving forward in pursuit of our own goals.

Environment Effect

Environment in which we grew up in plays a big role in what we do as adults. Generally, if risk taking or mistake making were viewed unfavorable in the environment that we were/are in, we would follow the same point of view as we grew older. For example, if all you see growing up is your parents and other people around you work regular 9-5 jobs every day, staying at their jobs for many years, usually in the same or similar position, and then eventually retire, your understanding of what is expected in your situation may be similar, whether that is the case or not. Expectation of securing a steady job, which requires you to put in 80+ hours per week and remain at that job for many years until retirement, whether you enjoy what you do or not. Therefore, if this is not what you want yourself, and you want to pursue our own dreams and do what you absolutely love, you have ability to change where you are, explore new opportunities and new experiences.

Points to takeaway:

Every person has an ability to seek what they want in life, what they want themselves, not necessarily what other people want or expect from them. You need to ask yourself what is important to you at this point in your life and whether you are willing to make necessary changes, make mistakes, face failures and hard work, to achieve what you want. If the answer is "yes," then you have necessary foundation to change your present and begin to follow your dreams. Also, as you are conducting self-analysis determining what may be stopping you from acting today, please review next section of this chapter on Fear of Change.

Fear of change – Inhibitor of Growth and Success

Mislabeling of Change

Change, even the word by itself sounds scary and gives a sense of discomfort. Change typically involves stepping away from the norm and business as usual way of doing things, and step into something new, unexplored territory, change in lifestyle, habits, business practices, way of thinking. When we think about change, fear of the unknown overwhelms us with wave of negative thoughts and concerns. But why do we immediately focus on the negative when we think about change? Is change something that we should fear or is it an opportunity to start new, start fresh, and re-create your life for a better?

Change in Our Lives

Change is a driver of growth and progress in any environment or phase of our life. Therefore, it should not be viewed or regarded as something negative or fearful. Change should be something that we look forward to versus trying to avoid. When we attempt to avoid change, we are telling ourselves and everyone around us that we are comfortable where we are now and do now want anything more, we are happy with the way life goes and prefer to keep everything the way it is. But is that really the truth or are we simply telling ourselves and others that we are afraid of the unknown. Now we know exactly where we are, what we have, how it is going to be in the next 5-15 years, but when change comes to play, we refuse to think about it or accept it as an opportunity to explore something new and different, perhaps something more fulfilling and exciting.

Readiness for change

When we choose to accept change, we tell everyone and the universe that we are ready for more, for something greater and not satisfied to continue sitting in the same place for the rest of our life. When we are open and willing to embrace change, we would notice changes in our life, new opportunities, new challenges, and new ways to invest into personal and professional growth. I am not saying that change is always simple and comes easy. Often, we are faced with challenges and obstacles along the way, especially at the beginning of a new journey. However, during these times of change that is when we learn and acquire new skills and enhance our existing strengths to prepare us for a new journey.

Exploring the world around us

When we change where we live from geographical perspective and move somewhere else, somewhere new, we meet new people, new cultures, new way of life, which helps us to expand our knowledge and introduce new and different perspectives into our character development while continuing growing as a person. Staying in one place all our life will never get us there unless we are able to travel around the world and explore multicultural and vibrant world around us on the regular basis.

Change in the mindset – 'Minimum Wage Mindset or 'Success and Growth Mindset'

The other way of experiencing change is by changing our mindset and go from 'minimum wage mindset' to 'success and growth mindset'. We often talk about how much we want to change where we are today - living paycheck to paycheck, never seeing world around us due to lack of resources or time, because we try to save few dollars to be able to buy basic necessities and for gifts for birthdays and holidays. However, someone with a 'minimum wage mindset' is not taking any steps to change where they are today and start doing something that sets them on a path of progress and change. By 'minimum wage mindset' I am not referring to someone who is broke, but to someone who's mindset is set on unwillingness to act or trying something new and different to change their life for a better, whatever that may be for them – more time with family and kids, more money, bigger house, better or newer car, etc. We all have different goals in life, therefore, what is important to me, may not be as important to someone else. Therefore, we must choose and go after what we want to achieve in life.

Change in Business

Change works the same way in business. The businesses that are unwilling or afraid to change their processes, policies, ways of conducting business, would eventually disappear and be replaced by the ones that welcome change, innovation, and respond quickly to changes in consumer wants, needs, and expectations. Business environment is always changing and evolving, new technology is introduced every day, consumer behaviors change, therefore, it is essential to keep moving and adapt to world and expectations around us, if our goal is to grow and deliver value to our customers for many years to come.

Do not be afraid of change

Change is not something that we should fear, instead, we should be open to and welcome change into our lives. Change is always present around us, all we need to do is recognize it and act on opportunities that it presents with determination and optimism. We are always in control what happens to us, that includes whether we are standing still or moving forward, the choice is yours. Stop being afraid of change and what other people may think, say, or do, you are in control. So, be in control.

Stop being afraid to try. People will judge you anyways

Setting limits to growth and development

Often, we are so afraid to try something new, something we are interested in, because, we are afraid what other people may think or say about us, when we do not even know who they are. We do not want to learn a new skill just because we do not want to be viewed as unknowledgeable or unconfident. We do not want to be placed in an uncomfortable state of being. However, by doing this, by being constantly afraid to try, we are limiting our personal and professional growth and development.

Our desire to fit in

We grow up wanting to fit in, be accepted, liked, and appreciated by every person we meet, whether it is in school, work, or at the local store purchasing groceries. That is what we want and expect, because that is what makes us feel good about ourselves and gives us a sense of value, whether it is real or perceived. But who really cares if it is real if we feel good about ourselves and feel the sense of acceptance? That is what we come to expect. When something goes against our expectations, we feel bad, get upset, and discouraged, we do not want to put ourselves in the similar situation again, and, therefore, we choose to avoid it at all costs. We know that avoiding the uncomfortable, new, unexplored, we set limits on our own personal development and growth, because we miss the opportunities to learn and create new skills that can only be obtained by trying something new, something that we want, but choose to intentionally ignore just to fit in.

We create our own fears

The fears of trying something new, taking a risk, trusting our "gut feel", exploring challenging unknown, are all fears that we choose to create and hold on to in our mind. First it starts with desire to fit in and be liked by others, then it is fitting into the company's culture and relationship building expectations, and then it is lack of desire to change and create new habits, because we have lived with the old habits most of our adult life. Therefore, we choose to create and hold on to our own fears that we had created, instead of trying to overcome them and begin improving our life and feel good not because we fit in, but because we choose to accept our reality, accept ourselves for who we are and be happy as a result.

People will judge you anyways

One thing that many of us do not realize is that regardless how hard we try to fit in, be the role model for our peers, be the best in school or place of business, leading by example, there will always be people who will judge you, even if you are doing everything right and for everyone's benefit. That is just how we are, that is unfortunate but true. When we see someone, who is extremely successful and wealthy, we say that everything that they have was handed over to them by their parents versus them earning everything that they have through hard work, education, and extreme dedication to reach their plans and goals. We immediately assign our won labels just because we may not have achieved the same amount of success, wealth, and/or fame. When we see someone, who is extraordinarily successful athlete, someone who has achieved many victories and have accomplished a lot in their life, we say that they were born to be a 'world class' athlete, not because they have trained for 15-17 hours each day, including weekend, not because they had to adhere to a strict diet versus eating everything they wanted. We think this way because it is easier for us to do so, since somewhere deep inside we realize that we would never reach such success.

We judge other people because we refuse to try to change our life for a better even when we really want to, doing what we genuinely love, or simply, because we are afraid of challenges and hard work. It is much easier to sit on a couch and judge and blame other people or situations for your own failures or lack of trying. If you really want to achieve something great in life, improve your lifestyle, physical and emotional state of mind, then stop judging others, and start investing in your growth and development, and most importantly, stop being afraid to try. Remember to celebrate your successes, but also remember to own your mistakes and failures. We grow personally and professionally by recognizing what we did well and what we can do better. That process of learning, personal development, growth, and ownership should never stop.

If not now, when?

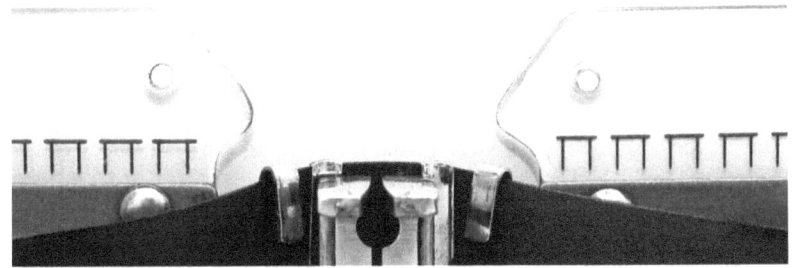

Owning your successes and failures – The challenges and benefits of the choices and decision we make

Throughout our entire life, we will face many choices for us to make and, of course, with each choice comes an outcome or result – good or bad, positive, or negative. Regardless of the outcome it is important for us to remember to own the result and learn from it. If we made a mistake or wrong decision, we do not want to repeat the same mistake again, because, if we do then it becomes a choice that we are making, and no longer a mistake.

Living with the choices we make

It is not easy to make a choice, especially if the choice you are making involves the potential outcome which would affect not only you and your future, but also the future of others. The level of importance of making the right choice increases significantly, because you obviously want to make the right decision and the right choice. So, you are probably thinking and expecting for me to give you the secret recipe for making the right choices, however, I am going to disappoint you here if this was your expectation. I cannot and will not give you a secret recipe simply because there is no such thing. If someone is telling you otherwise, I would think twice before accepting such guidance. Each choice that we make is individual ad unique to us, in our situation, on that day, at that time, with the circumstance which we are facing at that moment in time. No one has been in that exact situation that you had experienced and lived through, therefore, how can anyone tell you how you supposed to react and what choice you supposed to make? The answer to this question is simple – they cannot, no one can. Only you can make a choice and decide what is the right thing to do for whatever you are facing and dealing with. What other people can do is share their own personal experiences in perhaps similar situations, but that is about it, and then you would decide what piece of their example, if any, that you may use to help you to make more educated decision based on your unique situation. So, how do you know if the decision you are making is the right one?

Making the best decision – taking action and accepting the outcome

You would never know if the choice you are making is the best one until you take a leap of faith and move forward with what you feel is the right decision. Once the decision has been made, the next step is to analyze the outcome of that decision and see if it delivered the result(s) which you were expecting. If the outcome is positive and what you were expecting, then you can consider your decision as successful. However, if the result of your decision and choice is not what you were hoping for, or if you had failed as a result, then take some time and create a detailed step-by-step analysis of your decision-making process and steps you have taken to understand where in that process is an opportunity to make some changes, try something different and learn from those opportunities uncovered, address them, and try again. Often, we must try again and again until we achieve the outcome that we want and expect.

What if I am not sure if I want to try again?

If you ever find yourself asking this question, then whatever you are going after, the outcome which you are seeking is not something that you really want, you just kind of want it. Therefore, as soon as you run into an obstacle, challenge, or a decision which let to failure, you have no desire to try again, you have no interest to learn from your opportunities and improve, all you are hoping for is a quick win, and quick win is vastly different from long-term success and inner value-fulfillment. If you really care about something, if it is one of your most important values, then you will not stop trying, despite a series of failure, until you finally find what you are seeking. This is what separates passion, value, or dream, from interests and wishes.

Owing your successes and failures – decisions that either make us or break us

The decision we make in life either bring us closer to where we want and expect to be or they are taking us further back, away from inner personal and financial freedom and happiness. Regardless of the choices we make, we must be ready to own our decisions regardless of the outcome they yield. Same way when we make commitments to ourselves and others, we must own and follow through on those commitments, because that is what is building our character, confidence, trust, and respect. Therefore, when you make a certain decision, you must own the outcome, learn from each experience, and keep on trying until you are happy with a result in your own definition of success. If this is something that you really desire, if this is what helps you get up every morning and keep going, then you will not give up. If you choose to stop trying and give up, then you should ask yourself what is important to you and re-evaluate your values, because, whatever you gave up on what not important to you, not important enough to be considered as one of your value. As Niccolo Machiavelli said in his book "The Prince": "All courses of action are risky, so prudence is not in avoiding danger (it's impossible) but calculating risk and acting decisively. Make mistakes of ambition and not mistakes of sloth. Develop the strength to do bold things, not the strength to suffer."

Remember, when it comes to owning our decisions and actions, we must become problem solvers and solutions creators vs. running away from problems when they arise.

Becoming and being a problem solver & solution creator – Are you going to create solutions or create and run away from problems?

Being a problem solver is a unique skill that very few people have. However, almost every single person has the ability to find or create a problem and bring it up to attention of others without offering a solution. What value does that bring? None! All you have at that point is a problem without a solution. What we all should be thinking about is how to find a solution to a problem that you have uncovered before appropriate action can be taken to fix the problem or overcome the challenge that you may be facing. So, many of us a very quick in bringing and voicing our problem to the world in hopes that someone helps us to find the solution, and often we are ready to wait as long as it takes until somehow someway the problem either disappears or someone helps us to fix it. But why wait? Why not attack the issue head on and look for ways to overcome it? Why not explore opportunities that may be already available to us, all we must do just open our eyes and reach for it. This does not mean that we must solve all problems we encounter on our own, quite the opposite. There are people, subject matter expects, who might have encountered similar problem before, so all we need to do is just reach out to them for feedback and guidance. However, because we choose to ignore opportunities that may be already available to us, we put off taking action for another time, procrastinating, hoping to find a quicker and easier route to help us solve an issue or problem that we are facing.

Be a problem solver in everything that you do, no matter what you do professionally. When you encounter an issue or a problem, immediately begin searching for a way to solve it using tools and resources available to you already and reaching out to subject matter experts around you for input and feedback. Doing so, would help you to focus on issue resolution instead of complaining and excuse-making that nobody wants or need to hear. If you have a reputation as a problem solver, people will be coming to you seeking your help and guidance, which is a good reputation to have, no matter the type of business or industry that you are in. Nobody comes to a person who complains all the time asking for their help in solving a problem. Why? Because person seeing help only expects to hear is more complaining and reasons why a particular problem or situation cannot be solved, and then fall back to a typical tune highlighting how unfair the world is and so on. Do you find it helpful in any way? I certainly do not. It is like surrounding yourself with constantly negative people and expecting to receive a boost of positive energy. So, if you want to become a problem-solver, surround yourself with problem-solvers and work together towards finding most effective ways to overcome challenges and issues that you may be facing today or in the future. Running away from problems or pretending that problem does not exist is not a solution. Are you ready to become a problem-solver or will you continue to hope challenges that you may be facing today would disappear on their own?

With difficult problems or situations comes high pressure and high stress. How can one avoid conflict while remaining in the comfort zone? Keep on reading to find out.

Navigating high pressure and high stress situations – Ways to avoid conflict while remaining in the comfort zone

Avoiding conflict and remaining in the zone

Often, we are faced with difficult challenges, high pressure situations that push our patience and self-control to the max. So, how do we regain a sense of composure and calmness in such situation? Unfortunately, there is not a one good or right answer to this question. Why? Because each of us are different and we respond differently to various situations in life. However, before we choose to react one way or the other and take few minutes or even seconds and ask ourselves why certain questions are being asked, requests that are being made of us, or why we are being put on the spot and go through some possible reasons in our mind before we choose to open our mouth and respond back, this exercise alone could help us avoid many unnecessary conflicting and stressful situations. We tend to be very quick in responding and voicing our concerns and disagreements to other people, but we often forget to ask ourselves the question – "Why we are behaving in the way we do?" In some situations, the response or objection is not even warranted or appropriate and, of course, we would realize that if only if-and-when we tried and took just few seconds and ask ourselves some self-discovery and situation-awareness questions. This practice alone could help save many hours of our own valuable time and keep us from engaging in unpleasant conversations, and in some cases arguments.

Do not let your ego control you

Do not let your ego make your decisions for you. Please do not get me wrong here, I am not saying that you should allow other people to disrespect and walk all over you, however, in many situations our actions tend to be guided by our ego alone. In such situations, there is no time dedicated to think and analyze the situation we are in and whether the solution and best response is to keep your thoughts and objections to ourselves. Also, if we really take some time and think about why we may be placed into specific situations or why certain requests are being made of us, we will realize that our way is not always the best solution for a problem at hand, or that our skillset and experience may not be the best fit for a task at hand. So, why create problems, concerns, and unnecessary stressful situations out of thin air? Why not look for the most optimum and mutually agreed upon outcome or solution to a problem? No reason at all. We are simply allowing for our ego to take over our actions and responses.

Think before jumping to conclusions

Instead of jumping to immediate conclusions, take some time to think about a specific situation you may be in, ask yourself the question – "Why I am behaving/responding in the way I do?" Go through all possible reasons as to why you are the one who is being presented with such question, request, or problem to deal with. Do not forget to ask yourself about your level of experience and/or knowledge in the specific area. Are you a subject matter expert in the specific area or had possibly dealt with same or similar situation in the past? Lastly, think about possible outcomes if you were to respond in the positive and understanding manner, and if you were to respond with voicing your concerns and objections, where would your response take the conversation or specific situation. All this analysis needs to take place in your mind before responding in a written or verbal form. Following this self-analysis and situation awareness process could help many of us avoid unnecessary conflicts, arguments, and high stress/pressure situations, which in turn should create more pleasant and productive interactions with those around us, both at home and at the place of business.

Perhaps you have already mastered the art of an effective and productive conversation, now what? You have all these goals and ideas in your mind but not sure where to start. Goals you hope to achieve appear to be impossible to reach. Are they, or is you simply not sure how you would ever achieve them, creating limiting beliefs before you even start? So, let us discuss some of the way that you may use to achieve exceptional results with a simply changing the focus and how you view each obstacle or a limiting belief.

Going for the stars and landing on the moon – Focusing on what may seem as impossible to achieve exceptional results

Setting easily attainable target benchmarks

Often, we tend to set our bar way too low for ourselves, focusing on what we know that we can achieve with moderate effort and receive expected rewards as a result. However, what happens then is we are setting as easily attainable benchmark, that becomes our norm with all future goals and objectives that we may choose to take on or go after. After a while, our expectations change, we want more, we want better rewards for accomplishing set goals/plans, however, because, we have conditioned ourselves to target a specific easily attainable results, our rewards and results remain unchanged, what we receive is equivalent of the amount of effort that we put in. So, why would we ever expect something more, something better?

Shifting our mindset into performance overdrive

However, there also another way. We can train and condition our mind to go after goals and ideas that may initially seem impossible to achieve and give our all working towards reaching set goals and plans that everyone thinks cannot be reached. But then, even if we end up falling slightly short of reaching the top, we will still end up achieving great results, in most cases exceeding our own expectations. Why? Because we were not aiming at what we know can be easily achieved and setting easily attainable benchmarks, instead, we set our success benchmark high, put it everything we had in reaching it, wasted no time on things that took away from our main goal and objective, and as result achieved great success, even if we did not quiet reached the top of the 'tallest mountain.' Look at it this way, we've conquered multiple smaller 'mountains' during the journey, which we wouldn't be able to conquer otherwise.

Do not settle for a 'good' performance

Do not settle for a good performance, always go for the great. If we establish this habit early in life, we will hold ourselves to the highest performance standard and expect the best in everything that we do, or from the teams and companies that we may lead. Almost anyone, with some training and minimal drive can achieve good results, those that are acceptable by people around them, including the company or business they may be representing. However, good performance does not lead to exceptional results, therefore, if you are looking to exceed your own and your business expectations, then you should set your performance targets higher then 'good range' and go for the great. Even if you end up falling slightly short of reaching and exceeding 'great range' performance goals and targets, you will still meet the standard. But, if you set your performance targets for 'good' and then fall short then you will not only fail to meet required performance standards, you will also find yourself in underperforming in other aspects of your professional career. If you own your own business, then nothing less of exceptional should be accepted from your products, your services, and/or your employees to build and run a successful business long-term.

So, do not sell yourself short, you can achieve that what you set your mind to even if initially your goals and aspirations may seem out of reach. Go after the "impossible," have strong patience, determination, and focus on what you expect to achieve and work towards it until you exceed your own exceptions and achieve exceptional results.

Often, we tend to allow our past to dictate our future, and as result we procrastinate in taking action to change our present. Instead, why not try something new and different and stop creating excuses for our lack of inaction? These and other questions are coming up next.

Why allow your past to dictate your future – Creating excuses or trying something new and different

Self-creation of our own roadblocks on our path to success and happiness

How often do we allow our past to dictate our future and where we are today? Very often if you ask me. Most decisions that we make have some sort of connection to our past, both good and not so good. We make decisions based on your prior experience or the experience of someone else. Instead of leaving our past behind and focus what we have and do today, to keep moving forward, we continue to remain closely attached to our past. It is not a bad thing to use positive experience which we have experienced previously and incorporate our learnings in our life at the present time. However, we rarely look back to something positive that had happened to us, instead we rely on all the negative experiences, which often become roadblocks on our own path to success and happiness that we strive to achieve.

Why do we get so attached to the negative experiences from our past?

Mostly, it is because it is easier for us to come up with an excuse as to why we should not try something new, take a risk, versus doing it. Attachment to negative past does not require any action on our part, except for coming up with a clever excuse which we can use and point to the past, trying to prove why you should not try again, or try something different. Why waste time if something similar was already tried before, which resulted in a failure? Whether it was tried by you or not it does not matter, if you can point your finger to something, trying to justify your lack of action. These experiences could be really anything from starting your own business online while working full time, starting a new career, starting a new diet or healthier eating plan and lose weight, stick to a regular exercise plan long-term, become financially free or debt free, etc. These are just some of the most common goals that many of us start but then quickly give up on them and create all reasons as to why we should not have to start anything to begin with based on prior experiences and/or failures.

Leaving negative experiences of the past behind and starting over with determination and plan to succeed no matter what

Do you want to continue to be viewed as someone who tried, failed, learned from it, and eventually succeeded, or someone who gave up after the first major roadblock? I would think it would be the former. Most of us want to be viewed as winners, someone who does not give up on their goals and keeps their word. That is why to move past the initial roadblocks and failures, we must leave our negative experiences in the past, use what we have learned from those experiences, and keep trying, despite all difficulties and opinions of those who think that what you have started is not possible, and keep going with extreme persistence and determination until you reach your goal(s).

Only you know what you can and cannot do, so do not let someone else to second guess your abilities. Instead, find your path to success and prove everyone who was doubting you what you are capable of. We are as strong as our own confidence in ourselves and our abilities. So, do not get into a habit of giving up, instead get into a habit of finding solutions to the most challenging obstacles you may face over time. Your persistence and unshakable belief in yourself will help you find success, whatever that may be for you and happiness.

Have you ever asked yourself – What is the cost of inaction? I did, and what I see happening time-and-time again is a sense of disappointment and regret for not taking an action. So, why not take an action on your goals now, instead of waiting for the "right time?"

Cost of Inaction – A path of disappointment and regret

Inaction is usually the biggest reason for lack of change in our lives for a better. If we choose not to act and take necessary steps to keep going after what we want to achieve or have, then the result is typically – a disappointment, regret, and no change in where we are, in comparison to where we said we want to be

State of inaction that we live in – Why create New Year's Resolutions backed by excuses and false promises to ourselves and others?

So many people fall into this state of inaction every day, most frequently at the beginning of every year. Why? Because this is when many of us make New Year's resolutions and make plans to achieve the goals we have set. Whether your goal was to lose weight, build more muscular mass, run every day, go to school to keep pursuing your degree, learn a new profession, or any other goal, the main component in goal achievement is taking necessary steps to get you there, it requires you taking action. What happens instead is, we make all these awesome action-packed goals and never actually take any steps to do what we said we were going to do. Instead, we create excuses by finding reasons as to why we are not following through on our goals and commitments. Then why making New Year's resolutions in the first place, or why setting goals in general? There is no reason unless our goals and commitments are backed by action vs. just false promises to ourselves and others.

Start today, start now, not soon or next week – Doing what you can today with resources and time that you have left at the end of the day/week

In one of the prior blog articles, I have discussed the importance of doing what you can today, with resources and time that you have today, vs. waiting for the right time to come and find you. It is applicable here as well, because guess what, opportunity only comes to those you are ready and open to receive it. But more importantly, it comes to those who are taking necessary actions and steps to go after their goals and dreams. If you are not sure if you are ready to take required actions to go after your goal(s), then it usually means that you either do not really need it or want it bad enough. If you really want something in life, regardless how big or small this something is, you will find a way to go after it, and if you do not want it bad enough or need it, you will find every possible reason in the book why you cannot or should not pursue that one thing today.

Do I really want it? Important questions to ask yourself when setting a new goal

So, next time when you are setting a new goal, creating a New Year's resolution, or are looking for a change, ask yourself the question – "Do I really want and need it today, and am I ready to make necessary steps to start working towards this one thing or goal today?" Also, ask yourself: "How bad do I want it or need it?" If the answer is 'yes' and 'I need/want it now', then there should be no excuse not to try and start working towards that one thing, that one goal immediately, regardless how big or small those steps may be. What is important is to start now with what you can, and then learn and add to your action plan along the way. However, if the answer is 'no', or 'I do not really need/want it now', well, then take time to understand what you really want in life before making it as one of your goals and creating action plan around it.

In conclusion…

If you genuinely want something bad enough, you will find a way to reach it. It may take some time it may take a long time, but you will reach it. However, if you do not want to reach or achieve whatever that may be, you will find a list of excuses for not trying, or you will find something or someone to blame for your own lack of effort. So, what is it going to be? Are you going to take actionable steps today towards achieving your goals and dreams that you want to accomplish, creating the lifestyle and achieving the level of happiness you seek for yourself and those around you? The only person who can answer these questions is you!

Chapter 2 - Finding Happiness – Tips & techniques to deal with life's challenges

Unconditional Giving – Making a difference in lives of those in need

Unconditional giving is giving something of value to other individuals or a group of people without expecting anything in return or expecting a payback later.

I personally believe that many of us often forget about the possibility of giving something unconditionally just to help another parson that we want to help and care about. We often wait for something in return, because, in our mind that is how things are supposed to be. However, it is far from reality. If you are giving something and expecting a payback, it is not unconditional giving, that is called a loan or intentional giving. So, be sure that you fully understand the difference between the two before acting, as you always want to make sure that perception that you are fiving of yourself to others is the one you intend to give, the one that represents the real and honest you. Be honest with yourself always. If you truly, genuinely want to help someone in need, then please do so, as even the smallest gift of generosity could often help another individual to change his or her life for a better, even if it is only for a short period of time.

Many of us go through some tough times in our lives, and many face difficult times today. But, by being aware of people around us and their unique wants and needs vs only focusing on what is going on in our own personal world, can help us to be that source of hope and positive energy that other people are seeking every day. When someone reaches out to you offering help and/or support when you are going through some challenging times in life is an immensely powerful feeling, it is uplifting, motivating, and encouraging. It gives us that needed step to try harder, push ourselves to improve, develop, and grow personally and professionally. So, why not help? Why not offer your genuine unconditional help today to those in need, give someone else a reason to smile and create a happy future? You are awesome! Know it and believe it because you are!

Just like we should always look for good in people and share our positive energy with them, we should also remember that we are the ones who decide each day as to what kind of day is it going to be. Is it dark and gloomy or sunny and beautiful?

Dark and Gloomy OR Sunny and Beautiful

First impression is not always the right one – limited and obstructed view

How often do we judge someone or something by the initial appearance or very first experience? I would say most of the time. Rarely do we stop and ask ourselves if what we see is the only reality that exists. We often judge someone as a person by our very first interaction with them, by very first conversation, however, what we see on the outside may not be what is really going on inside that person. Perhaps what we see is what we were invited and allowed to see. Yet, we have already made up our mind about someone and the kind of person they are, which may be incorrectly.

Do not be so quick in judging a situation by the initial experience – what you see may simply be a cover protecting a beauty and awesomeness hiding inside

I want to share one analogy with you, which prompted me to write about true and perceived realities of our experiences. As my plane was taken off runway, what I saw through the window of the plane was dark and gloomy day, with clouds completely covering the sky. Typically, you see this type of weather outside when it is about to rain or if strong storm is developing. So, it made me think about all the things that I was working to overcome, all the challenges and obstacles that I was facing at that time, and what I needed to do to overcome them. However, as plane pierced a thick layer of dark clouds, all the sudden a beautiful picture appeared – lots of sunlight, beautiful white clouds, and endless blue sky. This image completely changed my thoughts and what was going through my mind just a minute ago. What I saw was peace, comfort, and re-assurance in the present and future. It helped me to appreciate once again everything and everyone that is in my life now and was part of my life before. So, this example brings me to my original point – do not be so quick in judging someone by the very first experience and/or impression when meeting someone new, by their outer appearance, their lack of smile, by how they communicate, or remain silent. You never know if there is another side of a person that you do not know yet, simply because they have not invited you in. There may be completely different person hiding behind the outer protective shell, visible to everyone, only selected few will be invited in to meet the inner personality.

Two side of the coin – All you need is to flip the coin on another side to see a change

The same goes for any situation that we may be facing in life. Regardless how complex, how impossible, or challenging something may look initially to us, it does not mean that there is no other more positive, encouraging, and full of hope side to any story or situation that we simply may not see just yet. Perhaps, we have not look hard enough, maybe we were so focused on the obstacles or negative, that we failed to see the positive side. Often, we just need to pause and look around, see past the negativity, and conflict and have confidence and belief that there are always two sides to any coin, and maybe all we need to do is to flip the coin on the other side.

Turbulence is temporary

Do not let temporary turbulence distract you from your goals in life. Turbulence will pass just like tough times in life, and beautiful and full of accomplishments, successes, and smiles path would appear. Be patient and keep on moving forward. Remember that happiness is a choice.

Happiness is a Choice – We all have an ability to choose our level of happiness every single day

I am going to start by saying that life is a ridiculously awesome and unpredictable thing. It is not going to be only filled with happy and exciting moments, there will be plenty of times when we will be tested by life, where things do not go as planned or turn out as we had expected. There will be times when we would face sad moments throughout our life that we would be expected to deal with and overcome. Why am I telling you all this when the topic of this article is happiness? Because I fell that it is important to understand that life is filled with both positive and negative moments, but what we choose to make out of each situation is up to us. Even in sad situations we can find some happiness, especially when we are going through some tough times. I know you are probably thinking, what is he talking about? How could one find happiness when we are faced with difficulty and challenges in life? How can one be happy when he or she is struggling on a personal or professional front? I know that it may appear or sound crazy, but it is possible to find happiness when life gives us lemons.

Each day we make a choice to be happy with where we are, with whom we are, and with what we have, or to be unhappy and displeased telling ourselves how bad or challenging our life is. This is the choice that we all make every day

Have you ever moved or know someone who moved across states or internationally, not because you or someone you know always wanted to travel and live in a particular state in U.S. or country, but because that is something that needed to be done due to various different reasons? So, when such move takes place, going where everything and everyone is new and unfamiliar, where you do not know what to expect or even what to do next, your mind could go wandering in many different directions. Some may begin to panic, some would be afraid of the unknown and unfamiliar, some would hate the change, and there are some who would be genuinely happy despite the chaos around them. But how? How can someone be possibly happy when they find themselves in situations or places where they have never been or experienced? How can someone be happy when they are faced with unexpected and often difficult moments in life? Remember when I said that happiness is a choice that we all make every day? That is exactly how it is possible to find happiness wherever you may be and at any point in time. You can choose to be happy and appreciate everything and everyone you are surrounded by in your life, or you can choose to be in what already may be a difficult situation.

Happiness begins in your mind

So, when faced with unexpected or challenging situation, you must begin by asking yourself how you feel about the situation that you are in, and if this situation be solved now or in the future, or can you adjust by changing your mindset and how you feel about each situation or problem you are facing. For example, moving into a smaller house or an apartment, having less bedrooms or bathrooms, living in the less desirable part of town, etc. The real question is – can you make the best out of the situation that you are in and be happy? Absolutely, if you make a choice to be happy. Some people would choose to complain and hate the situation they are in because their house is located too far from their favorite restaurant, grocery, or department store, even though they have a nice warm and beautiful home, they have food to eat and clothes to wear. And then, there are families that must move back and live with their parents because they are unable to afford the house or apartment on their own at the present moment, whether it is because of job loss or another unexpected life event that took place in their lives. Therefore, they must live in small quarters sharing space with other family members, and they had to downgrade to one vehicle or no vehicle because they could no longer afford their car payments. However, instead of telling themselves and everyone around them how difficult their life is, they choose to be happy and appreciate what they do have while working through life's challenges together one at a time.

Positive mindset leads to positive results, even if those results are not immediate.

In addition to positive mindset, planning and goal setting are also particularly important actions that an individual can take to create direction and pave the path to eventual goal achievement. However, goal-planning and setting is different from attempting to pre-plan your life. If you think you can pre-plan your life, you are fooling yourself and others.

Going through life one day at a time – If you think you can pre-plan life, you are fooling yourself

Going through live one day at a time vs creating and managing personal life's goals

What I have learned over many years is that life cannot be pre-planned, and instead, should be lived and enjoyed one day at a time. As much as we want to have complete control of what happens with us and to us every day and in years to come, it is something that we should let universe to do for us, because life is so fluid and unpredictable that we simply do not know where our life would take us at any given point. Now, this is different from having a plan for our personal and professional development, both short and long-term. We can and absolutely should have our goals and vision of our dream future clearly defined and written down. We should also regularly review, update, and add to our existing and future goals. Goal creation and management is our expected life's path in its ideal state. However, as you may have seen or experienced for yourself things often do not go according to our plan and often require detours and search for ways and new paths to get back on track.

Why it is important to understand the unpredictable nature of life?

When we know and understand that life can and often will change its course as we navigate through it, we are more prepared for various surprises, challenges, failures, disappointments, and successes that may be thrown our way. Sometimes, the challenges that we face in life could be extremely difficult to overcome and find a way to stay motivated and optimistic. However, we must always remember that there is always a way, regardless how difficult to overcome something may appear. Please do not get me wrong, I am not saying that it will not be difficult at times, especially when we are looking at ourselves in a mirror and asking how in a world would we overcome a situation or problem and not seeing an immediate solution. However, even though things may look unpromising or unsolvable, just know that it is only a perception based on where you are at that point in time. Since we truly do not know what may happen in our life tomorrow or day after, we must be patient, confident in ourselves and those around us, and remain optimistic that everything will be ok soon. As long as we are hopeful and optimistic of positive outcome, we will eventually get there. Look at the alternative – being negative and stressed out when life is taking us through challenging periods, what does it get us? Does being in negative and depressed state of mind help us in any way? No, it does not. It simply directs our mind to focus on how bad everything is, instead of forcing us to look for solutions and ways to overcome specific problems and challenges that we encounter throughout life.

There is always a way up, always!

Regardless how challenging things may seem, never stop the work of creating and following through on your set goals and going after your dreams creating the lifestyle you are seeking, while remember that life can and will throw challenges along the way where you would be required to change and alter your course. But remember that any challenges on your path are life's test of your strengths, determination, character, and commitment to your goals and future you are in the process of building. So, do not give up, do not get discouraged, do not lose hope. Difficulties you may be facing at this time are temporary, and there is always a way up after a period of difficulties, tests, and misfortunes, always. The more you focus on the negative, the more of negative you will attract to yourself, and the other way around. Be the one who creates a positive energy in a negative situation, and you will begin noticing positive changes in whatever the situation you may be in. Even though you cannot control life, you can control how you react to life's surprises. Learn to enjoy and appreciate every single moment as you go through life's events and experiences.

Life – Enjoy and appreciate every single moment

Breaking away from all the craziness and appreciating the life we have today

Do you ever stop and think how wonderful life is? Break away from all of craziness, business, problems, wins, successes, chase for the fame or title and simply appreciate the life we have today, despite how hectic or difficult things may be on the surface. Unfortunately, what many of us are struggling with is exactly that, we don't know how to take the time really stop and appreciate everything and everyone we have in our life today, and yes, some of us may not be in the best possible situation when it comes to our business, our job/career, or money, but at the end of the day you can see beautiful blue sky above your head and share your experiences, good or bad, with those around you.

Turning away or choosing to pursue our own dreams and aspirations

Many of us go through life without noticing anything or anyone around us, including those close to us. We tend to take life for granted, and 'poison' it with outside influences, such as: negative thoughts of others about us, expectations that we are expected to adhere to and follow every day whether we support those expectations or not, striving to do everything we can in order to fit in, in order to look and feel like everyone around us. We often choose to go against our own cultural and personal beliefs, just because someone said that we should to be accepted and understood. But what we do not think about is that by doing so, we turn away from who we really are, who we were born to be, and become another member of a larger group, losing our unique identity, and then go through life chasing after dreams and expectations of someone other than our own.

Pause and appreciate who we really are

One question that you should ask yourself is if this is something that I want for myself and my family, or do I want to be me, the person who I was born to be. I think that most of us, after asking this question, would choose the later. Why? Because we want to be ourselves, we want to be able to express how we feel and what we think, and we want to be in control of our own life. If this is the case, then why do we fall into this trap of going through life fulfilling everyone else's expectations and dreams but our own? I really think it is because we simply forgot what it is like to pause and genuinely appreciate who we really are and appreciate every single day and every minute we live on this wonderful planet Earth.

Stop waiting and begin doing

Many people wait all their life until they reach the end of their until they reach the end of their journey and only when they are at that point is when all lifetime goals, dreams, wants and aspirations come up to the surface. That is when they begin to show true appreciation for life, sharing most secret desires that were hidden very deep inside of them throughout entire life beneath the invisible mask of expectations, assumptions, and fake smiles and negativity of shoes who pretend to be someone they are not. The most important part is that in many cases time left to realize our inner wishes and lifetime dreams and everything that we wanted to accomplish quickly slips away from us when we reach that point of our life when our journey is coming to an end. So, why wait? Why intentionally add limits to our own life, our wants, and aspirations? Why live someone else's life vs. our own every day and watching life going passed us, only leaving us in the shadow of someone else's success?

So, stop living your life in someone's shadow, and begin living your own life today while enjoying every single moment that you encounter. Seek to find enjoyment while going through tough times as well as good. Find something positive in each situation, regardless of its complexity or how impossible something may seem. At the end of the day, remember to enjoy life from all its multiple sides and angles and simply live. Start living in the present vs. living in the future because you deserve it. Do not let anyone convince you otherwise. Remember, small happy moments in life that we experience, can make a big memorable difference in our lives. That is why we should appreciate those happy moments wherever we may be in life.

Small Happy Moments Can Make a Big Memorable Difference – Appreciating happy moments in life wherever we may be

Most of us strive for bigger, better, and more luxurious or prestigious things throughout the course of our life, and there is absolutely nothing wrong with that. There is nothing wrong with wanting the best for yourself, your family, and your friends. For example, one would much rather stay in luxurious 5-star hotel vs. a 2-star one, because he or she would like to have access to a multitude of amenities that may be available in a 5-star hotel, better location, closer to all entertainment, restaurants, etc. However, could we have as much fun with your family staying in a 2-star hotel? Absolutely. It is all how we look at each experience and our priorities and values. When the most important thing to us is being with people that we love and care about, and going on various adventures together, then it really does not matter whether we stay in a luxury hotel, motel, or somewhere else. Why? Because our attention is fully absorbed by our significant other and/or our child(ren). We can absolutely make the best travel or vacation experience with those that we love and care bout if our priorities are aligned with our values.

It does not matter where we go with my family on vacation, or where we end up staying, we always make the best out of each and every situation no matter what. Sometimes, when we go to a big event and when all hotels are sold out around the venue, we end up staying few nights in a nearby motel, and guess what, we always have a wonderful experience together regardless of where we are, because, our top priority is to have a great time together, so everything else comes second.

I often observe families have a particularly challenging time vacationing, because, either their plane was few minutes delayed, or Uber car was not as big as they were hoping for, or room at the hotel was on a lower level than expected, and so on. What is often observed in such situations is unhappy travelers, frustrated parents, disappointed children. But why? Why ruin your days, week, or month when frustration can be avoided by simply shifting our focus on what is most important to us – people that we love and care about and doing everything that we can to make them happy.

Now, I completely understand that we all have our own unique thoughts, opinions, and priorities in life. So, my goal with this article was to simply highlight one point that happiness can be found wherever we may be in life as-long-as we are surrounded by those that we love and care about and remember that even small happy moments in life can make a big memorable difference. Remember to live in the present and make the time for people whom we love and care about vs. living in the land of our memories.

Life Free of Regrets – Living in the present and making the time for people whom we love and care about vs. living in the land of our memories

How often do you stop and appreciate everything and everyone that is present in your life today? I know that in my case, I can certainly do a much better job at this than I have done thus far. So often we get carried away by the routine that we all live in, that we simply forget to pause and recognize everyone who is present in our life today, to appreciate their presence, their support, and their genuine love. Often, we take it for granted. Many of us, myself included, often take our present for granted and not making time to really appreciate and to think the universe for everyone who is by our side and have been by our side for many years. But why? Why not pause our extremely busy life for just few minutes and do just that? Why not send our thanks and appreciation back to the universe showing how thankful we are for having people that we love in our love? Why not share our thoughts with those that we love and care about every day, letting them know how happy we are for having them in our life? Unfortunately, I do not know the answer to this question. What I do know is that very often we wake up and realize that people that we cared very deeply about and loved are no longer there for us to tell them in-person how much we cared about them. So, why wait until it is too late? No reason at all. It does not take much effort or time to show our love and appreciation to those whom we love and care about. If we are not doing this today, if we are not making time, then we simply creating excuses for our own lack of action in making a first step in approaching those that we love and letting them know how much we care and appreciate them. You never know how much the display of genuine care and appreciation may mean to the other person, whether it is your spouse, husband, parent, child, grandparent, or your close friend. Perhaps that is what they have been waiting for all their life. Perhaps that is what they need to keep moving forward in life and fight through any roadblocks or challenges that they may be dealing with in their own life today. You never know. If you never take the first step and reach out to them, you may never find out until it is too late. So, do not wait for a better time, do not put it off for another day, do it today, do it now, especially if people that you love and care about are right by your side, and if not, if you are separated by a long distance, then pick up a phone and give them a call, as they may be sitting by their phone right now waiting for your call. If you have an ability to drive or fly and go see your loved ones in-person, then do so. It is not going to require much effort on your part, but it will mean a world to another person, probably more then you can possibly imagine.

One of the biggest regrets that I have is not making more time, creating more opportunities to go and see my grandparents in-person on the regular basis while they were still alive. I kept on telling myself that I can always to do so later, whether it was next day, week or month, putting my visits away for another time, because, either I was too busy or did not have financial resources available. Well, now I have one out of four grandparents alive, you bet that I make every effort to go and see him in-person every week or at the minimum every other week. I can tell you will strong level of confidence that there is nothing that puts a bigger smile on my grandfather's face than seeing his grand-grand children come visiting him and spending some time with them. How much move can I ask for then seeing him and my children happy.

Many of us have people in our lives whom we care about and love, so can we say that we spend time with them regularly or at a minimum call them on the regular basis? If not, then we really should think about our present and our past and do some deep searching inside of us, asking us one question – "Why not?" I vividly remember a scene from the movie – 'Home Alone' – where child had asked his neighbor, why doesn't he speak with his son? Why doesn't he give him a call? To which neighbor replied that he believes that his son does not want to speak with him, because, of long-standing disagreement they have had with him, which also kept him from spending time with his granddaughter that he loved very much. Only after the neighbor got enough courage to call his son, he realized that such simple step was the barrier between him and his son, him, and his granddaughter, one phone call was a solution to a longstanding disagreement and/or misunderstanding.

Earlier example is exactly how many of us create barriers in our own mind that may not even exist or may be completely irrelevant. So, let us remove those barriers in our own mind, let us overcome any hesitations and our own egos and make a genuine effort to reach out to those around us, those whom we love and care about today, letting them know how much we care about them and live the life free of regrets about our past, present, or future. We only live once, so why waste our time living in anger, misunderstandings, disagreements, or "what if." Be happy, be thankful for everyone that you have in your life today, and do not waste precious time living surrounded by walls built by our own doubts and fears anchored in our mind. Life is an unpredictable rollercoaster full of ups and downs, twists and turns, so always be prepared for a change when life takes an unexpected turn, while remaining focused, determined, and motivated, knowing that just like in rollercoaster ride, when ride takes a downward path, you know that very soon it will be heading upward once again.

Never Say 'Never' – Life is an unpredictable rollercoaster full of ups and downs, twists and turns

Our entire life is a composition of different, often unpredictable events, both good and bad, that we experience and live through all throughout our lives. Why good and bad? Because, as you had probably already noticed or experienced for yourself, life is like a rollercoaster, it is not only going up where we experience positive and happy moments in our lives, it also often takes alternative route or turn, or in many cases rollercoaster goes down. Unfortunately, when it goes down it is not the same feeling you when you are speeding downward on a rollercoaster, instead, you experience and go through some tough and challenging times in life. That is why we should always remember the concept of rollercoaster and how it travels along the track – going up, making slow and sharp turns, as well as going down extremely fast without notice or an opportunity to prepare.

This is exactly how life works, it goes up, takes turns for which we often not prepared, and in many cases, it takes us through paths full of challenges, problems, and disappointments. Why is it important to know and remember? Because life often takes such unpredictable turns and twists for which we may not be ready or can prepare for. Instead, we are faced with situations in front of us – good or bad – and we must overcome them no matter what. It is easy to accept good and positive changes, but it is not so easy and simple to accept and face difficult situations when we are faced with one. However, if we know and accept that life can and will take turns which we may not expect, like, or welcome, we will not be completely caught off guard and be ready to face specific difficulties and/or challenges vs. running and hiding away from them.

Many people choose to ignore points mentioned earlier and instead choose to pretend that their life can and will only go up, completely denying that there is even a slight chance that things may change, and life can take an unexpected turn for which they are not prepared or be presented with unforeseen difficulties and challenges. Even when by observing someone else dealing with a specific life's challenge at work, at home, business or personal, they are convinced that they could never face similar situation in their own life, until life takes a turn and presents its not so positive and unpredictable side. Then we realize that we should never say 'never,' because regardless of where we may be in life today, how much or how little money we may have, employed or unemployed we are, run our own business or work for someone else, life may present us with its challenges and its rewards alike, and we should always be aware and ready for such possibilities. So, do not get discouraged if you are going through challenging time in your life at this time, life is a rollercoaster, so what you are experiencing and dealing with today, may not be what you are experiencing tomorrow or day after. Be ready, be aware, and never, ever lose hope in good and determination to succeed in life. If you ever need a boost of motivation and inspiration, picture yourself in your 'happy place,' place where you feel relaxed, at ease, and simply comfortable. Then, draw your inspiration from your visualizations, and keep on moving.

Returning to a 'Happy Place' When Inner Peace is Desired – Living the life full of energy and motivation

Our entire life is a composition of different, often unpredictable events, both good and bad, that we experience and live through all throughout our lives. Why good and bad? Because, as you had probably already noticed or experienced for yourself, life is like a rollercoaster, it is not only going up where we experience positive and happy moments in our lives, it also often takes alternative route or turn, or in many cases rollercoaster goes down. Unfortunately, when it goes down it is not the same feeling you when you are speeding downward on a rollercoaster, instead, you experience and go through some tough and challenging times in life. That is why we should always remember the concept of rollercoaster and how it travels along the track – going up, making slow and sharp turns, as well as going down fast without notice or an opportunity to prepare.

This is exactly how life works, it goes up, takes turns for which we often not prepared, and in many cases, it takes us through paths full of challenges, problems, and disappointments. Why is it important to know and remember? Because life often takes such unpredictable turns and twists for which we may not be ready or can prepare for. Instead, we are faced with situations in front of us – good or bad – and we must overcome them no matter what. It is easy to accept good and positive changes, but it is not so easy and simple to accept and face difficult situations when we are faced with one. However, if we know and accept that life can and will take turns which we may not expect, like, or welcome, we will not be completely caught off guard and be ready to face specific difficulties and/or challenges vs. running and hiding away from them.

Many people choose to ignore points mentioned earlier and instead choose to pretend that their life can and will only go up, completely denying that there is even a slight chance that things may change, and life can take an unexpected turn for which they are not prepared or be presented with unforeseen difficulties and challenges. Even when by observing someone else dealing with a specific life's challenge at work, at home, business or personal, they are convinced that they could never face similar situation in their own life, until life takes a turn and presents its not so positive and unpredictable side. Then we realize that we should never say 'never,' because regardless of where we may be in life today, how much or how little money we may have, employed or unemployed we are, run our own business or work for someone else, life may present us with its challenges and its rewards alike, and we should always be aware and ready for such possibilities. So, do not get discouraged if you are going through challenging time in your life at this time, life is a rollercoaster, so what you are experiencing and dealing with today, may not be what you are experiencing tomorrow or day after. Be ready, be aware, and never, ever lose hope in good and determination to succeed in life. Regardless how challenging or complicated the roadblocks may seen on your path, there are ways to overcome them.

Motivation Roadblocks and Ways to Overcome Them

I am sure that we all at some point in our lives have struggled with finding motivation to keep going, keep trying to reach or accomplish a particular goal or task. You set all these interesting and important to your objectives that you really want to accomplish, and you work hard every day to reach them, but then one day you hit a motivation roadblock and not sure what to do or how to move forward.

There have been multiple times in my life where I was in this exact situation. One day I was very motivated and ready to do whatever it takes to achieve specific goal(s) set in front of me, and another day same goals but my motivation had left me. What do you do?

How do you restore the same drive and motivation that you had before, when you were willing and ready to do whatever was necessary to reach your goals?

This is where many people make unfortunate and sometime irreversible decision to give up on their goals and lifetime dreams, simply because they had lost their motivation and do not see it ever coming back.

Are you willing to give up on your dreams and forget all the hard work that you have put in, and all the time that you have invested working towards your goals and dreams?

I think you would agree with me that the answer to the question above is a definite "No." Of course, you do not want for all your efforts and ideas to go to waste. Often, the breaking point, where you begin to reap fruits of your labor, is closer than you may think, and all it takes is one more step, one more attempt, one more challenge to overcome. Now that we understand that motivation roadblocks are real and affect every person in some point of our lives, the question is: How does one overcome these roadblocks?

I am going to list several ways/steps that can help you overcome motivation roadblocks and bring motivation you need to keep going towards your goals and dreams. This is not an exclusive list, as I am sure there are many other ways to find motivation, however, these are some of the ways that work for me when I hit a motivation roadblock.

Ways/Steps to overcome motivation roadblocks:

Speaking and sharing your motivation struggles with a person whom you trust, someone who will listen to you and share their honest and valuable feedback with you

Sometimes you need to hear direct and honest feedback from another person who knows you better than anyone else, someone who knows what you went through to get to the point where you are now in your life

I share my motivation challenges with my wife, who will always listen to me and then remind me what I had to go through, how much time and effort I had already invested on the journey towards my lifetime goal. My wife will not tell me what I want to hear, but what I need to hear to find my motivation and keep going

Reviewing your written goals and objectives with respective timelines for each goal that you had set previously

In your mind you should remind yourself why you had set a particular goal several days, weeks, months, or even years ago

Re-create that same feeling that you had when you were setting each specific goal. How have you felt at that time and why have you felt that way?

Obviously, when you were setting each of your goals it was important to you, your family, or both. Bring that feeling and those emotions back

Write down everything that is going through your mind as you are recreating prior memories

Review the list that you had written, and it should help you to bring that needed motivation to keep going

When you face another motivation obstacle, go through this exercise again and capture your thoughts

Listen to your favorite motivational speaker. If you do not have one, you can easily find one by conducting a quick search online

Some of my favorite speakers are: T. Harv Eker, Anthony Robbins, Zig Ziglar, and Nick Vujicic

In addition to listening to great speakers, you may watch one or more motivational videos by conducting a search on YouTube

Some of my favorite motivational videos are: "Quiet Desperation" by Les Brown and "You owe you" by Dr. Eric Thomas

I really hope that steps that I had listed above help you to find your motivation whenever you face a motivation roadblock. These steps work for me. Sometimes one of the steps above is all I need to bring that drive and passion that I need, and sometimes I need more than one. You must find what works for you and use it whenever you can use additional motivation to keep driving towards your goals and dreams.

Remember, you may be closer to success than you think, so do not stop now, find that passion in you and keep going forward. In the next section of this chapter, I will share some positive mind-setting techniques, to help you keep negative thoughts out of your mind.

Daily Positive Mind-Setting Techniques – Ways to Keep Negative Thoughts Out of Your Mind

Why did I choose this topic?

Probably, because, I face the same challenge as many of you - the need to focus on the positive in every situation vs. the negative. Often, if you allow negative thoughts or emotions to take over, you will become controlled by them, and all actions that you would take will most likely result in negative outcomes. I have been guilty of allowing negative thoughts or situations to dictate my next steps, which never resulted in the positive outcome. Instead, negative actions led me to the negative results. However, when I acknowledged that negativity has taken over my action and re-focused only on the positive instead by pushing away any negative thoughts and emotions, all the sudden my day dramatically improved and productivity increased.

There are two primary ways that you may be exposed to negativity.

First, is your mind choosing to focus on the negative thoughts and see negative outcome in every action that you may take. Second, is being surrounded by negatively minded individuals, who are not happy or satisfied with what may be happening around them at any given point of time, almost every day. I will discuss both ways separately for further clarity.

Negative mind is your own enemy.

How does our own mind become our source of negative energy? Usually, it all starts with experiencing failures on the repetitive basis in our personal and professional lives. Most people would focus on the negative outcome before any action is even taken, just because that is what they had experienced in prior attempts. Therefore, the thought is, "well what is different this time, it will still result in the failed outcome." For example, a particular initiative was discussed and implemented temporarily in your business, it generated a lot of excitement and drive, however, in the few months the idea was placed on pause or stopped all together. Then, new, and exciting initiative is introduced again, but now instead of feeling excited and hopeful, your mind is focusing on the negative, thinking "well, this initiative will be forgotten in few months again, just like the one prior." Therefore, instead of focusing on the positive and presenting a plan of action to ensure that this time the new initiative becomes successful and long lived, our mind goes into negative mode which required no action on your part, and no need to present solutions - an easy way out. But is that an effective way that will help you and your business to be successful? Of course not, as focusing on the negativity will result in the negative outcome for all parties involved.

Negative people = Negative Thoughts = Negative Results.

What happens when you are surrounded by negative people? When you are surrounded by negative people, often their negative energy consumes you and begins draining your positive energy. The goal of negatively minded people is to convert your positive energy into negative, to ensure that your energy and way of thinking matches theirs. It works the same way when you are surrounded by positively minded individuals. Their positive energy and way of thinking will inspire you and refill your positive energy bank to the top, which usually would lead to positive and successful outcomes. Therefore, be mindful of the people with whom you surround yourself with, to make sure the energy you receive from them is the energy that you need.

So, what are some of the ways to keep positively focused mind and keep negative thoughts out?

When faced with a situation where you know that similar situation when tried before failed, instead of focusing on the prior negative experience, focus your mind on the positive

Break the situation down into smaller pieces and find something positive in each piece (ex. trying something new is better than staying in one place and not changing, or you contributing to the organization and flow by sharing your ideas, may lead to a positive outcome vs. not sharing and keeping your great ideas to yourself)

When negative thought enters your mind, refocus on something different, something positive, and do the same every time negative thoughts enter your mind. Eventually, this exercise will turn into habit

Always look for something positive in every situation, regardless how challenging or difficult it may be. If you focus on the negative (ex. telling yourself that you cannot do something), guess what is going to happen - lack of progress on a particular task, that is if any progress at all.

If you continue convincing your mind that you cannot do something, eventually your thoughts will become your reality. However, if you focus on what you can do, you will overcome any obstacle and find a way to get things done. Do not set yourself up for failure, set yourself up for success.

When you are surrounded by negative-minded group of people, seek to understand the reasons behind their words and actions. Often, it could be as simple as not understanding the bigger picture and their individual role in a particular situation, which could be critical to the overall success.

Many people do not ask questions to understand the "why" and instead create their own incorrect and often negative opinion about a particular situation.

When you are positive and other people around you are negative, they would want to understand why you are seeing the same situation from a different, positive perspective, and that is your opportunity to help them to see "why" behind it.

Daily Mantra of Positive Thoughts. This does not have to be complex, and the easier it is to remember and follow, the better. Your personal daily mantra could consist of 8-10 sentences at most

Example: "I am happy with my life and loving every day"

The goal of daily mantra of positivity is to repeat it at least once per day, preferable first thing in the morning, and use it every single day

Daily mantra of positivity helps to re-focus your mind on positive thoughts and your strengths

Try not to engage in the negative conversations and gossip, especially in your place of business. Even without you participating in the conversation itself, negative energy around you could take away from your positive energy. You do not want that to happen.

If you do not understand something or someone, be sure to ask questions to ensure accurate and complete understanding of the individual and the bigger picture. Do not create something which does not exist, instead focus on facts.

Lead by example by being always positive. People around you feed off your positive or negative energy. Therefore, make sure that you focus on the positive and help others to see that positivity in you every single day.

Listening to an inspirational and uplifting podcast, song, or watching a motivational video often helps to refocus your mind.

When negative thought attempts to enter your head, ask yourself, "why do I feel this way?" For every negative reason try to find a positive response.

Example: "This is very difficult and unattainable"

Positive response: "If this task is being assigned to me, then my business leader has full confidence in me, and knows that I will complete this task with high level of quality. I can and will get this done"

If you had received an email or other communication that is very direct in nature towards you and/or negative. It is best not to respond right away. Instead, take 5-10 minutes and step away from your computer, if you can, and then come back and respond while focusing on the positive, without matching the direct or negative manner in the original communication.

Follow through on your promises. If you promised something to your business leader or your subordinates, or peers, be sure to follow through on your promise(s). If unable to follow through, then explain the reasons why, do not just stop delivering on your promise without an explanation.

Begin writing your thoughts on the paper every day, either in the morning as soon as you wake up, or before you go to bed. This exercise should help you to get all your thoughts on paper and out of your head, while reflecting on the positive daily mantra or positive accomplishment that took place during the day (if you are documenting your thoughts before going to bed).

Use as many steps as you need to keep negative thoughts out of your mind and negative energy away from you. Focus on the positive in every situation and share your positive energy with others. Remember, positive thoughts lead to positive results, and practice make it perfect. Now, let us unleash the positivity within you.

The Power of Smile and Positive Energy – Unleashing Positivity Within You

Do you sometimes feel down or discouraged? Do you sometimes feel the weight on your shoulders that you have difficult time removing?

The reason why you may feel this way is due to negative energy accumulation, accumulated amount of stress and worry, or due to series for failures that you may have faced recently. You are trying to get rid of all this stuff that weights you down, but it seems to remain. Why? What am I doing wrong?

It is not necessarily that you are doing something wrong, you may simply need a different approach to address and alleviate your concerns, worry, and stress.

You have so much positivity stored inside of you that sometimes all you need is to unleash that positive energy and turn everything around for a better.

Before you can uncover the power of positivity, you need to recognize and understand what got you to where you are now, your current state. Without understanding the reasons or triggers that might have negative effect on your emotional state and wellbeing, it will be difficult to eliminate negative barriers and replace them with positive energy.

So, first, take some time and write down all your negative emotional roadblocks or situations that you are facing or had faced recently. You would need to list every negative situation or thought that you had experienced. It may not be the easiest thing to do at first, but this step is necessary to remove all that negative energy that you may be dealing with and transfer it on paper versus keeping it all in your mind. Once you complete your list, you should already feel better and more positive than you did before.

Next, you would need to take each item or situation written on your list and find something positive that you can list for each one. For example, one of your negative items may say something like this: "Everything seems to be going against me today, if it's not one thing it's another, it's just a very bad day." The positive response that you may list could be: "It's a beautiful and sunny day outside, I have everything that I need to be successful, one challenging day will not stop me." This is just one of many examples that you can list, and I am sure that you can find something good and positive to counter any negative thought or situation.

Once you have listed something positive for every negative, you should have an incredibly good and positive feeling inside of you. All the sudden everything is not as bad as you had thought initially, instead, everything is good.

You have what it takes to challenge and overcome any negative thought or situation with positive energy within you. It is important to remember that power of positivity and smile can help you to live a much happier life despite of occasional challenges that you may face thought out life. So, smile more every day, live in the moment, and unleash the positive energy within you.

Living in a Moment One Day at a Time

What is 'living in a moment' means to me?

It is being thankful for every single opportunity to be able to enjoy myself in a company of my family and friends. It is not complaining about little issues or problems that we face regularly, and instead turning a problem into an opportunity to learn and feel great about it. Living in the moment to me means being happy and appreciative for everything I have, every blessing and wonderful opportunity that I receive.

So often I hear from various people statements such as: "I don't have this or don't have that," "I wish I could have this or live there," etc. So, my question to someone who makes such statements is: "What are you doing about changing your current situation, if you are not happy?" If you find yourself in this situation, ask yourself this question, because, at the end of the day, if you are not happy where you are now, then change it. If you cannot change it, then ask yourself why you cannot. Remember, it is never a situation, or a problem, or a person that is keeping you where you are, it is always you.

The importance of NOW

Just know that everything that you have today is a direct result of your actions, that you take every day, whether it is at work or home. Please do not blame someone or something else for your failures, be happy for what you do have now. If your present is not your dream life, then work hard, and put in everything you have got to change your now.

Remember to say thank you for what you have and celebrate your victories, regardless how big or small they are. Success builds on success, and positive outcome comes from positive state of mind. If you are happy, positive, and appreciate what you have today, then in turn, you attract more good things and positivity to you. All the sudden great things start to happen, new opportunities become available to you and within your reach. Being happy and positive does wonders, but also remember that it works the other way around. You create your future, and that future could be everything that you can dream about and more, or future where you stand still and constantly unhappy with life, your choice.

Cherish your memories and save them in your 'memory bank'

Refill your 'memory bank' as you encounter new experiences. It is kind of like adding more money into your piggy bank. The more money you deposit into your piggy bank, the more money you save. It works the same way with positive experiences, good memories, when you were happy, and you 'deposit' your positive memories into your 'memory bank'. The more positive memories you deposit in your 'memory bank', the more you can reflect on and feel great again in the future. Your 'memory bank' can be simply mental notes in your head, it can also be physical notes that you write and then save in a jar. When you need to improve your emotional state and put smile on your face, you can review notes from your 'memory jar' anytime you need it.

So, be happy, work hard for what you want, be in control of your future and continue to grow your 'memory bank/jar' with happy and positive experiences. If your memory jar is full, you can always get another one started! Be happy because there is no reason not to be. To help you stay motivated and inspired you may use affirmation, visualization, and/or vision boards anytime.

Do Affirmations, Visualizations, and Vision Boards Actually Work?

I am a firm believer in affirmations, visualizations, and vision boards. However, just because this is something that I absolutely believe in and think that they work, it does not mean that you should believe in them as well. Practice of using affirmations, visualizations, and vision boards is completely option and is unique for each person. Additionally, I am not aware of any scientific study which proves that practice of using affirmations, visualizations, or vision boards somehow directly attributing to results achieved by people who practice them.

With I personally strongly believe in power of affirmations, visualizations, and vision boards because I use them every day to help me get closer to and eventually achieving my goals. I will discuss each one of these practices listed earlier in more detail a little later, but before I do so, let me share my opinion as to why some people may not see any results from using affirmations, visualizations and/or vision boards.

Why use of affirmations, visualizations, and vision boards may not yield any noticeable results?

I believe that the main reason why many people do not notice any results is due to lack of consistency and commitment. Consistent use of affirmations is a habit that must be developed and practiced daily, otherwise it makes no sense to waste your time to start such practice. Specific affirmations and visualization should be used until the goal has been reached, and once one has been achieved new visualization and affirmation should be created, and everything starts over. As long as you still have goals and dreams, use of affirmations, visualizations, and vision boards could help in your journey to reach those goals.

Other reasons why many people give up on using affirmations is the expectation of immediate results, which is not going to happen, unless you just happened to be the luckiest person in the world, and the awkward feeling while practicing them, especially affirmations, since affirmations require you to say them out loud.

The awkward feeling of affirmation use

Sure, initially when you begin practicing affirmations, you may have that awkward feeling that someone may hear you and what that person may think about you.

There are two potential solutions to this not so problem.

One, which is the one I prefer personally, is not caring about what anyone else may think of you if they happened to hear or see you practicing affirmations. Why does it matter what anyone may think, it is your life and your future? So, what if they hear you, let them, and perhaps your affirmations may help them in some way.

The other potential solution is to practice your daily affirmations in private, such as in your car or home, where there is no chance for you to be overheard by other people. Choice which option is completely yours, if you take necessary steps that get you closer to where you want to be.

Now that we have covered potential reasons why many people do not practice or believe in affirmations, visualizations, and/or vision boards, as well as obstacles that some may be facing at the beginning states of practicing them, let us discuss each one in little more detail. You may see or hear different explanations/descriptions of each one in other resources available to you, but I want to share my understanding of each one based on many years of self-education.

What are Affirmations?

Affirmations are one sentence-long statements created by you verbalizing you reaching a specific goal or set of goals. They could consist of anywhere from two to multiple words in length. Affirmations must be specific to your goal. Here are some examples of affirmation statements: "I have one million dollars in my checking account right now," or "I am my own boss and successfully run my own business in the field of (specific field of business)." There are just some examples of affirmations that can be used, depending on your goals in life. You may have multiple affirmation statements that you use and verbalize, you are not limited to one specific number. Lastly, affirmations must be repeated verbally out loud daily until you have successfully achieved the goal in mind.

Now, it is important to remember that affirmations, visualizations, and vision boards are just an additional tool that you may use in addition to other steps that you are taking while working to get closer and eventually reaching your goals.

What are Visualizations?

Essentially, visualizations are affirmations but in the visual form, mental images of you achieving a specific goal that you create in your mind. Just like affirmations, visualizations must be utilized daily. Good thing is you can practice visualizations without saying a single word, since everything is taking place in your head. One example of visualization may be you visualize yourself reviewing your checking account balance, and the available balance is showing $1.000.000.00. This specific example ties in with one of the affirmation examples shared earlier.

When is the best time to practice visualizations and affirmations?

You would have to find the time(s) of the day that works best for you. I personally practice affirmations and visualizations at the same time each morning. You may choose

to practice them when you wake up, before going to bed, or at another time more convenient for you.

How frequently should I practice visualizations and affirmations?

There is no specific number that you must hit every day, if you practice at least once per day. If you want to visualize several times during the day, you may absolutely do that, the choice is yours. The key is consistency, not frequency.

What is a vision board?

Vision board is an actual physical board that you create where you add images and/or small physical items that represent your goals which you want to achieve. This could be as simple as an image of the car that you wish to own and drive one day, or an image of $1M that you want to have in your checking account.

Vision board is representation of your goals in the physical form. It also does not have to be in the form of an actual board. For example, I created a small clip binder where I inserted clear plastic sleeves with pictures of my goals, things that I want to have. Therefore, instead of looking at the board, I flip through many images in my 'vision binder.' This technique also helps to visualize myself achieving those goals a little easier. I have seen some highly creative vision boards, but since I am not highly creative, I chose to create something simple and different that works for me, the choice is always yours.

Do I have to use all three – Affirmations, Visualizations, and Vision Boards?

Not necessarily. You should use what works best for you in your specific situation. So, if right this moment you do not have vision board created yet, that is ok, because you can still practice affirmations and visualizations, or one of the two if you are pressed on time. The important part is taking the first step and use what you have and can do now, everything else can be added when it is possible. Remember, it is not quantity but consistency that matters. Of course, once you have all three, I believe, the energy that you can potentially create multiplies and expands, and you begin attracting more positive energy to yourself to help you achieve the goal(s) in mind.

In addition to using affirmation, visualization, and vision boards to stay focused and motivated on our journey towards reaching that what we see as success, but also once we get there and live the life that we have been dreaming about.

Unhappiness Caused by Too Much Success

Why do some people feel the sense of unhappiness once they have reached their lifetime goals and are extremely successful? Shouldn't we be happy that we finally achieved the highest level of success personally and professionally? The simple answer is yes, we should be happy. So, why then some people experience unhappiness?

I believe that one of the reasons for unhappiness when you are at the very top, is that now we have everything that we wanted to have and achieved everything that we wanted to achieve. So, in our mind the question is: "now what?" What do we do when we have everything? We have spent all our energy and time to achieve our dream(s), and now we are there.

Once you are at the 'top', what are the next steps?

Once we achieve all our personal and professional goals, it is important to remember that we can invest our energy, time, and resources to help others in need, and not necessarily only from the financial standpoint, but also from personal development perspective.

There are so many people who need guidance and for someone to mentor them as part of their personal development, that there is always an opportunity for individuals who have achieved success to offer their assistance.

What is the outcome?

Keep driving to achieve all your goals and dreams, and once you are there, once you have reached the top, then look for opportunities to share your knowledge and wisdom with others who may be seeking hep and need someone's guidance.

There are always ways to contribute and make our world a better place. So, personal goal achievement is just a beginning of the exciting journey which opens so many ways and opportunities to keep driving your vision forward. With all this in mind, how does one become the source of motivation, especially when going through some rough patches in life? Let us explore that in the next section of this chapter.

Dealing with Stress – Self-Inspiration and Motivation

Sources of stress

We all experience stress in our lives. Sometimes it is as simple as sitting in traffic with important meeting time approaching, and sometimes it is more serious, such as being let go from a job and not knowing how you are going to pay bills moving forward. Regardless of the sources of stress, we experience it, and many people experience it regularly.

How is stress affecting us?

Continuous experience of stress may also have a negative effect on our physical and emotional state. We often forget to recognize stress as something that is affecting us when we are down and/or facing challenges, thinking that if we try not to focus too much on what is going on, it will pass without us taking any actions to address it.

Even though we know about negative impact of stress on our wellbeing, we do not know how to deal with it on our own and, therefore, choose to ignore it until it gets difficult to manage. But why? Are there ways to recognize and manage stress?

How to recognize and manage stress?

First and foremost, it is important to be honest with yourself and to recognize the period of time when you may be dealing with stress, regardless of its complexity or timing. Typically, when a person is experiencing stress, they are asking themselves the following questions: "How do I deal with specific situation at hand? Or "Am I capable of accomplishing a particular task or project within expected timelines and quality?" or "How do I deal with situation at hand?" These are only some examples of questions that may be going through a person's mind when they are faced with uncertainties and stress.

So, how to you deal with stress once you recognize it?

One method that works for me every time is asking myself: "What is my lifetime goal and dream that I want to achieve?" It may seem like it is simple or even unrelated question in relation to stress experience, but it certainly is related. Once you ask yourself this question, it helps you to refocus your thinking on the bigger picture versus continuing to focus on temporary setbacks you may be experiencing.

Temporary setbacks and reasons to keep moving forward

There is always a good reason to keep moving forward despite occasional setbacks in our lives. For example, losing a job, as bad as it may be temporarily, refocusing your mind on bigger goal may prompt your mind to look and create ideas and ways to address temporary unemployment, coming up with some ideas you had never thought of before when you were employed, and often with higher financial gain opportunities, such as finding a higher paying job or even starting your own business.

Believing in yourself and your abilities to overcome anything on your path

In addition to refocusing your way of thinking on the bigger picture and goal, the other particularly important ingredient in dealing with stress is to remember that you can accomplish anything that you set your mind to and come out of any challenging situation on the top. All you need to do is remind yourself that you can, and really believe in it.

Be in control of your mind

Unfortunately, our mind usually focuses on what we cannot do, doubting our own strengths and abilities. However, please remember that we are the ones who allow thoughts to enter our mind whether they are positive and motivational or negative and doubtful. So, if you are in control of your thoughts, focusing on the positive outcome, remembering that you can accomplish anything if you really believe in it, you will begin looking for opportunities available to you versus continuing looking for ways to create more problems and more stress.

You control what goes into your mind and how you respond to what your mind receives. Do not let anyone tell you what you are capable of, the only person that really knows what you are capable of is you, and you are the only person who is capable of setting or removing barriers in your life. You are also the only one who truly knows what is important to you, what your values are. With many thoughts going through our mind at any time, how do we prioritize our values to live a simple and fulfilling life? I will address this any other questions in the next section of this chapter. So, keep on reading.

Value Prioritization – A Way to Live a Simple and Fulfilling Life

Many of us know what is important to us, what we value. However, have we prioritized our values based on their level of importance? We want to dedicate our time and energy to what matters to us the most first and distribute remaining time and energy to other values accordingly. I know that this may sound like a lot or be confusing, so let us pick this topic apart and make it digestible and easier to follow and understand.

What are Values?

In one of my blog articles, some time ago, I discussed the topic of values, what values are, and what do they mean to us. We all have values that are important to us. For some, it is family and everything that evolves around our family, such as: health, money, lifestyle, fun, and security. For others, it may be career. Therefore, what we would consider important to us are thinks like: working for a right company, career advancement and growth, location, personal development, and people. These are just some of the examples of values that we may place as the most important to us. This does not mean that these two values listed are what most people have on their list of values that they care about, some people may value completely different things in life and, therefore, their list of values could be rather extensive. You may be asking yourself; well can I value family and career at the same time? The answer is, absolutely. However, even though both family and career are important to you, they would never be placed on the same exact level of importance, one would typically be more important or valued than another. That is where the importance of value prioritization comes into play.

What is Value Prioritization?

Value prioritization is prioritizing your values based on their level of importance, where two different values never equal each other on the importance scale. Value prioritization helps us to understand our values better and laser-focus our energy and time on most important values first, versus spreading it across multiple values at the same time, potentially missing on what is tremendously important to us, when it is most important to us. Value prioritization is not a static list of values, it is ever-changing, growing or shrinking list. Values change over time, so should our value prioritization list, where the most important values stay at the top and rest of the values are organized based on their level of importance.

Goal Setting and Value Prioritization

Even though goal setting may appear to be similar to value prioritization, they are actually different or at least how they are defined. Value prioritization focuses on prioritizing your values based on their level of importance to you at a specific point in time, whereas goal setting is a roadmap to achieving each goal that you have set, which may or may not be related to your values. For example, your most important value may be family, however, one of your goals is to go on vacation to Bahamas. Are they related? Not necessarily unless your goal is to take your whole family on vacation to Bahamas and spend time together. Goal setting, if done correctly, and in accordance with your top values can serve as a vehicle to fulfilling and living out your most important values.

As in example with family vacation, taking your whole family on vacation may be one of many things that you can do to invest your time and energy in what matters to you the most – your family. Perhaps, the other goal you may have is starting your own business. How is this goal ties to your top value – family? You have freedom in creating your own schedule, spend more time with your kids, attend important school events, which otherwise you would be unable to attend, creating the lifestyle you want for your family. So, hopefully these couple of examples helped you to see how smart-set goals can help you in achieving things in life that support your most important values versus being goals without meaning or value behind them.

Why is value prioritization important?

If you had ever felt that you are doing a million of different things to support what you viewed as important, and then feeling as if you have not accomplished much, with feeling of being spread too thin, with no energy left to enjoy what is really important to you, then you are most likely spreading you time, energy, and resources on many different wants and needs, versus one or two values that are most important to you right now, and spending the remainder of energy and time left on other less important values. This does not mean that other values on your value prioritization list are not important. All this means is that you should be investing most of your time and energy in what is important to you first, and then distributing remainder to other wants and needs that you may have. It is a way to live a simpler and more fulfilling life that many of us desire.

What about abundance and the material wealth? Exploring the topic of alignment of your priorities based on what is important to you in the next section.

Seeking Abundance and Material Wealth or Genuine Down-To-Earth Happiness Created by Support and Care

Seeking material wealth

For many of us obtaining a great amount of material wealth, such as: luxurious houses, prestigious cars, great amount of money, etc., is a number one goal in life. Everything that we do is to support our goal of acquiring more, bigger, and better, more luxurious, and prestigious. We seek new employment or business opportunities just to put ourselves in a position of power and unlimited wealth, to satisfy our craving for more stuff, and not just any tangible items, but only the best. We are not satisfied with average or what other people came to appreciate, we want better, more expensive, something that only available to us. All our life we are chasing a goal that could never be fulfilled. Why? Because there is always more 'stuff' for us to go after, something new and better, something that we may not already have in our possession. Just look at the example of new cell phones or tablets become available on the market. As soon as new smart phone is out, we are rushing to the store to upgrade our existing phone and continue paying more every month. But that does not matter, because now we have the latest model of the phone that others may not have yet. So, where is a stopping point? There is none. We will continue to seek more and acquire more for as long as we live.

Material wealth – Good or Bad?

There is nothing wrong with wanting something better, newer, more luxurious. It is normal to want to improve our life and lives of those around us for a better by improving our lifestyle. Lifestyle improvement could include many different items, such as: moving into a nicer and safer neighborhood, purchasing a home, and moving out of apartments, or buying a more spacious house to have more space for children to play, purchasing newer and better-quality vehicle so that we can stop throwing money on repairs or existing ones, etc. So, are all these lifestyle improvements bad? Of course not. It is normal and expected to want a more comfortable life. However, what we often forget during the process of material wealth accumulation is creation and appreciation of our non-material wealth – that what makes us happy and peaceful inside, that which carries us forward and creates a balance in our lives – support and care of our family.

Seeking and protecting our non-material wealth

Have you ever met or know someone who has bare minimum material possessions, just enough to live comfortably, not in luxury, without expensive cars, houses, and other material items that many of us seek, yet they are some of the happiest people you know? Why? How can they be so happy and satisfied with their life when they have just enough to live a simple life? The answer to this is simple, they have what some of us do not, and that is unconditional support, love, and care of those who are close to us, our husbands, wives, children, and of course, our parents. They genuinely appreciate everything that they have in life, and less on the material side of things, but more on the non-material. They know that regardless of what happens in this unpredictable thing we call life, they will have those who they love and care about by their side, both when life throws us challenges and when we are presented with opportunities. People who come to appreciate and cherish what and who they have in life versus living in a constant stress and desire for more, then to be happier and excited about opportunities that each day may bring. Why? Because they know that even if everything else fails, they will always have those who will support and encourage then not to give up but keep moving forward. Also, because their life does not solely dependent on acquiring more material wealth, they focus on finding opportunities to grow and develop themselves every day in anything they do, and as result, material possessions and lifestyle improvements come naturally. Even if those successes are small, someone who recognizes the importance of non-material wealth, appreciates, and welcomes each opportunity as it enhances already happy and fulfilling life.

True wealth that we all seek

Regardless of where you may be in life, remember that there are more to life than material wealth accumulation. Remember to pause, look around and appreciate everything and everyone you have in your life at any given moment in life, because, at the end of the day that is the true wealth that we all seek.

How do we go elevate and maintain our desired happiness, focusing on achieving our goals and dreams in life? This any many other topics are discussed in the Chapter 3 of this book, so, let us dive right in.

Chapter 3 - Get Up and Grind – Hard Work & Persistence as a Way to Achieve Desired Results in Life

A Unique Way to Look at Goal Planning and Achievement

I know you have heard and read about the "I can, and I will" approach to goal planning and visualization. However, even though I still believe that stating what you can and will do to achieve your goals is important, I feel like it leaves a room for an escape and/or a way out from staying focused on your goal(s) and doing everything that you can to get closer and ultimately achieving that what you said you can and will do. Why, because, by stating that you can and will do something does not commit you to taking necessary steps today to get you from sinning on your couch and just envisioning the outcome in your mind, vs. getting up from that couch and doing what you said you are going to do now, not tomorrow, not a month from now. Therefore, I think there is an opportunity to modify the goal setting and achieving approach here. I call it "I can, and I am" approach

What is "I can, and I am" Approach? Why should this approach be used daily when setting new, and working toward existing goals and plans?

What "I can, and I am" approach does is it requires you to commit to a specific action that you are doing now to reach a particular goal of yours. When you say that I can and I will do something, it essentially allows to take that action now, tomorrow, or year from now, there no specific commitment from you and no insight into what are you doing to achieve or get closer to what you have said you are going to accomplish. When you say: I can and I am dedicating 2 hours of my time each day/week to write high quality content, which then would be incorporated into a book, which is ultimately a main goal of yours, you are calling out the immediate action you are already taking to achieve your dream. Can you see the difference between both approaches? "I can and I will" is self-motivating and confidence boosting, where's "I can, and I am" is action-oriented, plus encompassing the benefits of the first approach.

So, next time when you are ready to set a new goal or when you are reviewing and updating existing goals or plans of yours, ask yourself one question: "What am I doing today to achieve that specific goal or dream of mine? What immediate steps that I am taking today to get closer to the goal accomplishment?" Use "I can, and I am" approach to help with adding clarity, accountability, and laser focus to understand that you are doing today and what you can be doing. At the end of the day, you choose whether you wish to remain where you are today without expecting for thing to change or taking one step each day to create the life that you want for yourself and for those around you. Remember, there is never the 'right time,' to begin pursuing your goals, do what you can today using what you have, while celebrating small wins along the way.

Do What You Can Today Using What You Have, Celebrating Small Wins Along the Way

Setting non-existent limits in our mind

So many people quit on their life-time dreams simply because in their mind they have convinced themselves that reaching their dream is impossible or would require such a great deal of time, energy, resources, and effort, that pursuing it would be unrealistic in their current situation, or from where they are today. Newsflash, our minds are always designed to protect us, therefore, as soon as we think about taking a risk or trying something new, which has even a small chance of risk, our mind's protective function kicks in and convinces us that it would be difficult, challenging, unreachable, or impossible. We, of course, believe and listen to what our mind is telling us. Why? Because it is easier this way. We do not have to try, do not have to risk, or put in any effort. Basically, we can stay where we are, even if it is far from where we want to be, but hey, it is easy and does not require us changing anything that we do today. We can continue to sit on our couch and dream about our dream life, about new car, new house, or a house, new or better job, more money, higher position, well, I think you get the point that I am trying to make here.

Creating false sense of possibilities to stand still

One thing that we fail to realize, is that it does not always have be to be extremely challenging, unreachable, unattainable, require a lot of resources or money that we do may not have at this time. We create false realities in our mind to create a reason not to try to go after our goals in life. Even though we really want to, we tell ourselves that because we do not have x, y, and z, we cannot or should not change anything or even try. The reality is, we can absolutely start something that we are passionate about, follow our goals, and dreams, pursue lifestyle that we really want, without having a lot of money, time, resources, or experience. The key is to start today with what we have and do what we can.

Required ingredient to fund success in life

You do not have to have a million of followers today to be a successful blogger. You do not have to live in a multi-million mansion to enjoy the lifestyle that you want, at least not right this minute. You do not have to invest thousands of dollars into your online business to begin creating a successful business with loyal customers. What you do have to have is willingness to simply try. You do have to have is a strong desire to learn, and I mean learn from your failures and mistakes, because they will take place. You must understand that success, may and typically will not happen immediately, it takes time, effort, and quality content and/or product that you deliver to your audience and your customers. If what you are presenting to your audience is kind of good, well, you should not expect for your business to take off right away after launching. However, it does not mean that you cannot get better, you can, all you must do is be patient and continue to work on improving your skills and content/product. Do not have a lot of available time to start your online business? Well, guess what, you can start your online business while working full time, you can also spend hours working on your business on the weekends, or days off. Any reason you create for not pursuing your goal or dream today is just another excuse for not being willing to try and put in the work.

Small wins matter

The other important component of starting and sticking to a specific goal, is to celebrate small victories along your exciting and often challenging journey. Do not wait to treat yourself only when you reach your lifetime goal or dream, as that may take months or years. Instead, celebrate small victories with small rewards along the way. You have got to make it fun and rewarding for yourself. That is what will help you to keep going, keep it interesting, and give you a reason to try harder, until you reach that one thing that you are going after. Do not stop when it gets difficult, keep going, keep trying, because it is not over until you say that it is over. If you honestly believe that achieving a specific goal or dream of yours is possible, then you make it possible through your actions. Remember, you are always in control.

It is Not Over Until You say It is Over – Uncovering our inner strength and determination when up is the only way

You are not alone

Being in a place of desperation when nothing seems to work for you, where opportunities seem to avoid you at all costs, where money and wealth seems so far that you cannot even see it in your imagination, may be the trigger you need to act and begin turning things around for the better.

If you think that you are the only one in such unfortunate and non-promising situation today, you are greatly mistaken. There are many people who are in a remarkably similar or exact situation as you are, where up is the only way, you just choosing to act and begin marching in the opposite direction from misfortunes, failures, lack of progress in search of opportunities, success, wealth, and lifestyle of your dreams.

Do not quit on yourself and your future – simply wanting is not going to cut it, doing is the name of the game

Regardless how difficult things may be today for you, regardless how broke you may be living paycheck to paycheck, or even worse, unable to pay your rent when it is due or put gas in your car, running on empty until your car stops running, just know that your current situation is only temporary if you genuinely believe that it is. Listen, the only person you can make failure or success permanent is you. You are probably thinking, "well, it's easy to say than actually getting it done", and that is true. Many people say that they will do something about their not-so-great situation and will work on turning things around, but then take no action just because it is hard. It is much easier to do nothing and complain to everyone how bad your life is, how broke you are, and how unfair everyone is to you. Where is it takes all, and I mean all you have got to go the other direction, to take steps in choosing to design your ideal present and future. Wanting is not going to cut it here, you must know that you will get there, regardless of what anyone thinks, says, or does, and regardless of where you are now. Life is a beautiful and unpredictable thing, it tends to change for better or worse very quickly, and often unpredictably. But if you know what you want in life and have unshakable confidence that everything will be exactly as you envision it in the end, then that is exactly how it is going to be.

How much do you really want it?

I can speak from my personal experience. I have come to U.S. 20 years ago as teenager without knowing English language, culture, traditions, expectations or where to start, but what I did have is unshakable knowledge and determination of where I wanted to be in life and the lifestyle that I wanted to create for my future family no matter what anyone thought or said. Long story short, in the last 20 years I have developed many extraordinarily successful teams and helped many talented people to reach their true potentials that were hidden within them. Also, I live with my wife and two kids in a beautiful state of California, just few miles away from beautiful beaches and blue ocean, while continuing to take steps forward in creating the future and financially-free lifestyle for my family. I know that I will get there, there is no doubt in my mind, and if I can, so can you. The question you should ask yourself is, how much do you really want it?

Discovering our inner strength and creating opportunities in life

Please remember, if you now where you want to be in life today, do not get discouraged, and know that we tend to discover our inner strength when we think that all options have been exhausted. As Bob Marley put it: "You never know how strong you are until being strong is the only choice you have." Believe in yourself and you will create success wherever you may find yourself in life. Stop living in the fantasy world of your wishes and procrastination, begin creating the life you have always dreamed of now.

Stop living in a Fantasy World of Your Wishes and Procrastination – Hard Work and Extreme Persistence Is What Is Required to Succeed in Life

The importance of really hard work and persistence to get you where you want to be

I think many of us underestimate the importance of hard work and persistence when it comes to reaching your goals and objectives and get what you want. We say that we work hard, but are we? Or are we simply want to impress someone by saying things that are not necessarily true, but sound good. I think so. It takes everything you have got to keep pushing and driving to get to where you want to be. A lot of energy, and determination is required, especially when you face obstacles on your path. This is usually where most people give up on their goals, just because it is too difficult, or something is not going according to their plan. Things normally do not go according to plan, and that is ok, that is part of life and struggle that we need to overcome before we reach something great, a place where you really want to be.

Persistence – A way to get from point A to point B

Persistence is that driving force, your fuel, that moves you forward. Persistence plus hard work is required to break through difficult and hard to reach objectives that initially may seem unreachable. But remember, nothing is unreachable, it really depends on how much you really want it. How hard you are willing to work to reach your dream lifestyle? How many hours of your personal time are you willing to invest every single day, to continue moving a needle toward that one thing you are working towards?

These are all especially important questions to ask yourself BEFORE you embark on your journey. The truth is, if you are not willing to invest any available time that you have during the day, and in some cases night, regardless of whether you are working a full-time job or not while pursuing that one thing, then you will not get far. I wish that I can be incredibly positive here and tell you that you will reach your dream if you just wait for it, but I cannot do that, and I cannot and will not lie to you or set false expectations. Yes, patience is particularly important, especially if you are expecting great things come to you right away, they will not, you must work for it and be persistent on getting there.

Personal Example of Hard Work and Persistence

I have personally faced many, many, struggles and difficulties in my life, both personal and professional. One example, attending high school when I could barely understand or speak English. Many people were laughing at me, making fun of my accent, I would be

going to and registering for wrong classes to only find out later that I was in the wrong class and having to unregister. I translated every homework problem using electronic translator at night, while everyone was sleeping, then sleep for 3-4 hours and go back to school again. Despite all these difficulties, I graduated high school with honors, completed all required credits, and was accepted to one of the best universities in the nation. What got me there, were a lot of hard work and insane persistence.

Tools, Resources, Action Items

I am a firm believer that reading or listening to books in your field of interest is a must. I am talking about reading and listening many books, and never stop reading and searching for new content, to continue learning and growing your knowledge base. Some people say that they have read 1-2 books on leadership, and that is great. But, when they are asked what they have done with the information that they have learned, in response you receive silence or "nothing yet." If information is not used to get you closer to your goal, then there is no value in it. Using what you learn is a key to success.

Let us be realistic about your accomplishments and focus on what you will do!

Do not create false reality for yourself or others. Focus on your accomplishments, your goals and plan of getting you to your dream career and lifestyle and put in everything you have got until you get there. Do not create excuses, anybody can do that, instead talk about what you have done and what you will do until your mission is fulfilled.

How do you determine what do you really want? I am glad you had asked, because this and other questions will be covered in the next section.

What do I Really Want in Life?

When I was growing up, I was asking myself this question many times – "What do I really want in life?" Many different ideas come to mind when you ask yourself this same question. For some, it is finding a good high-paying job, to live in comfort, and for others it is helping and supporting other people through volunteering and non-profit work. But what you I want to do? That was the top question on my mind for many years. I did not want to be in a job where all I do is collect a paycheck and stay miserable. It was not until college when I knew what I want to do in life, and it was not due to classes that I attended or lectures that I sat through. Somehow it came to me naturally thinking through my prior failures and all the mistakes that I had made in the prior years as a teenager who was born and raised in another country, and now living in the United States, going through all the difficulties of someone who is new to the culture, lifestyle, expectations, and country in general. This was me in my first year of college. I am sure that many of you who are reading or listening to this can absolutely relate if you ever moved to live in a different country or even different state within United States.

So, going back to my failure analysis. I knew that I want to help other people to avoid making similar mistakes in their life by sharing my experiences and my knowledge acquired over the years. And, I am not saying here that mistakes or failures can be eliminated completely but, perhaps, the impact of those mistakes can be predicted or better calculated and reduced to the minimum. I found my passion, my passion for personal development, learning, and leadership.

One question that helped me to uncover and understand my passion was: "What do I wish I had or done as my younger self?"

The response came to me almost immediately – I wish that I would have invested in my personal and leadership development earlier, several years earlier, so that I did not have to wait several years of my life searching for my passion. To some this comes naturally, but with me it was not the case. It took many years and many failures and mistakes, and long hours of self-reflection and searching somewhere deep inside of me, until I asked myself the question mentioned earlier. It was the question that had changed my life because I finally knew what I want to do, I knew my lifetime dream.

I feel that self-learning is a particularly important for anyone interested in personal development and growth. So, learn as much as you can, anywhere you can. One thing that should never stop is your desire to learn.

If you are still asking yourself: "What do I want to do in life?" then ask yourself the same question I did: "What do I wish I had or done as my younger self?" and see what kind of responses, you will find somewhere deep inside of you.

It does not matter where you are in your life today, what career you had chosen, or how much money you make at this time. If you are not happy where you are today, then you still have not found your passion in life. As Mariah Carey once said: "If you believe in yourself enough and know what you want, you're gonna make it happen"

Also, if you think that there's not enough time in a day to invest into your passion, pursuing your goals and dreams in life, you are looking at time and time management the wrong way. Let us dive deeper into these points in the next section of this chapter.

Weekend – Time to Grind or Time to Play?

Once on my way to the library on one of Saturday mornings, one thought would not leave my head, so I want to share it with you. You probably thinking why library? Well, because library happens to be the quietest place, I can find to gather my thoughts and put them on paper.

So, anyways, let us talk about weekends and how we may view them differently. Many people view weekends as an opportunity to relax, sit on the couch and watch tv the entire day, go to the movies, or go shopping. Next thing you know is two full days went by, you have not accomplished much, if anything at all, spend a lot of money on the things you may not need, utilized credit cards, and now it is time to go back to work to your full-time job. By the way, you are still tired and feel like you need more time to rest. Well, guess what, the weekend is behind you and it is time to work until the next weekend. Some may not even have Saturday and/or Sunday off to rest, because you may be working on the weekends and all you have is few hours in the evenings to enjoy and use them how you see fit, most likely do the activities I had mentioned earlier since you are tired and do not feel like doing anything at all.

Why am I telling you this?

Because I used to do the same before I realized that what I was doing, was not getting me anywhere at all, I was staying in one place, far from my goals and dreams. At the same time, I dreamed about improving my and my family's lifestyle. But how could I do that without doing something about changing my situation and unproductive behaviors? You cannot change your life and tough situation you may be in unless you are ready to act and work hard to get to where you want to be.

What does weekend have to do with this?

Weekend is the time to grind. Yep, you heard me correctly, weekend is the time to grind and hustle, if you want to change where you are today.

If you always dreamed about starting your own business full or part time while working your regular full-time job, then weekend is when you can accomplish most of your tasks to set yourself up for productive and successful week ahead of you.

You can take the same 5-8+ hours on Saturday and Sunday to focus on building solid foundation for the next several days, weeks or even months, by completing writing projects you needed to complete, podcasts you needed to record, work on your website, begin writing a book you always wanted to write, or other activities to help you to get closer to accomplishing your personal and professional goals. Ultimately, accomplished goals would lead you to your lifetime dream, whatever it may be for you – better lifestyle, more vacation time, more money, ability to spend more time with your family, etc.

Taking time away or adding more?

As I am writing this, sitting in the library looking outside thought the window, other people are playing at the part with their kids and enjoying the time outside in the beautiful weather. Of course, I want to do the same and spend this time with my family versus sitting in the company of bookshelves. However, I know that even though it may feel like I am taking this time away from my wife and kids, I see it differently. I see it as adding more time to spend with my family in the long run, maybe not right this minute, but in the near future. My reasoning is simple here, I am investing my time and energy to do what I love, helping other people, just like me few years ago, to find themselves somewhere deep inside of them, find their strength, confidence, and courage to keep working towards their goals and life they want to create for themselves. I do so by sharing my extensive experience and knowledge in the field of personal development and leadership which is based on my experiences, my successes, and failures, as well as lessons learned from each of my failures. My passion for self-development helps me to build solid foundation for my and my family's future, the time when I would be able to dedicate all my time, including the weekends, to my family while doing what I love – helping others grow and develop personally and professionally through my work.

Why am I telling you all this?

I simply want to highlight the importance of utilizing every minute of available time, including the weekends, and work on getting you from where you are not to where you want to be. Yes, it is absolutely a lot of hard work, but what was it ever easy to reach the top. So, how are you going to spend your weekends?

One important part of everything that we do in life and how we do it or do not do it, are habits that we form throughout our life. Whether we create new habits or replacing old or bad habits, our life is controlled by the choices that we make. So, how do our habits control and dictate everything that we do? That is exactly what we will discuss in the next section, so keep on reading.

Consumed by the Routine – How Our Habits Control Our Lives

Are you being consumed by the daily routine or habit of yours?

Do you follow essentially the same or very similar steps every day, such as: eating breakfast, or if you are like me – someone who does not typically eat breakfast – drinking a cup of coffee or two, getting ready for work, driving/walking to work, coming back from work around the same time after spending good amount of time sitting in traffic, if you are driving, eating dinner with family, watch tv, go to bed, then repeat next day? Do you feel like you are being consumed by the routine of daily busy life? Do you take time to pause and appreciate your present, people around you, your family, kids, happy moments in life? Unfortunately, many of us often forget to do so, because we are being consumed by a routine and our daily habits that control what and when we do what we do.

There's time and place for everything

Sometimes we may go on a family vacation that we have waited for an exceptionally long time, however, instead of spending quality time with our family, our kids, we turn our attention to the cell phone or a laptop to catch up on few work emails. I know that many would agree that as soon as we turn our attention to the email, we might as well forget about rest of the day, since we will most likely spend it working vs. spending the time with our loved ones. Please do not get me wrong, work is important and staying caught up is equally important, especially when an urgent report or project must be completed with extremely strict deadline. However, there's time and place for everything. There's time to work and there's time to relax and unwind. That is why it is important to take time to pause, break away from the routine for some time to spend time with and appreciate those around you in the specific point in time at the specific place.

Being aware of what is happening around us

Routine and our habits will always be there and will continue to take us through life in predetermined paths. So, if we want to have a positive, fun, and exciting memories to reflect on later in life, we must remember to always be aware of what is taking place around us at any given time. We need to give our undivided attention to people with whom we are communicating with at work, at home, and in the social setting, to ensure that they feel valued and heard. This especially applies to our family members and our close friends. How many times have you spend time on your cell phone browsing Facebook or other social media platforms while your kids were trying to get your attention so that you can play with them? But because we are so focused on following our routines which consume us completely at times, we fail to recognize those important and critical moments which we should spend doing other activities, rather than being glued to the tv screen or our phones.

Pause and Reflect

To avoid being consumed by our routines and habits, which often are the same, we must be aware of everything that is happening around us and what role, if any, we play in the process. This often requires us to pause what we may be doing at any given point in time, such as working on a specific report, which may not be due any time soon, and spend few minutes on other activities such as: playing with your kids, taking your dog for a walk while enjoying a beautiful weather, or sit down and chat with your significant other about something not related to work. If you are at work, take few minutes to walk around the office, if you can, and socialize with your co-workers.

We can never get the time back which has already passed, but we can focus on the future, and begin adding more great memories to our "happy memory bank" and enjoying life to the fullest.

So, how do we design and live the life that we have always dreamed about? How do we go from planning to action, challenging the status quo? These and many other questions and topics I will be covering in the next chapter of this book.

Chapter 4 - Designing and Living the Life that You Want - Challenging the Status Quo

Do not Let the Lack of College Diploma Stop You in Finding Success in Life

Finding success in life without college degree

Can one find success with incomplete college education, or in other words, without a diploma from a college or university? I think so. However, it may be more challenging and will take much longer to get there without one. Finding success whether it is as entrepreneur or working for another company, requires extraordinarily strong work ethic, never-give-up attitude, extreme persistence, and strong willingness to learn. By learning I mean self-education on the regular daily basis. This includes finding courses online, both free and paid, attending educational conferences, workshops, and seminars conducted by various successful business and world leaders. The key is to attend training courses that you find most interesting, informative, and most importantly, applicable in your area of interest and focus. I found that taking a specific training or attending a conference that others believe you should attend is not the best way to invest your hard-earned dollars. There are also a ton of free and paid resources available both online and offline. One of the great offline resources that everyone can utilize is a library with hundreds or thousands of books for us to choose from. So, do not let the lack of internet or computer stop you on your journey of personal development and growth. Those of us who continuously invest in our own development through self-learning and discovery, are part of the lifelong education program which never ends.

Critical personal qualities that one must have to succeed in life, especially without college diploma

The other especially important attributes of an individual who is likely succeed even without college diploma are extreme persistence and extremely hard work. Why? Because, you may not have the benefit of starting at the higher-level position within a company, unlike someone with a college degree. You would most likely have to start at the very beginning of a 'corporate ladder', and through extreme persistence and hard work move yourself up the 'ladder'. It is not an easy process, and there will be many obstacles along the way, but if you are committed to delivering excellent results wherever you may be working, and do so consistently, while depending only on your own knowledge, experience, and confidence, you can reach the top of that 'ladder' and become successful in whatever you do.

Mindset of commitment and persistence

Who is a person with a mindset of commitment and persistence? This is someone who knows that there is nothing impossible in this world regardless of where they may be in life, and someone who fully believes in themselves possible. This is also someone who is not distracted by outside noise and opinions of others and is marching towards their goals and dreams despite occasional challenges of everyday life. Therefore, I believe that if you are someone who possesses these qualities and do not currently possess a college diploma, you can still be successful wherever you may be in life today, regardless how complex your unique situation may be. Have unshakable confidence, believe in yourself, and you will find success that you are seeking. Even when you do not see an immediate progress based on actions you are taking, have confidence and believe in yourself regardless. Do not give up no matter what.

Finding and Supporting Your Passion in Life – Not giving up on your dreams regardless of circumstances or lack of immediate progress

How many of you thought about giving up on your goals and dreams in life, or your lifetime passion and/or hobby, just because you did not see any progress whether you were hoping to monetize your hobby or attract people to support your vision and sharing your passion with them? I know I have. But then I reminded myself why following through on my goals and passion is important and what it means to me and my family. It is easy to give up, and that is exactly what takes place whenever someone loses patience, gets discouraged due to lack of results or progress, loses motivation. But why? If it is our lifetime passion, whatever it may be for you, that we are pursuing, it is something that we deeply care about, there should be nothing that could stop us from following through on our goals, dreams, and live our life with unbreakable determination of reaching that what we set to accomplish. Isn't that is what we love to do? Isn't that is what we care about? I would assume that the answer here is a strong "Yes.' So, let us not forget that regardless how slow the progress may be, how many challenges or problems we may have to face along the way, regardless of what other people are telling us of what we can or cannot do, trying to discourage us, we know what we want to accomplish in our life, we know the lifestyle we want to create for ourselves and for those that we love and care about. So, let us get after it. At the end of the day our passion, our hobby, is what we have created in our mind and we know how it would make us feel once we accomplish it. We must believe in ourselves, motivate ourselves, and never give up on our passion and our dreams.

Even if you are far from being great at what you love to do, for example, being a writer or blogger, keep working on it, keep honing your skill, keep learning, because every day we get more experienced and more knowledgeable. So, keep learning and exploring something new daily, and eventually everything will align just like you had envisioned it in its ideal state. Often, you will find yourself going against the flow, and that is ok. Just because other people do you share your desire to reach specific goals and objectives in life, it is their prerogative. If you know what you want to accomplish, that is what matters.

Going Against the Flow

What is it like swimming against the flow when river's current is moving at an extremely high speed, heading towards the ocean, and what would happen if you choose to stop and resist the flow?

It should not take much to understand that you would most likely get swept by the strong current. This analogy is an illustration of what happens when we choose to resist the expected, the norm in our personal and professional lives. That is why so few people choose to go against the flow, and instead choose to follow that what they believe is right vs. that what is expected. This small group of people choose to stand up for what they believe and trust. This is especially difficult when one is immersed in the environment where popularity and social and financial status is the only attributes that are valued and cared about. What if you are the one who does not share the same values as the rest of the larger group? What happens then? Are there any options for those who choose to live by the book, those who choose to be themselves and live in tune with their own values vs. someone who they are expected to be? Of course, there is. I am going to oversimplify here, understanding that each situation is different. However, the main concept and steps that one would take are the same.

So, what can one do when he or she finds themselves in toxic environment that is draining them of any positive energy and expectations for positive outcome they had in a specific situation and/or team environment?

First, remember that you are not a number on the company's payroll or roster. You are an individual with your own thoughts, beliefs, opinions, and feelings, and no one can take that away from you, unless you choose to give it away. There is nobody in this world like you. We all bring something unique to this world. So, do not trade your uniqueness for place in the group that chooses not to recognize your unique set of qualities, talents, and your value as a person and as an employee.

Second, do not feel like you must hold your valuable opinions inside of you. Do not be afraid to share your thoughts and opinions that bring value as soon as opportunity presents itself to you. But make sure that you are sharing with those who can do something about it and act on your feedback. Sharing your thoughts and opinions with those that do not care, not ready to listen, and/or cannot do anything about feedback and thoughts shared, would only create an empty noise in a loud room. However, those who are ready to hear you out and act on the feedback provided should be your audience.

Third, just because majority thinks that something is right thing to do, it does not mean that it is the right or the only option/solution in a situation. So, do not be afraid to express your opinion(s) when appropriate, focusing on the facts, prior experiences, and observations, and do so in a manner that is neutral in tone. Those leaders who are ready to listen and open to feedback of others will listen, and those that are not, would still do what they feel is right, regardless of opinions shared by others. Do not waste your time and energy if you feel that your feedback/opinions go nowhere, just move on.

Fourth, do not allow opinions of majority to squash the inner you. If you strongly believe that something is wrong, do not hesitate to voice your concerns supported by the answer to question "Why?" Stating concerns or problem without being prepared to provide a solution is not a problem solving, it is called complaining, and that is not what is being discussed in the article. You do not want to be viewed as complainer, but you do want to be viewed as a problem solver in all situations, both at home and in the place of business.

Finally, always remember to be yourself, the person you were born to be, and if everything else fails, go back to this step, and remind yourself of who you are. You are unique and awesome individual! So, what are you going to do today to live the life you had always dreamed of in the future?

Living Today, Living Now – What are you going to do today to live the life you had always dreamed of

Are you going to wait until December 31st to create and write down your goals on paper, then being acting on your goals on January 1st? Or are you going to create and work towards accomplishing your goals, bringing your life's aspirations and dreams closer to their fulfillment, and eventually reaching them?

I hope it is the latter. Because many of us live our lives hoping to change our circumstances, our lifestyle, our future for a better every day without doing anything about changing our present and taking action, whatever that action may be, and regardless how big or small that action is. We wait for a better time to act. But the truth is, there is no such thing as a better time. We will always be busy, there will always be problems that we must deal with, there will always be people in our lives who will support us, and those that will try extremely hard to point us in the wrong direction. So, why wait? Why not begin working on changing our present and future today, regardless of how challenging our present situation may be?

Even the smallest and easiest step or action that we can take now is still a progress and change in our present situation. The point here is not completely changing our life in one day, one week, or month, the point is to start doing something that creates a motion, creates energy and drive in creating change. Then, with time and continuous effort, goal setting and follow-through on goals set, again regardless of their complexity or size, things will begin to change, our life will begin to change and point in the direction where we want to go. It may take a long time to get there, or we may reach our goal(s) much sooner than anticipated. What is important is to keep moving forward, keep ourselves focused, energized, motivated, and focused to stay on the path that we are on, heading in the direction where our dreams eventually become a new reality.

So, how do you stay focused on the path to goals' accomplishment and not getting derailed and pulled in the wrong direction as we go through life?

1. Create a plan – Create a plan, and not just in your head, but a concrete plan written on paper that you can refer to every day. Such plan should include your short-term (1-day, 1 week, 1 month) goals as well as long-term (6 months, 12 months, 3yrs, 5yrs, etc.) goals. Make sure that your goals are extremely detailed with dates, times, and specific measurable benchmarks/success stories all outlined for you to see and follow-through.

2. Create a daily schedule – Create a daily schedule for yourself, listing action items that you will complete each day – your 'To Do Checklist.' Examples of to do items may include - a). Reading or listening to a book for 25-30 minutes each day, b). Listening to an online training of the subject/topic you are interested to learn more about or an area you would like to improve in (ex. negotiation skills, sales, etc.).

3. Create and keep a daily journal – Keep and write in your daily journal every day. Example of entries in the journal could be: a). reflections of your day; b) Plans for the day; c). Something new and interesting you have learned; d). An important thought that you have had during the day. Journaling is a way to capture your thoughts and ideas on paper, free your mind from thoughts and ideas you have been thinking about, brainstorm about everything that has been on your mind. Remember, your daily entries do not have to be complex or extensive. Make it as long or as short as you would like.

4. Follow your plan and stick to your schedule every day

5. Motivate yourself – Motivate yourself to always keep energy and drive in the high gear. Watch motivational videos, listen to motivational speakers, read inspiring success stories and blogs. Remind yourself why reaching your goal(s) is important to you now and in the near future.

Create the life you want to live today and stop waiting for a better or 'right' time. Actions that you take each day are either help you to build the strong foundation for the future of your dreams or weaken that foundation piece by piece at a time should no action be taken. The route you take and the choices you make each day are the decisions that we all have an opportunity to make as we go through life.

If today you do you have all information or resources that you need to accomplish your goal, do not let that stop you. Focus on what you do know and resources that you do have and just start, then seek out and acquire what you need along the way.

Manifesting Tomorrow Today – Focus on what you know and believe in manifesting the life and future you desire

Self-limiting thoughts and beliefs, planting seeds of doubt in our mind

Have you ever been told that you cannot do something because of x, y, or z? Of course, you have. All of us have heard such remark at some point in our life, unless you choose to continue living in imaginary world, then, of course, everything and everyone is perfect. But the real question here is, did you agree with such statement? Unfortunately, many people do listen to and agree with such statements, especially if it comes from someone they look up to and respect. But did you ever stop and ask yourself how accepting self-limiting beliefs can limit your personal growth and future, both personally and professionally? I hope that you did, because only you can truly know what you are capable of and have potential in achieving in life. So, the less we focus on what other people think of us or our abilities, then more opportunities we must find success and happiness in life.

Where did our confidence and decision-making power go?

Why do we continue to listen to opinions and recommendations of others when they do not take our wants, needs, and goals that we care about? Because it is easy to simply agree and move on with life. We do not have to prove ourselves to those that doubt us, which means less work if any at all for us. In the meantime, we are making a choice to stay where we are, stop seeking anything more, stop learning and growing ourselves. Who wins in such situation? Well, most definitely not us since we have made a choice to give up on our dreams and aspirations.

How can we change? How do we go from a place of low confidence and self-esteem to a place of winning and proving everybody wrong, by achieving everything that you said you were going to achieve?

A good place to start is to listen to what your heart is telling you, not someone who expects you to fail or question your abilities. Do what you feel will help you to move forward in achieving your goals and dreams regardless how difficult or far away the finish line may be. What is important is knowing and reminding yourself every day that you can achieve that what you know and care about deep inside of you. Nobody knows you the way you do, so do not sabotage your future by creating limiting beliefs that do not exist. Also, by accepting the statements that you cannot do or achieve something, you are telling the universe that you are not ready for anything more at this time, if ever, and close a window for new opportunities to find you while remaining where you are. You can do that or take your own future in your hands and show everyone who is or has doubted you all that you can achieve.

Listen to your won heart and mind, and not interpretation of your goals by others. You can achieve that what you honestly believe in

Please do not listen to me of what to do, listen to your heart and mind. I do not know your unique goals and dreams, so who am I to tell you what you should do. Only you know what perfect life and future looks like in your own mind. However, what I am sharing with you here are my own personal struggles and experiences I had to learn, recognize, and overcome to get crystal clear on what I expect and will achieve in life and career, regardless of what anyone thinks, says, or does, trying to convince me otherwise. Create your own motivation, do not wait for help to come, and find you. Seek out opportunities, do not be afraid of new and unknown when your current ways do not yield expected results. Change them, create your own opportunities, and go after them without doubt, because you can achieve that what you believe in. Focus on what you know and believe in. Only you know your limits and what you can achieve. As Walter Bagehot put it: "A great pleasure in life is doing what people say you cannot do"

We live in an instant gratification society and expect immediate results based on actions that we take or words that we say. However, things just do not work that way. It takes time to achieve or create something great.

Instant Gratification Society – Would you stop pursuing your lifetime dream if you know that success may be just around the corner

Where did our patience and persistence go?

Society that we live in wants and expects everything that we hope to have or achieve immediately. We do not want to wait; we want it today. Same applies to goal setting. Once we have set a goal, regardless of its complexity, we expect to reach it immediately even though our brain clearly understands that it is not possible, and that achieving set goal takes time, persistence, and organized focus. So, where did patience go? And how does lack of patience with expectations of immediate gratification affect the outcome?

Instant gratification society

Many of us, when instant gratification is not received from set objective or goal, we lose interest in whatever it may be. Take for example New Year's resolutions. We set goals for the upcoming year, understand its value to us and important of reaching them, however, because we are not seeing immediate results, and good examples here would be – healthier eating, regular exercising, debt management and budgeting – few days of weeks later we lose interest in our once ambitious and important goals and revert to the old ways of doing things. We switch back to less healthier food options, we stop going to the gym regularly, we stop working and looking for ways to reach our lifetime goal and passion in life, whatever that may be for us. So, what happened? Is the goal that we have set became less important to us? No. We simply lost interest due to lack of immediate gratification in the form of immediate results that we were hoping to see. Well, I hate to break this out to you, but most things in life worth pursuing do require time, energy, and a lot of patience before satisfactory or expected results can be achieved and visible to us. Nobody said that it is going to be easy, but it would worth it in the end. If you stick with a plan long term regardless of what you are working on or towards, results achieved when goal is attached would help you appreciate your persistence, hard work, patience, and often sacrifice.

So, when setting new goals or re-setting existing ones, stick with your plan and give it all you have got until expected results or outcome has been achieved and, yes, it may take several months or even years to get there. Just do not stop halfway or near the finish line, because, you never know how close you may be to reaching end goal and finding success. Stay tough, persistent, focused on the goal, and determined of reaching it, and you will get there. Why? Because you can, and because you deserve it. The big thing to remember is to stop wasting precious time and being building the future that you want today.

Stop Wasting Time – Begin building the future that you want today

Since we are now at the beginning of a new school year in the U.S., whether you are starting in the first grade or your senior year in college, this is the time when new expectations are set, new goals are created, and new futures are formed.

If you are the one who spent most if not all your summer months on something other than preparing for a new school year reading books, going through and reviewing schools' materials from previous year, looking for opportunities to expand your knowledge in various subjects, then you would most likely find yourself not ready or unprepared as new school year begins and would spend first few weeks or even months catching up. Is that the position that you wanted to be in? I am sure the answer is "no." However, it should not come to you as a surprise that those that prepare and spend their time on activities that help to increase the amount of information that was acquired through school education and/or self-education by investing your free time in activities that contribute to your own personal development and growth, such as: reading, writing, learning new information, creating, designing, etc., tend to be much more prepared for what's waiting for them in the future, whether it's in school or outside of the classroom. Why is that? Because individuals who take time to prepare, learn and use every opportunity available to invest their time and energy into their personal development, they typically have a noticeably clear vision and understanding of exactly what they want and expect to achieve in life now and in the future. They know and understand the importance of preparation and hard work, and instead of wasting their time on unproductive activities such as playing video games or watching tv, typically watching shows that have zero educational value, they spend that time working towards their lifetime goals and dreams.

Now, do not get me wrong, it is still important to spend some time doing fun things that a person may enjoy doing, such as playing sports, playing outside with friends, even playing video games, however, there is a big difference between spending all your free time on these activities vs. dedicating specific periods of time throughout the day on such activities. What is also important to note is that if playing sports is your passion in life and that is what you strive to do as your career in life – being a professional athlete, then you should ask yourself – Am I doing everything that I can today to help me get closer to my goal? So, in your free time are you learning more about activity or subject you are passionate about, expanding your knowledge in a particular area of interest as well as practicing it on the regular basis, or are you just saying that you do because that is what everyone wants and expects to hear from you?

Everybody says that they want to be successful in life, acquire great amount of wealth, travel the world anytime they choose, driving luxurious cars, and living in a place they've always dreamed about, but then the question is: "What are you doing about it? What steps are you taking every day to help you get closer and eventually achieving the future that you genuinely want?" I am sure that the answer to these particularly important questions is not – "I will start tomorrow or next week" or "I don't have time today." Because the answer to these questions looks something like this: "I am taking the following steps x, y, and z, every day and use every opportunity I get to help me to get closer to reaching my plans, goals, and dreams." Does your answer look like the one I just listed?

Remember, time does not stop just because you are not ready to act, it keeps moving forward. Therefore, you have a choice every day to either use the time that you have and invest it into the activities that help you to grow personally and professionally, or in the activities that are holding you back from creating the future that you say you want.

Sacrificing Time Now While Investing into the Future

Sacrificing time now while investing into the future

As I was sitting on a plane and seeing other people around me watching various movies, playing games, reading, I was tempted to do the same, especially since I have many movies that I cannot get to in my Netflix list. But, instead of falling for such temptation, and spending 2-3 hours watching shows, I remembered that by doing so I will not learn something new and would not continue to invest in my personal and professional growth, and growth of readers and listeners such as yourself through my writing. What else helps me to stay focused and keep moving forward towards my goals in life without taking any breaks to rest, even while sitting on a plane in extremely uncomfortable middle seat, with AC barely breathing, is my family and the life that I want to give them, the financial free and comfortable lifestyle, the lifestyle that they deserve.

Finding your motivation?

Most of us have something or someone who help us to stay focused on our goals and dreams. So, anytime I think about relaxing and just do nothing, seeing my wife and kids helps to set my priorities straight in my head, and instead of wasting time on activities that do not contribute to getting me closer to my goal(s), I dig in, re-focus, and continue to keep working, keep writing, and learning something new every day. In case you are wondering, yes, I am also workaholic, which some may view as weakness, however, I see it as a strength, strength that does not permit mediocracy and procrastination.

What is your motivation in life? What keeps driving you forward towards your goals?

Next time, you think about spending your time on unimportant, non-beneficial activities, think about motivation of yours and all the reasons why it is important to you. Ask yourself what you are doing every day to get you closer to fulfill your goals and dreams, whether they are yours or those that you care about. If what you are doing is not getting you to where you want to be, think about what you can do to change that, and I am not saying to quit your job, but activities that you do daily that either bring you closer to where you want to be, or taking you further away. We often must sacrifice free time now, while investing our time in building our future.

Having clearly outlined plan of action is a must when it comes to goals-setting. This important key to success is often underutilized by many, which often inhibits the progress of goal achievement.

Planning is Obvious but Often Underutilized Key to Success – Creating and applying the habit of planning in all aspects of our life

How many of you who are reading this enjoy planning? You don't have to raise your hand, just kindly check off 'yes' or 'no' in your mind. I hope that most of you have checked off 'yes,' because, I certainly did. I love planning every project, every trip, every vacation, or road trip must be planned. Why so, why do I so strongly believe that planning is something everyone must do before taking on an important action or project? The answer here is surprisingly a quite simple one – planning helps us to make what initially seemed like a complex task into an amazingly simple one.

Let us take vacation planning as an example. How many of you plan your vacations? Ok, make another note in your mind. I plan my family's vacations to the smallest detail, from transportation to food, lodging, entertainment, finances, etc. You may be thinking why go to the extreme? Why not just go and see what happens? Because peace of mind and mine and my family members' happiness is important to me. The last thing that I want is to find myself trying to do is figure out the logistics during the vacation, which often causes frustration, confusion, unhappiness for everyone involved in the absence of a clear plan.

Take for example a family trip to a Disney World in Orlando, Florida. Many people would find it an overly complex and often anxious experience, especially when you are traveling with little kids. I have personally observed several families with kids having an exceedingly difficult time, being upset, disappointed, and frustrated while at Disney World. Why? I would say that the biggest reason would have to be the lack of planning before the trip. However, when you plan everything out well in advance, know where you are going, the attractions you want to see, rides you want to ride, reserve fast passes to the rides and shows that you absolutely must see and experience, purchase meals well in advance, securing transportation and lodging, then the entire Disney experience will be very enjoyable for the entire family. So, that is why I view planning as an important key to a success and happiness for all involved.

By the way, planning does not only apply to vacations, but it also applies to virtually all aspects of our personal and professional lives. When you are assigned a large project at work, the very first step that one should take is to break down this project into smaller sub projects, and then create a plan of action – how will you tackle each sub project along the entire timeline to ensure that complete product is delivered before the deadline, while meeting and often exceeding quality controls and expectations set by the business. Remove planning out of the equation and you are stuck with big unknown, with a challenge that you do not know where to begin in handling, or if you can even complete it before the requested due date. This creates unnecessary stress and pressure placed on our shoulders. So, why not planned it out and tackle the task or project in smaller, much more manageable chunks?

I would challenge you to look at each task, project, or event as a planner. Have a plan clearly outlined listing step-by-step action items to be completed over time without preestablished guidelines or requirements should they be present in your specific situation. Write down you detailed plan on a paper, and if you choose not to user paper and pen, then have it typed up on a pc/tablet/phone, where you can easily access it at any time. Remember, if you are working on a project for your employer and you happened to run into an obstacle or a roadblock along your project journey, be sure to raise your concerns to the appropriate individual(s) proactively, especially if/when you are at risk of missing a deadline. Do not wait until the very end, as it may be a difficult and often impossible to address any of the concerns near or at the 'finish line.'

So, if you have previously viewed planning as a non-important or unnecessary task, hopefully you now see how important the process of planning is in all aspects of our lives and will begin viewing planning as necessity and part of everything you do in your personal and professional lives.

Part of planning is to pro-actively look for solutions and find ways to prevent or minimize the impact of problems and issues that will be encountered along the way. Pro-active planning and issue resolution are different from simply creating and empty noise telling people others that they want to hear just to fill the air, however, empty noise does not create solutions or resolve problems encountered.

Creating the Empty Noise

Should you be sharing your challenges or issues with others or keep it to yourself?

If that makes you feel better by sharing your frustrations or challenges that you are facing with someone else, then go for it. However, you should keep few things in mind – how you sharing your negative energy with another person affect their day? Probably not in a positive manner. And is the person you are sharing with able to help solve your problem? I believe that unless the person you are speaking with can help you in solving a particular problem, then there should be no reason to occupy their time with something they can do nothing about.

Some people share their problems or issues with others just to receive some understanding or compassion and that is great, but is the compassion received is genuine or was something said to you just to make you feel better? Does the person with whom you are sharing something person understands your problem on a very deep personal level, as much as you do? Most likely not. At the end of the day the problem still exists, or a particular issue already had taken place in the past and there is nothing you or anyone else can do anything about it now.

What to focus on vs. creating the empty noise?

You should be focusing your attention and energy towards problems/roadblocks that you can do something about, and not by sharing it with others, but by pro-actively looking for a solution or finding ways to prevent a problem from occurring in the future. Always own your mistakes and failures, do not push them over onto someone else's shoulders to deal with, even if you are simply telling them how you feel about a particular situation.

Be the person who looks for and finds solutions when problems arise, do not be the one who always talks about their problems just to share them and feel better at that point of time, and then when finding out that when the next day comes around that the problem is still there and needs attention. Always be the problem owner and solution-finder, not the complainer.

What about thoughts, opinions, and feeling of other people? What happens if your goals and values do not align to the expectations of others? Great, question, let us explore it in the next section.

Conformation to Others' Thoughts and Feelings is the Ultimate Downfall. What do You Think and Want?

Daily grind

Do you know what you want out of life? Do you know your lifetime goal or dream? If not, then most likely you are spending your time and energy to fulfill someone else's goals and dreams.

I feel that many people are so overwhelmed with life's daily challenges, obligations that we have, and just daily grind, that we completely forget about our wants, wishes that we have desire to fulfill, our dreams, things that we talk about with those that know us for who we are and where we came from. We tend to lose our voice and opinions and conform to the opinions of others. Why is that? Why is it easier for someone to conform and go along with what other people think versus following our opinions, and voicing them when appropriate?

Conform or Create a New Path?

I think the biggest reason for this is because it is simply easier to conform, then create your own path, and implement your ideas into action. Why should we try or work harder if someone has already done that and paved a pre-determined path for us to follow – the guided path, where you do not ask any questions and just follow directions given. It is easier, sure, but what do you accomplish by following preset path? Not much, if anything at all. You do what other people want and expect you to do, get paid for your efforts, whatever the predetermined rate is, and nothing more. You cover your minimum monthly obligations and repeat the same path every day. On the rare occasion when someone asks you for your opinion you are almost afraid to share because of being afraid to be held accountable for your suggestions or to add more work for yourself. Therefore, you stick to status quo and keep your thoughts and opinions to yourself, supporting others who are brave enough to say something, which may or may not be the best option for you. You are ok with it because nothing needs to be done on your part, except to continue and follow someone else's path.

Complain vs. Act?

Then you go home and complain how unfair life is and how you can never get out of the situation that you may be in, or to improve your and your family's life style – get a bigger house, purchase new car, go shopping and actually buy whatever you or your significant other wants, without checking your back account to see if there's enough money to pay rent for the apartment you may be living in and put gas into your car.

Why do we continue to do this to ourselves and continue live the life helping other people reach their dreams, versus working towards reaching ours?

We are afraid of challenge, changing our safe and known lifestyle to something new, unknown, even though this is what we secretly want. A lot of times we are afraid to put in more work than what is being asked of us. We want better life for ourselves and others that depend on us, but we do not want to put in everything we have got to get there. Well, here is the thing that you probably do not want to hear or think about, to achieve the lifestyle that you want and to have the things that you want to have, you must put in everything you have got, all your energy and time, every available minute to work towards that goal.

Learn and invest in self-development or wait?

Things do not just happen on their own where all the sudden you are extremely wealthy and happy with life; you have got to work for it. Whether it is learning everything you can about the position that you want in your company without waiting until someone comes to you and asks if you are ready to learn, which will almost never happen, or starting your own business and begin pursuing your dreams on your own terms. Whatever it may be for you, the key here is moving forward and taking steps on your own path versus path that someone else created for you.

Do not give up on your goal

You can be extremely successful working in the corporate world if you are ready to work hard to reach the position that you want to reach in the company. Sure, you may be at bottom of the organization chart and far from where you ultimately want to be, but it does not mean that you cannot get there when you choose to invest in self-development and becoming an expert in each role you hold until you reach your goal. The question is, are you willing to work for it? If so, there is nothing impossible on unachievable. Everything starts and end in your mind.

If you are ready to create your own path and start your own business by doing what you genuinely enjoy and love, then make sure you are ready to fully dedicate your time to building your business, put in extra-long days for months or even years, be ready to face obstacles on your entrepreneurial path that you would need to overcome while counting mostly on yourself. Sounds scary and uncomfortable, doesn't it? It sure does. But guess what, nothing worth having is easily achievable.

What does it take?

To reach greatness and success, you must dedicate your time, energy, and resources to get to the top. That is why very few people reach the top, because it is exceedingly difficult to get there, it requires dedication and extreme desire to reach your dream no matter what you may encounter on your path to success. It also requires you to follow what you want, think, and feel versus conforming to thoughts and opinions of others while keeping your wants and needs to yourself.

So, what do you hope to achieve and what are you going to do to get there?

Reaching the top also requires the ability to listen and look for opportunities when other people choose to ignore them and, instead, allowing noise to distract them from their goals and objectives. How does one focus on important thoughts and ideas that help us to move forward, eliminating the noise? Did you know that silence can be immensely powerful? These and many other questions are addressed in the next section.

The Power of Silence

Difference ways in which we communicate

If someone you know can hardly ever stay quiet, and instead is always talking about something, telling stories, jokes, giving suggestions, there is usually nothing that remains unsaid or private. You typically know everything that this person would say or what they think before they even open their mouth, because, you have already heard and know all their opinions, since you have heard them before. So, there is no secret, no mystery, nothing more that you want to uncover through conversation. You also know that as soon as this person begins speaking there is no stopping them, and you do not even need to ask, because they will tell you what they want to say, whether you are ready or want to hear it.

And then there are people who are patiently waiting, going through their thoughts, formulating them, removing unnecessary fluff, and only if they are asked for an opinion, that s when they share their point of view on a specific topic.

Communication preferences and behavioral styles

Big part that plays a role in which one of these groups you may fall into are the behavioral styles that we naturally gravitate towards throughout the course of our lives. Of course, there are more than just two behavioral and communication styles that exist, however, understanding what may drive one person to speak all the time, while another to remain quiet and reserved could be the starting point in creating productive and positive working, business, or even personal relationships with someone who does not respond to daily interactions the same way you do

Understanding individual communication preferences

Our brains are all wired differently, therefore, we all think and digest information differently. Also, we respond differently to the information received. Some of us who are more direct and expressive may respond immediately or start the conversation with the group because that is what we prefer, enjoy, and comfortable with – to be in the driver's seat and have the spotlight shining on us all the time. However, some of us prefer to remain quiet and reserved and are very selective of who we let into our mini world. We may not respond right away because we simply need more time to think and digest the information. So, understanding individual communication preferences and behavior styles plays a noticeably big role in creating environment of trust and mutual respect.

Cultural upbringing component in communication

The other component that plays a big part in how we communicate and interact with others comes from our cultural upbringing. In some cultures, it may not be common to speak before you are asked to do so. However, in other cultures speaking freely and openly may be encouraged and expected. Therefore, it is important to understand and respect another person's preferences and how they prefer to communicate, versus putting them in situation where they feel out of place and uncomfortable, which typically does not encourage healthy communication and relationship building.

Silence can be immensely powerful

As strange as it may sound but silence can be immensely powerful tool in any environment and setting, whether it is negotiations, delegation, management, or being introduced to a new group of people in the new environment. Listening to another person without interrupting, while taking mental or written notes could be a sign or respect and strong character. Do not feel that you always must say something when you believe that remaining silent would be more beneficial for all parties involved, especially if by you remaining silent can help to de-escalate a conflict or and to move conversation further towards a more positive and mutually beneficial outcome. Often, we say things that we do not always mean, words that may be out of place, or words that do not contribute any value. What is important to remember is that it is difficult to take something back that you have said and did not mean without any negative consequences. Words have power, so choose your words and when to use them carefully. As Mandy Hale said: "Don't waste words on people who deserve your silence. Sometimes, the most powerful thing you can say is nothing at all."

Just like words, your thoughts, opinions, and values also have power over actions that we take in life, both personally and professionally. Would you overstep your own values and principles, just to please others and to fit in, or will you stay true to your values in everything that you do, remembering what is important to you and why? Let us explore this topic and address questions raised in the next section of this book.

'Fit-In' Culture – Overstepping Your Own Beliefs and Principles in Order to Fit In

Why fit in?

Whether you like it or not but unfortunately, we all live in the "fit in" culture, and it is not just in U.S., "fit in" culture is being lived and expected in many other countries around the world. What does this mean to us? This means that there is generally an expectation for you to fit in with the crowd whether it is school, college, place of employment or even social gathering. Everyone expects you to act, speak, and look like those around you – your friends, colleague, and your peers. As soon as you are observed not following the crowd, their opinions, interests, actions, then you are viewed as someone who is out of their group or circle. So, do you want or need to fit in? The choice is completely yours. If you prefer to think for yourself, make your own decisions in life, creating your own life versus following what everyone else is doing, then the answer is obvious – no.

What are the drawbacks of following a "fit in" culture and way of life?

There are multiple drawbacks of living and embracing a "fit in" culture. Some of those reasons are overstepping your own beliefs and principles that you have acquired over many years, including the knowledge and experience acquired from your parents, teachers, and other important figures that were and are still part of your life. Because the expectation of a "fit in" culture is to do and act as everyone else around you, you are essentially expected to forget your true goals, interests, and principles just so that you fit in and get accepted by others. Any goals and plans you had become irrelevant since you are now expected to follow someone else's goals and plans. You are losing your uniqueness and individuality as a person once you decide to follow a crowd versus following you own path.

What are the benefits of embracing a "fit in" culture?

If you choose to embrace a "fit in" culture you will most likely see and experience almost immediate acceptance by like-minded groups of people, acquiring many people in your immediate circle who call themselves "friends," when the reality is that they would be happy to leave you behind show their interests or beliefs change. You would most likely experience a much smoother career advancement path with minimal roadblocks, since you will be performing everything exactly as requested, regardless of whether you like them or not. Less friction created by not expressing your own opinion, you are generally more liked and accepted by others.

Being you or being part of the crowd

We all make a choice how we want to be viewed and the life that we want to live. Each choice that we make ultimately creates a specific path in our life. You can choose to live the life powered by popular opinion and expectations, or the life that you build by being genuine and true to your goals and beliefs – by being unique and awesome you.

It is also equally important to do what you want and enjoy in life, not what somebody else is telling you that you should do. You are in charge of the life that you create, no one else, so why not go after the future that you see in your mind, feature that you want. These and other questions I will cover in the next section.

Doing What You Want and Enjoy Despite Opinions of Others. Living the Life That You Create, Not the One Created by Others

Very often we hear from other people – business leaders, friends, "coaches", speakers claiming that they know what you want and need to be happy and successful. But how? How do they know what you want, like, and need to be happy and successful in life? They do not, no one does, except for you. Only you know what you like and enjoy, what your goals and aspirations are, and what you see yourself doing in life. Now, this may not always be the best and brightest ideas that visit us, but at the end of the day that is what motivates, inspires, and brings a sense of happiness to us.

We are conditioned to think and act as everyone else because that is what is popular. For example, getting your full-time job and travel the world in search of exciting adventure and inspiration, seems to be an extremely popular thing to do now, and, therefore, everyone is encouraged to do the same. It sounds great and all, but what about commitment to your employer, commitment to your family to provide for them. How do you expect to do that if you are just going to get up, drop everything that you had worked so hard in building and travel to some remote tropical island, spending the money you do not have, after selling all your possessions to buy one-way tickets and to pay for the lodging for the first few days or weeks? It sounds like a fun vacation, but vacation from which you still need to come back into reality.

It does not mean that you can eventually do exactly what I had just mentioned earlier, but there's time and place for everything. Dropping everything by quitting your full-time job that pays your bills and buys food for you and your family, sounds like a big problem waiting to happen as soon as you run out of money and do not have any backing in the form of long-term savings or supplemental income.

It is important to think for yourself, going after what you want versus what someone else is telling you, and doing what is right for you and your family at a specific point in time. There may be a time when quitting your unfulfilled job, which only brings you frustration and negative emptions, is the right thing to do. However, when this is the case, you typically know and ready to take the next step after securing another opportunity that you are excited about and are looking forward to, because you find what you like and enjoy doing hopefully for many years to come. That is called taking a calculated risk. Why risk? Because you are taking on something new and not fully explored, therefore, there is an element of risk present. Thus, before making an important decision that affects your and lives of your loved ones, ask yourself if this is something that you want to do, despite any recommendations you might have received from other people, and if it is the right thing to do at that specific point in time.

You will hear and see many different things that sound or look good on the surface. But one thing you do not know is what had to transpire in someone's life to achieve what they have achieved, what sacrifices that they had to make to get where they are today. Before they could talk about success and happiness that they now have. So, think for yourself, live your life, go after what you want, and create your own opportunities in life.

Not sure where to start? In the next chapter topic of self-reflection and discovery is covered in great length, diving into ways that you are invited to explore to help you find motivation, drive, and determination to act in pursuit of goals and dreams that one day you hope to achieve.

Chapter 5 - Self-Reflection and Discovery – Stop Worrying and Start Doing

Do not Sweat the Small Stuff – Directing energy and attention to what matters the most

We go through life focusing our attention and energy on things and situations that may or may not matter in our lives. Why? Because it is natural to react to whatever we face and encounter on our life's path. That is just what we do, that is what we have been conditioned to do since birth. When we are little and want something that we see, we cry to let our parents and everyone else around us know that we want it. Did we really need that one thing that looked interesting and shiny? No, not necessarily, and shortly after we receive what we thought we wanted, we forget about it completely and move on to something else that we find interesting, the next shiny thing. Then, as we become teens, we focus our attention and all energy trying to fit in and be a part of a "cool" group, to be accepted by everyone around us. So, when something does not go as planned, ex. haircut that we just received did not come out exactly how we envisioned it, and that, for some reason, turns into major drama. Why? Because we worry that everyone we know would notice some imperfection in style we had chosen. However, what we do not think about is that it is all in our mind, and that nobody else may or ever care to see what we are unhappy and worry about. Generally, what we fail to understand is that other people do not really care about what is going on in our head.

Why do we spend our precious time and energy on thinking about things that do not even matter or have any major impact on what is profoundly important to us - our family and our future?

Even after we become adults, our values, habits, and perceptions are deeply engrained in our minds, and we simply do not know that there may be other, much more effective, and productive ways to look at each situation, look at it from a big picture perspective vs. completely relying on our habits and emotions that we are so familiar with. There are so many things, situations, and people who need and deserve our full attention vs. sweating about small stuff in life. By focusing our time and energy on what really matters, we could be so much more effective in everything we do, because we are able to see our plans, goals, values, and objectives clearly and organized in our mind. We can see exactly where we are, where we need to be at any given time, and people that we should surround ourselves with, people who need us and we need them. What unfortunately happens a lot is that we choose to focus on things that do not matter in the long run, we miss critical opportunities in life that do matter.

One example that I have is being so focused on our own career, growth, and creation of financially free lifestyle, that we miss out on things that take place in the lives of our loved ones – our children, parents, wives, husbands, significant others. Then, one we finally reach the point in life when we are satisfied with our career and financial success, these precious moments are no longer there and are long gone, our kids have grown, and those who loved and cared about us may no longer be there.

Is this what we want? Do we want to find ourselves in situation in our life where precious, one-in-a-lifetime experiences are gone and so are the people who were in our life when we were too busy, focusing on our own success, wants and needs, that we simply did not notice anyone else around us?

If the answer to both questions is a "no", then we should seriously take a look at our own actions each day, things that we focus on, as well as people around us, and ask ourselves: "Am I focusing on what is important, or do I worry about little things that are not important in my life today?" See what you are focusing on and worry about, see where you spend most of your time and energy each day, to understand where you are and if lifestyle or priorities adjustments are needed to focus on what truly matter to you.

This is where the question – "Are you playing to win or not to lose?" in terms of mindset come to play. The thoughts and ideas that you introduce in your mind do matter and play a big role in determining which actions you take in life.

Mind vs. Mindset – Are you playing to win or not to lose? Resetting mindset blueprint

The difference between success and failure

Why it is important to understand the difference between mind and mindset? Isn't both words essentially mean the same? In my opinion, even though both originate in your head, I feel that there is a big difference between the two, especially when it comes to personal development and growth or lack thereof. I also believe that if we understand the difference and apply our understanding correctly then this easily could be the difference between success and failure both in personal and professional arena. So, what is the difference?

Mind – overprotective and perception driven data gathering and storing repository

Mind is an engine and library where data, ideas, thoughts, opinions, perceptions are created, formulated, polished or not, and then released to the outside world. Also, this is where we store all the previously mentioned elements, plus more. This is where all important and not important information resides, often sitting in the "storage files" for many years. As we encounter various situations in our lives, we check in our mind to see if we have experienced something similar before and do we have on opinion or perception already stored that we can draw from to proceed or retreat. Our mind analyzes each experience or opportunity to see if it is safe for us to act or take advantage or stay away without risking. This is exactly, in my opinion, where fear of trying, fear of new and different, fear of change is originated and stored. Therefore, whenever we are facing change or risk, defense and protection mechanism of our mind activate and tell us to wait, pause, think about, and stay in the risk and change-free zone, because this is where we are safe, and at the same time often in desperate need of change.

Mindset – play it safe and maintain status quo, or try something new and re-shape our future

This is where mindset comes into play. We can choose to rely on our mind's interpretation of the opportunity, risk, change, and stay where we are in life without an opportunity of achieving or trying something new and different, with potential to change our life for a better, more successful, happy, and potentially life-changing future that we have always dreamed of. This is where we make a choice to play it safe and stay where we are, possibly in situations that we know, somewhere deep inside of us that we must change to see a change for a better, improve our own lifestyle, as well as lives of those who depend on us. Yet, because we are so focused on listening to our overprotective mind, we procrastinate on taking any action or deciding and choose to stand still. We continue telling ourselves that there will be another opportunity later and create excuses for our lack of action and fear of change, unknown, and risk.

Playing to win or playing not to lose, what is it going to be?

On the opposite side of the coin, those of us who choose to welcome the opportunity and try something new and different, from what we have done before, welcome the change into our life and give it our all with the expectation of successful outcome, often end up succeeding personally and professionally. Is the end result always positive? Absolutely not. There are times where despite our maximum efforts in making things work, we end up failing. However, if you have a mindset of a winner, someone who does not give up at the first sign of difficulty or failure, you will use the failure as an opportunity to learn something new, gain new experience, make changes, and try again and again until success is finally achieved. This may take multiple attempts before we arrive at expected outcome, but those that do not try typically do not achieve anything new. How would you, if you choose to stand in one place and keep telling yourself that everything is exactly where it needs to be, and if new and better opportunities do not present themselves to you than it must be how things, or your life is supposed to be? This is an example of 'minimal-wage' mindset. If you would like to learn more about 'minimum-wage' mindset, please look at one of prior blog articles – "Minimum wage mindset". Essentially, summing up in few words, it is a person who chooses to live their life in the safe and never-changing zone, despite verbally expressing their desperate need for a change, but not taking any action to trying to get there. There you go, now you do not have to search for a blog article mentioned earlier.

Mindset - a 'blueprint' of our life today and a powerful engine of creating change

To sum everything up, mindset is something that we have from the minute we are born, it's or life's 'blueprint', where's mindset is something that we create throughout our life and have an opportunity to change and/or modify if we have the courage to take a step into the unexplored territory of change and trying something new and different with potential opportunity to change our lives and get us closer to happy and exciting future. The question is, are you willing to put your fear of the unknown behind you and try to do something you have always dreamed of? Wait, do not answer this question just yet, allow your mind to convince you that this may not be a good idea and that there is really no need to change. Or, perhaps, this is your opportunity to change your mindset, re-focus, and go after your goals and dreams. The choice will always be yours to make. Speaking of re-focusing, it is important to remember that there is a difference between a focus and a wish. So, what is the difference and why does it matter?

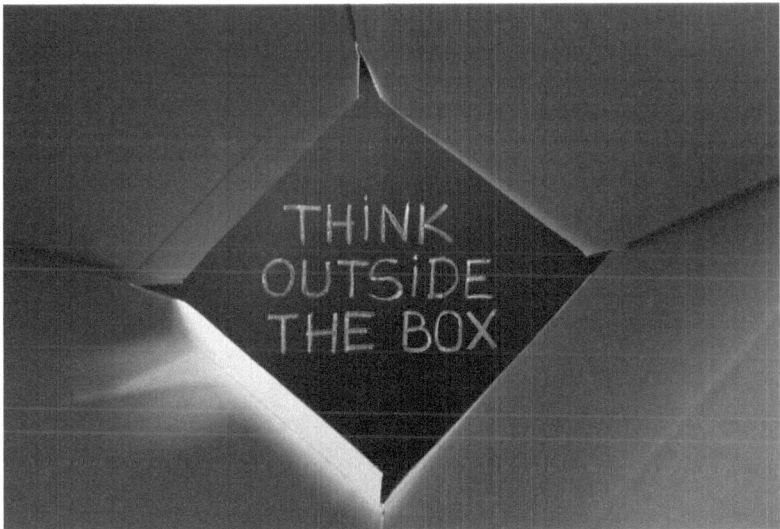

Organized Focus vs a Wish

What is organized focus and how is it different from a wish? Why should you care about understanding the difference?

It is important to understand the different if you ever hope to achieve your goals in life, instead of keeping them as goal that would never come to fruition. You can set all kinds of goals and New Year's resolutions, however, if you are not practicing 'organized focus' when setting new and/or working towards reaching existing goals, then you shouldn't expect for opportunities open up to you.

So, what is 'Organized Focus'?

Organized Focus it is your thoughts, ideas, goals, objectives, and priorities, organized in your head in a specific order, based on level of importance, urgency, and complexity.

As you can see, based on my definition of organized focus, how critical to exercise it whenever you are setting new goals or if you are stuck in the same position with an existing goal that you have set previously. Organized focus is in some way a reset point if you are unsure where to go or what to do next, as it helps to clearly prioritize your actions, determine required resources and time necessary to reach whatever you set your mind to vs. trying to expand all your energy, resources, and time on several goals at once. Without organized focus you are spreading yourself thin without giving the required attention to each goal's need before it can be achieved. It is a good skill to have overall, however, whenever you are trying to tackle multiple tasks at the same time, the quality of your product suffers as a result, plus you may be also missing multiple deadlines, because your focus is scattered vs. focused on one item or project at a time.

How is a wish different from organized focus?

Wish does not have a plan, time frame, order, or urgency. Wish is a goal without an organized focus. It is like electric car without a charge, nice to have but completely useless until you charge it. Goal without organized focus is something that is nice to have or achieve, however, the likelihood of a wish becoming a reality is extremely low to non-existent. Unfortunately, what most of us do whenever we set so called goals, which includes New Year's resolutions, we are expressing our wish and not a goal that we are committed to work towards. Because wishes are missing structure, commitment, and organized focus, typically we give up on our goals and New Year's resolutions shortly after creating them. So, next time you are creating a new goal, New Year's resolution, or pushing reset button on existing goals set, remember the key component of every goal – organized focus, otherwise, your goal would turn into a wish without a focus.

What are your thoughts about organized focus? Do you use organize focus when setting your goals/New Year's resolutions, and what results have you seen?

Also, when setting goals do not hold-on to the present, be ready to move on.

Do not Hold-On to The Present and Always Be Ready to Move On – It is Life

Holding on to the present

What does holding on to the present will get you in the long run? I will tell you; it will get you periods of frustration, worry, hopelessness, anger, and after, depression. Why is that? Why holding on to the present can, and often will lead to negativity and disappointment? Often, it is because of our inability to control what is always happening around us, good and bad. We think that we are in control, we think that nothing can happen to security of our jobs, our careers, style of living, and quality of life. But then life happens to us, things do not go as we had envisioned them, such as we lose our jobs, whether it is due to unexpected layoffs, getting fired due to underperformance or failure to meet boss's high expectations, fail to fin into the company's culture, or face unexpected and unplanned expenses – car breaking down, even though everything was working like a clock a day prior. What happens then when we are faced with unfortunate but possible situations mentioned earlier? What often happens is, instead of moving on with life and look for solutions, we choose to hold on to the current, keep our mind focused on what is happening 'inside the box', subconsciously knowing that there is nothing that we can do with what already happened. We fail to recognize that life goes on, and so should we.

Looking for someone or something to blame

I have seen so many great people missing out on great opportunities in life, because they simply were busy looking for someone or something to blame for their temporary misfortunes, and often those temporary misfortunes ended up lasing for long periods of time due to fault of our own. When one opportunity often even more beneficial with greater rewards would come. However, to notice the new opportunity, we need to be ready to see it and accept it. It can be difficult to do when your mind is filled with frustration, anger, and/or negativity in general. When our mind is closed to something new and different, and operates in constant state of worry, we tend to perform poorly on interviews when searching for a new opportunity. Why? Because, we are not present in the moment, we are not giving our 100%, and as result we sound less confident, unfocused, and unsure of ourselves and our own abilities and skills even though we know that we have them and can accomplish objectives outlined in the job description with ease. These verbal and physical queues get quickly noticed by others, such as hiring managers, and potentially great opportunity that you thought you were qualified for and wanted slips away from us. So, we go back to what we know best – blaming everything and everyone that got us to where we are today. But instead of looking for what we can to do to change, we hold on to the past, simply because it is much easier to blame life vs. fixing whatever that may be holding us back.

Life is full of surprises and challenges – are you ready for them?

We cannot and should not expect for life to always be the same without its surprises, challenges, tests, wins, and upsets. That is what makes life interesting and fun. I know, often we are faced with very tough situations which can take a lot out of us. However, any tough situation that we are or will be facing is temporary, not permanent, unless we choose to make it permanent. If we choose to remain in negative state of mind, then we should not expect for good things just begin happening to us. We must go out and look for opportunities, which could and often would help us overcome life's challenges. Any tough situation that we face in life is a test on toughness and test of our character. Will we beat ourselves up while negatively affecting those around us, or will we take control of situation(s) and turn it into a positive one. This often can be difficult to do, but it is not impossible. It takes time and energy to achieve great things in life, so be patient and never lose hope.

Every day is a new day – Life your head up and see the wonderful world around us

It is important to always remember that every day is a new day, and things change all the time, just like we change every day as we get older and wiser. Knowing and remembering this can help us to be ready for change wherever and whenever we may face it. But when you are not attached to present, and always ready for things to change with and without notice, we prepare ourselves mentally, and are not angry, frustrated, or defeated when life happens, because we are always ready for changes to come.

The Real Face Behind the Mask – Hiding our true personality and character behind fake persona build on views and expectations of others

The real face behind the mask – hiding your real personality and who you are behind fake smile

Why can't we just be who we truly are with others? Why do we need to pretend and play a character that we had created to suppress our true character, our values, views, likes and dislikes? Why do we engage in conversations that we do not enjoy, just because someone says that we must? Shouldn't we be able to decide for ourselves? Well, I think what happens most of the time is that even though we know who we are, we know what we want in life, but we simply do not want to expose that side of us to those around us, because we are afraid to appear less confident in our own abilities, we are afraid to expose our weaknesses and insecurities, we do not want to be judged based on who we are. Instead, we prefer to play in a theater where everything and everyone is ideal and perfect, and it does not matter how hard we must work to play by rules and expectations set by others, it does not matter hard we must work on suppressing our inner selves, if we make those around us happy with our actions, our looks, and material possessions that we have, even if we can afford them.

World would have been a much simpler place if everyone would be themselves, displaying sincere and genuine smile when greeting others, show honest care and genuine appreciation for things and people in our lives. Unfortunately, it ridiculously hard to tell if someone is genuinely interested in speaking with you and meeting you behind the artificial smile and personas that help protect our true selves. You may have an interesting conversation with someone, you may even find some related interests and hobbies during conversation, however, as soon as you disconnect from conversation because you are no longer interested, you then hear things about yourself that are told behind your back that you wished that were told to you in person instead to avoid false perceptions and false interpretation of your character and words.

Many people forgot what it is like to have a real conversation. Instead, they would go online and learn about you from other sources, such as Facebook and LinkedIn, or your resume. Is social media and online comments are considered a source of truth of who we are? What if someone does not have a social media profile, because they still appreciate true and genuine in-person conversations? Many would automatically create their own interpretation of someone else's life, situation, present and future in their own way whether perception that is being created has any sense of truth in it. That is how our artificial characters, our masks get created by those around us, whether we agree or not. We, however, then have a choice whether we continue to play according to someone else's rules and expectations based on their interpretation of who we are, or we show to the world who we really are, what we stand for, what we believe in, and live the life on our own terms without the mask covering our face. It is difficult to do, and that is why most people choose to continue living their entire life behind the mask vs. being themselves, being happy and enjoying every moment regardless of where they may be in life today, regardless of their social or financial status. We make our own choices of who we want to be and how we expect for others to view us every single day, and we either choose to live our life without a mask and be ourselves or continue to live inside a false image of ourselves created by expectations and perceptions of everything and everyone that surrounds us each day. How are you choosing to live your life?

What specific actions are you taking everyday to bring more good to your life and to those around you? Are you expecting for good fortune come to you based on the positive actions you are taking in helping other people, or do you feel that negative energy and thoughts had an impact on what you do and how you act towards others? Let us discuss karma as an invisible but always present life's justice system in the next section.

Karma – Invisible but always present life's justice system

Do you believe in karma? Do you believe that life has a natural way of rewarding those that do good in the world and penalizing those that negatively affect lives of those around them? If not, then perhaps you should look around more closely and see how your life or life of people that you know has been impacted in a positive or in a negative way based on specific actions that were taken by you or those that you know. I believe that life has a natural way of resolving and addressing actions that we take as people every day, whether it is doing or saying something bad or mean to intentionally hurt another person verbally and then walking away like nothing has happened while watching another person struggle to find a way out of a negative and difficult situation, or receiving unexpected reward, opportunity, acknowledgement. Why? Because some time ago you helped another person in need. That is why when one does something good, he or she should expect that someday something good and positive will happen in their own life, usually when we do not expect it. Conversely, when one does something bad, damaging, negative towards another individual or a group of people, he or she should expect for bad energy, bad karma to come back to them at some point in life. That is why when somebody hurts us verbally or act to make our life more difficult, damaging our reputation or image, just know that such negative behavior will be addressed by karma someday naturally. We do not have to engage in similar type of negative behavior just to hurt someone back, we should instead walk away from such situation or person and allow life and karma to address it someday.

What we can and should do is to focus on creating positive moments for others, helping those in need when we can and have an opportunity to do so, whether it is helping financially, by giving a useful advice, listening to another person's needs and concerns, and working together to find to overcome such concerns, motivating and inspiring someone to keep moving forward in life, and continue pursuing their goals and dreams in life. It is also particularly important to offer such help with genuine intentions to help without expecting something in return. Wouldn't you want to help someone who has done something good for you and others, just because they wanted to help and were able to do so when need was there? Someone who gave you their last dollar when you really needed it, even though they knew that doing so would create a major challenge in their own life? Of course, we would. That is exactly how karma works, it creates opportunities and situations in our life to mirror our actions that we take as we go through life's journey. So, why not live the life being surrounded by positive energy, knowing that good things will come our way, if we add more positivity in the lives of others while helping them to deal with difficulties encountered along the way? It is so much easier to go through life while having positive karma surrounding you vs. knowing that one day your negative actions or words will come back to you like a boomerang. That is why people that focus on making a world a better place for themselves and others never worry what is going to happen tomorrow, because they only see and believe in good in people, life, even if other people do not see it or refuse to see it in their actions.

So, remember, that our actions both positive and negative have reciprocal consequences. If you want good, then you should do good, that's how invisible but always present life's justice system – karma – works in a wonderful thing called life.

Also, please remember who you are as a person regardless how high you climb in life, achieving the level of success you have always dreamed of, and how low you fall should life throw a wrench in your plans.

Remembering Who You Are Regardless How High You Climb or How Low You Fall

Many if not all of us strive for a better life for ourselves and these around us – our family and close friends. But whenever we get to the top many people forgot who they really are and where they came from. Why? Because association to a different, less than exceptional lifestyle becomes unacceptable, at least that is what it seems like to me when observing individuals who have achieved great success and wealth in life. Of course, I am going to caveat this statement by saying that not every person who finds great success tries to distance themselves from their past, from who they really are. Why is that? Typically, this is because it is not popular to expose your true self, your challenging past, that may be much different from those in the new and successful circle of friends. All the sudden your old, less successful friends become forgotten, even though they were the ones who supported you and encouraged you to work harder, seek opportunities, overcome challenges, and not giving up when their support was desperately needed. What happen now? You are still the same person on the inside, but with more expensive outer image you wish to present to everyone one around. Here is the sad part in all of this, life is very unpredictable, and you never know what tomorrow holds. Today, one may be extremely successful and wealthy, then unexpected changes take place in one's life, changes in business, career, economy, etc. and all that wealth and success evaporate into nowhere. Then one begins to look around in search for support among old friends, but that support is no longer there as result of one's actions. At the same time new friends also disappear, because they no longer want to associate with someone who is unsuccessful or has necessary financial resources to maintain prestigious and luxurious lifestyle. So, you are back to where you once were, but now the support you once had is no longer there.

Now, look at this situation from a different perspective. If you find yourself in a situation where things are not going as expected in your life, you are broke, all of you once friends abandoned you, you do not see an immediate opportunity to reverse the situation where you are now, struggling to make a living every day. What many people do in this situation is to focus on the negative and everything that is wrong in their life, thereby, attracting more of the same. How can one expect for their situation to improve with such thinking and negative mindset? Here is what important to remember when you found yourself in such situation – remind yourself who you are, the strong person that you are. Remind yourself about all challenges you had to overcome in the past and how you managed to find your way out of difficult situations with strength, determination, and extreme desire to succeed. You have done it before. Yes, perhaps last time your specific situation or challenge was different, however, it was you who had to claw your way out of it and find success in what initially seemed as impossible. That is what many people forget when they are faced with challenges or after suffering a defeat in their personal and professional lives. They forget and, therefore, need to remind themselves that they are strong, and capable of achieving success regardless of where they may find themselves today or regardless how difficult their present situation may be or appear to be. Many people were able to achieve great success and wealth after finding themselves at the very bottom, and it was not because someone came and rescue them, it was them finally realizing that the only person capable of changing/improving your life and your situation is you.

The point in two, what initially seem like completely different situations, is the importance of remembering who you really are, no matter the situation, lifestyle, or the amount of success you had achieved. It is also important to remember where you came from and who was there for you when you needed support and guidance. As mentioned earlier, life is very unpredictable and today you may be standing on top of the pedestal, swimming in wealth and success, and tomorrow you may be at the bottom of that same pedestal, looking for help and a way to make a living. Lastly, remember that you have what it takes to create change in your life no matter how challenging your situation may be. Believe in yourself, have confidence and strength to keep going by reminding yourself that you can and will be successful every day, and opportunities to make a difference in your life will present themselves when time is right.

Do what makes you happy every day. Just because someone has a lot of expensive material possessions and money, it does not always translate to being happy.

Feeling Poor on The Inside with Luxury Material Possessions and Lifestyle

Have you ever met someone who has a lot of money, expensive, house, luxury cars, and great and phenomenally successful business, however, they feel poor and lonely inside? You would think that having everything that you want should make you feel great, make you feel happy and excited. However, it is not always the case. We tend to label someone who is wealthy and successful in life as someone who is also incredibly happy with life and could not with for anything more. But is that always true? I have seen many successful people who have all material possessions that they wanted and wished for growing up, however, once they have acquired everything they wanted – living in a beautiful house, driving prestigious and expensive cards, traveling around the world, there was a pig piece of something missing inside of them. So, everything looked great on the outside, but not so great inside. Why would someone who had everything feel so poor inside? Because, having all material possessions that you dreamed about is great and satisfying, this, however, would not replace how you see yourself from within, outside of the expensive image that you have created.

Leaving happy and joyful life within us

There are many people in this world who have nothing outside of bare necessities to live, and yet they are happy with life and enjoy every day to its fullest filled with joy and happiness. Why? Because that is how they truly feel inside. They appreciate what they have today and grateful for everyone who is part of their life. So, it is all about how you feel with what you have, regardless of where you may be in life, and regardless how much money you currently have. What is important to understand here is that I am not saying or trying to imply that having a lot of money and other luxurious material possessions is bad. It is quite the opposite. Having everything that you want and living a luxurious and comfortable life is great, and it is much more enjoyable if you also feel great inside about where you are, what you have, and people with whom you can share your success and inner happiness. For example, if you have an ability to help other people who may be less fortunate than you are and share your wealth with them, then not only will you feel better about yourself inside and receive a boost of positive energy and satisfaction knowing that you did something great, but you could also make a significant difference in lives of others, helping them improve their lifestyle. In turn, receiving gratitude and appreciation from those that you help can be an inspiration in taking your philanthropy efforts to make a world a better place on a global scale, while creating more wealth for yourself and helping those in need.

Benefits of positive energy

It is amazing how powerful positive energy can which has a potential to not only help someone to feel good about themselves but can also change their life for a better one act of kindness at a time. At the end of the day, it is important not only feel great about what you have, but also matching your level of satisfaction and happiness within to that outer image of yourself that is visible to those around you. Find and harness the motivation within your own mind.

What Do You Want for YOU – Finding and harnessing motivation within our own mind

Do I want to attract positivity or negativity towards myself? That is the question that we all must answer every day when we wake up and begin with our day, week, month, year, and the answer that we give largely depends on the answer to even bigger question – What do we genuinely want for ourselves?

Of course, you are going to say - "Well, of course I want good things happen for me every day," but did you ever stopped and asked yourself if decisions and choices that you make align with what you think and do? Or are you hoping for one thing – positive change in your life, your career, your financial situation, but thinking and focusing on all reasons why it is impossible or difficult to achieve the things that you want?

Unfortunately, many of us self-sabotage our goals and dreams. Instead of focusing on all possible reasons why it will happen for us and plans on achieving that one thing we have been dreaming about, we look for everything that may not be working out for us today, all problems and obstacles that we may be facing today. But why? Why not decide to only focus on what we want for ourselves and those that we care about, tuning out the noise of daily problems that we all face in one way or the other? Here is the thing, if we focus on what is wrong or bad in our life, we will only attract more of the same. So, if we are constantly negative and complain about the things that are not happening for us, we should not expect for things to magically change for a better, because everything beings and ends in our own mind. Similarly, if we focus on the positive, expecting and honestly believing that good things will happen for us very soon, even if we do not exactly know or see how, then somehow our life begins to realign in a positive direction over time.

Do not take my word for it, try it for yourself, especially if you are going through some challenging time right now. Try to change and focus your mind, your thoughts, and your actions in the positive direction. If you want to achieve something that you have been dreaming about, tell yourself that you will, but more importantly, believe with every cell in your body that you will achieve it, and remind yourself of this every single day when you wake up and before going to bed. Act, regardless how small that action may seem to help yourself get closer to your goal achievement. So, if you wish to write a book, begin writing, even if it is just few sentences each day, because any action is still better than standing still hoping for things to change. Finally, have fun with what you do. If we lack motivation or no longer enjoy what we are doing or pursuing every day in a professional, career, or personal development arena, then we should really ask ourselves – Is this something that I genuinely want for myself? Do and focus on the things that excite you and bring you a feeling of joy, happiness, and satisfaction, because, if you do what you enjoy every day, you will have no reason but to be happy and appreciate every single moment as you navigate your way through the rollercoaster of life. Remember, you are the one who is holding key to your own future.

You Are Holding Keys to Your Own Future

You are holding keys to your own future. When opportunity comes knocking on your door and you choose to ignore, it is nobodies' fault but yours. Why? Because you were not prepared for it and not ready to receive it or to pursue it. I know it probably sounds harsh, but that's reality.

This is especially important to remember that keys to your future are in your own hands when you choose to ignore what your parents trying to teach early in life. When you are young and unexperienced, the entire world is like an opened book that has been read yet. Therefore, you have an awesome opportunity to write your own story. Story where you do not necessarily have to go through some painful difficulties of facing challenges or roadblocks of life that perhaps your parents already went through, learned from them and now they are trying to teach you so that you do not have to waste your time on going through similar difficult experiences, and instead focus your time and energy on things that help you to become successful in your life.

Now, do not get me wrong, there will still be challenges and difficulties in your own life that you would need to overcome and learn from, however, if you pay attention to what your parents are teaching you, and reminding you about every single day, your path to success, however you are envisioning it, can be that much quicker.

So, what is it that we can all do when we are young to be more prepared for the real life that is ahead of us?

Read. Read every day, no matter the number of pages you read, but reading every day will help you to keep your mind focused on learning something new daily, whether you are reading something for school or for your own pleasure, fiction or non-fiction, business or comedy, reading is reading and the more you do it the better. Keep feeding you brain with new information and keep expanding your horizons.

Create. Limit the time you spent in front of tv, whether you are playing a game or watching a movie, and instead, create something new. This could be a simple as a new drawing, building something fun using materials you and find in your home, or using one of many fun projects you may purchase in stores like Hobby Lobby or Michaels.

Write. Just like reading it good to get into a habit of writing on the regular basis, daily would be best. What do write? It is easy. Get a copy of your own daily journal and begin capturing your own thoughts, opinions, and dreams on paper every day. We often choose to keep everything hidden inside of us allowing our worries, concerns, and thoughts to accumulate. But what it does it all these thoughts do not allow us to focus on anything else, because we continuously are thinking about everything that store in our heard day after day. Why not release those thoughts on paper, freeing your mind of worries and concerns, and instead download your mind with information that can help you grow personally and professionally? Plus, if you ever want to revisit your thoughts and ideas later, they will be there in your journal waiting for you.

Seek new knowledge and opportunities to grow yourself every day. Never be satisfied with what you know or have achieved, because there is always an opportunity to add to what you already know and add, enhance, or improve that what you have already achieved. If you have not achieved much yet, then look for opportunities to change where you are, focusing on where you would like to be or where you see yourself go in the near future. Again, you are the one who is holding key to your own future, and the sooner you realize that the sooner you can begin building the future of your dreams.

It is also especially important to remember, that everything mentioned above it does not only apply to school age individuals, but it applies to everyone at any stage of our life. It is never too late to begin reading, writing, creating something new, and seeking new knowledge and opportunities helping you grow personally and professionally.

Be happy and enjoy life every single day. Take care of your health and move past the obvious.

Make Time for What Matters

Take Care of Your Health and Move Past the Obvious

Do we see and understand the obvious?

I hope that we all know the obvious, that is maintaining a good health and taking care of yourself is important. However, do we understand the reason why it is so important? I think many would say, well, maintaining a good health is important because we want to feel good, we want to enjoy all the beautiful things that life has to offer, and so on. But is that really it? Is there something else, something that sums up all different reasons into one? I think so. In my own humble opinion, I believe that one main overarching reason is to live and enjoy life. It may sound obvious, but we often tend to focus our attention on the immediate, on the first things/reasons that come to our mind, such as: maintaining a good health so we can work, make money, go on vacations, grow our careers and businesses, etc. But, instead of focusing on some immediate reasons, it is important to realize and remember that good health is much more than that.

Focusing on the bigger picture vs. on the immediate, easy to see reasons

That one is a particularly important reason to maintain a good health and to take care of yourself is – without strong health many if not most other immediate reasons become irrelevant. When our health is in poor condition, all other reasons disappear and are replaced with one and only focus – get well and get well quick. However, because of our failure to maintain our health in the optimum condition and/or not choosing not to see a doctor when we are not feeling well or adhering to poor diet and lack of regular exercise, we often realize the importance of a strong health when our health state is in extremely poor condition. At that moment we recognize that something needs to change, we need to change and how we view our health and health of our loved ones. That is when we also recognize that all other little things that we thought were important to us, are no longer so important, and all we want is to get better, that is all.

Why are we waiting vs. choosing to act?

Why do we wait? Why don't we always take care of our health? Why do we continue to follow our bad habits, even though we know that some of our habits are diminishing our health day by day? It is all, because we simply choose to focus on the wrong reasons mentioned earlier, instead of the one most important reason of all – live and enjoy life every day, not some days. So, if you have not been taking care of yourself, your health, your diet, recognizing and changing habits and behaviors which do not add positive value to our health and lifestyle, then you should consider a change, change for a better, stronger, and healthier you. Start today, do not wait until tomorrow, as there is no better time to change than now.

The Beautiful World Around Us – Do not let time slip away, make time to appreciate, recharge, and reflect every day

Have you ever stopped and think about the beautiful world around us? Have you taken a break recently in your extremely busy schedule to look around and appreciate the nature around you? If you are surrounded by building without a single tree in sight, have you admired beautiful and unique buildings around you, the unique and astonishing architecture? If you live near the ocean, when was the last time you went to the beach and just peacefully sat on the sand admiring the beautiful and magnificent ocean, and its powerful waves?

I know it is a lot of questions that I ask for you to answer, but they are all centered around one thing – the importance of appreciation of the world and beautiful nature, surroundings, and people around us. Now, you may say that "I don't have time in my busy and hectic schedule to pause and just enjoy peaceful nature around me." However, if you are working in the office all day, have you taken just few minutes throughout your day to spend outside, perhaps eating lunch or grabbing a cup of coffee, leaving office environment for a period of time? If the answer is no, then perhaps you need to analyze your daily schedule and look for opportunities to optimize your work, meetings, projects that you are working on, so that you may be able to take just few minutes to step outside of your office and enjoy the beautiful day. Look, I know it is easier said than done, but if we do not create such experience for ourselves, we will continue being consumed by our busy lives without allowing ourselves to simply pause, reflect, think, and fill ourselves with the positive energy of nature.

I am sure many would agree that we often get so busy with our daily tasks, problems, issues, concerns, projects, work, etc., that we allow it to consume us completely day after day, and when we eventually find a minute or two to stop and look around, we notice that things have changed, our surroundings have changed. I often hear people saying – "I don't know where time went, but I didn't even notice how quickly summer went by and next season came." That is a great example of us being so busy that we do not even notice time passing us by, seasons changing, our surroundings changing, even people around us changing, while we are working extremely hard to create a better future for ourselves and those that we love. Why not try to combine hard work with some time for ourselves to pause and interact with our surroundings and people around us? If you can substitute driving your child to school with walking, not only will you enjoy the company of your child, learn more about what he or she are passionate about, but also spend just few minutes surrounded by nature, even if your route consists of walking through busy streets and buildings, you are still interacting with world and people around you vs. the interior of your car.

I hope that after reading this section, you thought of ways to add some inspiration to your busy life and motivated you to find ways to spend just few minutes each day enjoying beautiful world and people around you, helping you to re-charge and fill yourself with positive energy for the entire day, making it a little easier to deal with and overcome challenges and difficulties that we all face in our busy lives. Review tasks that you do every day and see if they can be optimized.

Something Must Change – Common mistakes many of us make performing specific tasks repeatedly in a consistent manner and expecting a different result

If things are not going according to set and expected plan, or you are receiving the same repetitive result, different from what you were expecting on the repetitive basis, then something must change. What you do not want is keep on repeating a specific process or action repeatedly without introducing any changes or modification within that process and expecting a different result.

Why is this important to remember with everything that we do in our professional and personal lives?

Because most people do not want to be stuck in continuous, never-ending loop or actions that lead to zero results, unless our goal is to deliver zero results. But I personally do not know any situations where this may be an objective. Therefore, let us focus on finding ways to break out of continuous cycle and create new ways of doing to begin adding value to everything we do and creating more effective and often efficient processes which help us to make progress in activities that we do daily at home and in the place of business.

How do you do that? How can one break the repetitive cycle of 'zero progress' and explore new possibilities and become the creator of change?

First, I would begin with analyzing a specific process that you are working on or responsible for managing and leading. More specifically, think about each step that you take in that process and capture it on paper or on the computer.

Then, think about steps and actions captured as part of the process flow and ask yourself an important question – "Is there an opportunity to make improvements or change specific steps in the process flow to make it more efficient, effective, and create a change for a better?" But please remember, if you are not seeing results that you hope to see, or you are not receiving results as quickly and effectively as you would like, then the answer here is obvious – typically there is always an opportunity to improve, enhance, and be creative.

If you are not sure where to start, or if you do not see where opportunity for improvement may be, why are not you ask your peers, colleagues, family members, friends, or your customers. Who would know what needs to change or improve better than people who are purchasing and using your product or service? The answer here is obvious – no one because your customers are eager to share with you what you may want to change in your daily business processes and ways of doing things, all you need to do is ask them for help. I know this can be extremely uncomfortable process at first, because you perhaps do not want to give others the impression that you need help, however, if you cannot find the best solution on your own, why not be open and seek feedback and help from those who are ready and willing to share it with you?

This works the same way when we are faced with roadblocks and challenges in our personal lives. You have been doing the same thing over and over with minimal to no result, so why not ask your family members or your friends for their input, their ideas, and feedback. Perhaps, the solution may be right in front of us, but we cannot see it because it simply takes another person to point us to it. I have dealt with so many situations where solution to a problem that I was looking to solve was right in front of me, but I did not see it, because I was busy with routine and repetitive tasks and simply did not have time to pause and analyze as I should have. As result I have wasted a lot of precious time running in the circle vs. creating new ways of performing a particular task.

So, next time when you are stuck in the process that does not yield expected results or results and rewards you were hoping to receive, pause and analyze each of your steps within a specific process and outlined above and look for creative ways in improving or enhancing the process, and most importantly, do not feel like you must do this on your own. Remember to ask for help when appropriate, because, help may be waiting just around the corner, but our ego may be preventing us from reaching for it. Often, our own ego can be our own worst enemy, so keep it in check and begin creating change in your professional and personal lives when it is needed most.

Additionally, if multi-tasking is your thing, ask yourself if it is a plus or a minus when it comes to goal achievement and performance quality.

Skill of Multi-Tasking – Is it a plus or a minus when it comes to goal achievement and performance quality

Multi-tasking can be a particularly useful skill if one can use it effectively while delivering the highest level of quality. However, very few people can perform at their best, maintaining highest levels of quality possible, and do so consistently. What can be observed most of the time is many attempt to multi-task, because that is what they believe can deliver best results with highest performance output, only to find out that performance drops after a period of time, because our mind is having difficult time focusing on multiple tasks at once and very quickly we get into a high stress and burnout.

Sometimes we are required to multi-task, trying to assign equal amount attention and focus to several tasks, projects, and other things that we need to complete. However, these situations are more of an exception than a rule, and they often take place involuntarily. For example, you are working on an important project at work, all your attention and energy is dedicated to that project. Then, one day something happens on the personal front that needs your immediate attention, perhaps, more than one thing, and, therefore, your focus and energy is now split between two, three, or more different items. Did you plan for this to take place? Of course not, but you are not expected to give your undivided attention to multiple projects or tasks at one, trying to maintain the same high level of quality between all of them, which is extremely difficult to do especially long-term. After a period of time, as some of the projects/tasks we are working on get completed, our focus is once again resets and prioritization of tasks occurs. However, this example is once again an exception, as we should not find our mind spread across multiple projects/tasks at once to maintain high quality and high output performance.

So, what can one do when they find themselves in such situation where multi-tasking between several projects, tasks, requests are required?

First, just like when setting multiple goals at ones, create a list of all your projects/tasks/requests that you are expected to focus over a period of time, including both personal and professional items to this list.

Second, prioritize your items based on level of importance and urgency. I am sure that not everything is at the highest level of important and priority, listing more urgent and critical tasks at the top of the list.

Third, assign due dates for each item on your list, including check in dates along the way. So, if you are required to complete a particular task by the end of the week, and it this is Monday, then your check in date should be mid-week – Wednesday, to reflect on your progress towards task's completion.

Fourth, create a 'To Do List' in Excel for each task with due dates, and check in dates, as well as descriptions of each project/task/request, so that you can clearly see what you are working towards and by what date.

Fifth, keep you 'To Do List' updated every day, marking your progress, accomplishments and, if needed, re-evaluation and updating the check in dates and due dates as appropriate

Sixth, once task has been completed, delete it from your 'To Do List' and move on giving your full attention and energy on remaining tasks until their completion.

Once again, multi-tasking is a useful skill, but only when that skill is used correctly and in line with your goals and priorities in your personal and professional lives. Are you skilled at multi-tasking and using it strategically to move yourself closer to accomplishing your goals in life and helping those around you?

Often, when we create plans and set new goals, a sense of doubt enters our mind, and we begin asking ourselves if we can really do what we want to accomplish, allowing self-doubt and low self-esteem to take over. Do not let doubt derail you from pursuing your goals and dreams in life. Focus on what you want to accomplish and go after it no matter what.

Constant Self-Doubt, Low Self-Esteem, and Ways to Overcome Them

In my opinion, doubt originates somewhere deep inside of you already low self-esteem, lack of belief in yourself and your own abilities.

Why do we put ourselves in such situation and such emotional and physical state?

Low self-esteem can build up quickly, it can also continue to grow and build over time, affecting everything that is happening to you negatively. The truth is, we allow doubt in our own abilities and lower our own self-esteem every time we decide that we cannot accomplish a specific task or reach a specific goal, regardless of its complexity.

Many say that something bad is happening to them because of someone else's actions, when it is them who decided to allow something negative to take place. We make decision for everything that is happening to us, whether it is something negative or positive. However, instead of owning our decisions and do something about it, we choose to transfer the blame on someone or something else.

When we decide to focus on negative and how bad everything is in our lives, we in turn attract all the negative energy to us and everyone around us. That is when you hear a person complaining that they cannot get out of from bad or negative things happening to them. By sharing all the negatives, more negative energy is being attracted to us vs. pushing it away. There is no place for positive energy to exist and develop in such environment.

The other thing that is happening is lack of positivity and excess of negativity creates more opportunity for failure, and in turn, development, and growth of self-doubt. Do you believe anything positive can come in such emotional and physical state? Of course not, only more of negativity and doubt.

Few steps that you can take to go from feeling down to feeling great again

To turn things around for a better, to replace negativity with positivity, and begin improving your self-esteem, one needs to do the following:

First -

Believe in yourself. If no one else believes in you or your abilities, do not worry about it. If you believe in yourself and know what you are capable of, that is what really matters. You are the one who creates your future, and you are the one who chooses if it is filled with positive or negative results. No one knows you better than yourself.

Second -

Do not let temporary failures or setbacks to affect your future actions. Failure is an opportunity to learn from and grow stronger and more positive

Third –

Believe in positive outcomes and they will take place. It may not be immediate, but great things will happen if you honestly believe in it.

Fourth –

Avoid negativity. Negatively minded people need someone to listen to them complaining to release their negative energy. At the end they will feel better, and you will feel worse. Be around positively minded people and you will charge with positivity from them and feel good about it

Remember, you are in control of your current and future physical and emotional state. If you want for positive and good things for yourself and others around you, then you need to believe in yourself, your abilities, maintain high level of self-esteem, and continue to spread positive and good energy to others. You are the only one who can set limits to your personal and professional growth!

What if challenges that you face along the way do not seem to have a solution, or at least the solution that you can immediately see, what to do then? Do you give up or keep fighting, moving forward against all odds?

Winning Against All Odds

Do you believe that you are capable of accomplishing something great, even though you have never done anything like it before? Do you think you can climb mountain Everest, running and successfully completing a marathon, become a New York Times bestselling author? I hope that your answer is, of course I can, because you are capable of achieving anything that you set your mind to.

If you are telling yourself in your mind that something is impossible to achieve, you are right, it is impossible to achieve something you do not believe in. In your mind you have already determined the outcome. If you think that something is impossible or too difficult, you are correct, and unless you change your outlook on a particular situation or task, it will remain unattainable in your book.

You, and only you control the final outcome

No one is capable of setting limits to your growth or control the outcome of a particular situation that you may be dealing with, only you can. So, if you are thinking about writing a book and want it to make the New York Times bestselling list, it may look as something way out of your reach, especially if you had never written anything before, but who says that it is not possible. Anything is possible. If you have extreme desire to succeed, passionate about the topic, and are willing to work hard, then even the most challenging goals can be accomplished.

Keep going until you reach the finish line

A lot of times we set out to do something that we feel passionate about and want to accomplish, put in hours or days of hard work, energy and out time, and everything seems to be going great. But, then as time goes by and passion wears off, we begin to dedicate less time and energy to keep driving towards our goal, and then eventually we simply stop. Why is that? Why do we give up on our goals so easily? Of course, the reason may vary from person to person, but in most situations, it means that task or goal you were working towards before was not critical enough to you, and therefore, was easily forgotten. You may say, well, there were reasons x, y, z that contributed to you abandoning a particular goal, but the reason underlying reason is that you may no longer be interested in what you were working on or, perhaps, you found it to be much more difficult and time consuming than you thought initially.

In this instance you had chosen to stop before the finish line was reached. The crazy thing is, we often do not know how close we may be in reaching a particular goal of ours. It may be so close that one additional step, one additional attempt, one more failure may lead us to success. But, because we choose to stop halfway, we would never find out how close we really were. So, what

I am trying to say here is that if you genuinely want and need to accomplish something, then do not stop and give up on that goal when you may be one step away from the finish line.

Give your 100%

Successful goal accomplishment requires 100% of your effort and energy. You may say, well, I always give my 100% in everything I do, but what I find that this is often too far from the truth. We say that we did everything we could, but if that is the case then why wasn't a goal accomplished? It was not accomplished, because we perhaps were willing to give it all, give it our 100%, but wanting and doing are two different things. Many people want to be successful, want wealth and fame, but only few are accomplishing these goals. Why? Because, one group wanted to get there, and another group made a firm decision to reach their goals and give their 100% no matter what. Remember, only you can set limits to your growth, success, and future.

Takeaways

Do not set limits to your growth and future. Give your 100% when the decision is made to reach a particular goal

Do not give up on your goal no matter what. If you said that you will accomplish something, then accomplish it, do not create the empty noise

Do not stop half-way on your journey. You may be much closer to the finish line than you may think, so keep going until the finish line have been crossed

Do not commit to a challenge or goal if you had already made a decision in your mind that it is impossible to reach. If you have made such decision, you have already lost. Only commit if you have made a decision to win, regardless how challenging it may seem

Do not be disappointed if it takes you longer to reach your goal than you anticipated. Be persistent, keep going, and eventually you will be rewarded for your determination and hard work. Believe in yourself.

What happens if/when we find ourselves in the place of desperation and uncertainly? How do we find motivation to face our fears and find strength and energy to crash any hesitation and fear created in our mind? Let us explore such situation in the next section of the book.

The Place of Desperation and Uncertainty Can Be Scary or Extremely Motivational

What happens when we are in desperate state?

Typically, when we are in desperate situation, we start looking for a solution, something that can help us to solve our immediate need or get us out of the situation that we may be in. During this desperate search, we begin exploring all possible solutions and options, something that we have not explored before. We are willing to take higher risks because there is really no room to fail, the only way that we have is up, and potentially finding success. Could we still fail? Of course, we can, and in many situations we do fail. However, because we are in desperate state already, we keep trying and searching to find the winning option to our roadblock.

Does every person succeed in locating a winning solution?

No, and in many cases, it is not due to lack of solution available, but it is likely due to one giving up too early and stop trying. That is why it is critical not to give up, regardless how difficult or unpromising the situation may be, but instead keep going forward, exploring all possible and previously ignored or unexplored options until the solution is found.

What is in it for me?

What does usually work well when we are in a desperate state and cannot seem to find a solution to whichever critical problem or situation that we may be dealing with, is somehow, someway uncovering the strength, energy, and determination that we did not think that we had before. This is in turn encourages our mind to look for plans x, y, z versus already tried a, b, c…, to get out from the desperate situation that we may be in. In many cases we find the answers that we were seeking, and then look back questioning why we did not see this solution before. The answer is usually quite simple, we got comfortable and stopped utilizing our critical thinking, resourcefulness, and relationship built over time.

Ask to understand

It is extremely important to always ask questions to understand where you are, what is happening around you in your business and/or situation to remain in control of your future, keep driving the business forward, and not falling in the place of desperation.

However, if you are in a place of desperation now and are dealing with uncertainty, remember to stay positive, focus on the main goal, do not give up and keep trying and searching for a solution until you come out victorious. You can accomplish anything that you set your mind to, the question is how hard you are willing to work for it, even if sometimes you may need 'helmet and face mask' to face challenges in front of you.

Helmet and Face Mask May be Required

We often face situations that from initial look appear extremely challenging to overcome. However, every situation, regardless of its complexity, has a solution attached, the challenge is to dig deep and find that solution. In some cases, to avoid being hit in the nose by life, while searching for a solution, we may need a 'helmet and face mask' to protect ourselves from various roadblocks along the way.

The thing is it is all about how you look at any given situation. You may say that there are some situations which have no possible positive outcome, or you may say that clear outcome may not be in plain sight and you must really look for it with magnifying glass. But, at the end of the day there is always an outcome. In some situation it may differ from our expectations, but less favorable outcome is still different from no outcome. There is always an opportunity to keep seeking the desired outcome until you are finally able to achieve it.

Do not be afraid to reach out for help

It is important to remember to keep those around you, your close friends and family, in mind when support and feedback is needed to re-focus. Often, we simply need for someone that we trust to listen to us vent, to release that pressure that has built up inside of us over time. Once, that is done and we laid out everything that we may be dealing with and obstacles that we may be facing, we can look at any challenging situation from a different angle and different, positive perspective. So, do not hold everything inside of you, do not let stress build up, just remember that there is someone who is always willing to hear you out regardless how busy they may be.

Positive and optimistic outlook is the key

Always remain positive and optimistic. Do not let negativity to get inside of you, because negativity spreads very quickly and adds a toll to our emotional and physical state in the form of stress. It helps to stay away from the source of negativity whenever possible. Instead, taking nice walk and clearing your mind from any negativity you may have involuntarily accumulated, while listening to some music that you enjoy.

It works the same way when you receive a very direct written communication via email or text. Before responding immediately, just walking away from your desk for few minutes, because, when you return the communication that you had in your mind earlier will no longer be applicable, and more positive communication will be delivered. As one of my previous bosses used to say: "be a bigger person."

Remember, you a-re in control how you view and feel about any situation. So, if you believe that something is 'unfair,' all that means is that you are looking for an excuse not to act.

Remove the Word 'Unfair' From Your Vocabulary

How often do we hear people use the word 'unfair' in their day-to-day conversations, or how often do we use it when interacting with others? I would say regularly, wouldn't you agree? We expect from people with whom we interact to change their opinion or decision on something. Do they? I have not really seen any situation to be turned around when someone used the phrase 'it's not fair'. What you typically hear in return is detailed explanation as to why it is 'fair' based on facts, situation, or arguments presented at that point in time.

What perception the use of the phrase 'it's not fair' may create?

When someone responds to the direction or assignment given with 'it's not fair,' the perception given to the person giving direction may be that this person is not ready for such assignment, needs more development or training, has love confidence or competence, and prompts the desire to re-assign the task or project to someone else. The original recipient of the project in question may be deeply knowledgeable and competent to handle the task, however, the use of 'it's not fair' may give a completely different message, and in turn, an opportunity to shine and show skills present may slip away rather quickly. Is this the type of reaction we are looking for from our colleagues and business leaders? I do not believe so. If your goal is to learn and continue developing personally and professionally, then you may want to think twice before responding with 'it's not fair' statement.

Be ready to face 'unfair' life situations

We cannot and should not expect for life to be 'fair' to us and must be prepared to face life challenges when necessary. As John Spence said once: "If you expect the world to be fair with you because you are fair, you're fooling yourself. That's like expecting the lion not to eat you because you didn't eat him." This works the same way in business, there should be no expectation of fairness, instead, there should be mutually agreed to terms and success measures on by both sides, to ensure that business and revenue goals are met by both parties individually while working together as a team.

When the word 'fair' may be used?

The word 'fair' could also be immensely powerful when used in the proper context. One way to use 'fair' is when creating mutually agreeable terms between two business partners, to ensure that both parties agree and feel good about the agreement itself. For example: "To ensure that terms we agree to are fair and in line with our mutual business goals, the following points need to be clarified…" The use of the word 'fair' in such context creates a sense of trust and respect by both parties as you are not only considering own interests but also interests of your business client or partner. You are stating that being 'fair' is important to you, versus just getting the deal done regardless of consequences.

Self-reflect when you feel that someone is being 'unfair' towards you

When you ever feel as if someone is being 'unfair' to you, remember the quote about the lion mentioned earlier, and ask yourself why the person in question should be 'fair' to you. Ask yourself the following questions - why is this individual act a certain way towards you or why specific words are used that make you feel 'unfair' while interacting with you? Perhaps, it is not the other individual who is being 'unfair', instead, something that you are doing or saying that causes them to act in such manger or use certain words during interaction. In most situations by going through self-reflection exercise you will uncover situations, words, or actions created by your which allowed a specific person to think and act as they do. Here you have an opportunity to correct any prior misunderstandings and establish productive and positive working relationships with other people.

So, what is it going to be: "life is unfair", or "I create the positive life I live in, not situations or people I encounter in life?" As always, the choice is yours.

Focus on what is important to you and take action to achieve that what you seek, stop telling yourself that something or someone is unfair and stop wasting time in a constant 'worry state of mind.'

Stop Wasting Time in a Constant 'worry state of mind'. Focusing on What's Important to You in Life Every Day

Have you ever asked yourself how much time you are wasting on things, situations, and people that do not contribute any value to you or what you are going after in life – your goals and dreams? If I had to take a guess, the answer is most likely 'no'. Why? Because that is many of us do, we worry about things that do not contribute any value or help us in any way all the time, we focus on situations and temporary problems, which are not even our problems. Then we spend hours, days, or weeks, thinking about these situations and how we were unable to do anything about them or help in any way, because the situation and resolution were simply outside of our control. It is not that we ignore others when they come to us for help, we do try to help or guide other people towards a solution. However, when something does not go as planned or when the person, we attempted to help chooses not to pursue the solution we had recommended, we continue to think and focus on the problem, even though it has nothing to do with us. We spend great amount of time thinking and focusing our energy on these things, which hurt us in the long run. We waste precious resource, which we will never get back – time. Time goes past us where we are spending our energy and resources on acquiring negativity, frustration, anger, and disappointment, because things just do not go as planned.

Who cares if you missed your boat on purchasing some freshly caught crab?

Here recently, I have decided to go to a local fish market which sells freshly caught fish, shrimp, crab, and other sea inhabitants. To purchase some fresh crab, you must be in the line to the fish market at 3:30-4am, if you want to get your hands on the catch of the day, more specifically crab, as they do sell out very quickly. So, instead of leaving my house at 3am, as I was supposed to, I left around 4:30am, just to make it to the market by 5am, keeping in mind that fish market opens at 5:30am. When I got there the 'crab' line was already long, as expected. However, I took a chance and still got in line. Fish market opened in 30 mins and line started to move. In short period of time, 30 mins to be exact, and with a lot of anticipation, I finally crossed the line into the market and approached crab stand, just to find out that they had just sold out of crab. This is when I noticed a great example of people sharing their frustration, anger, and deep disappointment with others, even though they knew that there is nothing that can be done, unless of course they are willing to go out to the sea on their own in hopes of catching some crab. There were a lot of people standing in line behind me, same people who arrived after 5am when they knew that the time that they needed to be in line was 3:30-4am.

So, the whole time they were complaining to the fishermen, I was thinking why everyone is upset even though it was their fault for showing up late to the party. It is like keep swinging your punches after the fight has already ended. Nothing will change in this situation, so why worry about it, why spread your frustration to people around you, affecting their day in the negative way. All you must do is let it go right away and move on with life, focusing on something that you can still have an impact on versus wasting your time on things or situations from the past.

Going back to my story. While we were still in the line of complainers, I smiled at my son, he smiled back, and we proceeded to move forward, purchasing some awesome fresh fish, enjoying the moment and beautiful morning. Then, we drove back home with the catch of the day and smiles on our faces.

Why am I sharing this story with you?

Because I want to help you see that there are so many beautiful and important things and people in our life for us to invest our time and energy with, versus focusing on things that are outside of our control, situations from the past, people from the past, and anything or anyone that is not adding value and positive energy into our lives. Cherish every moment with those that you love and, enjoy your life to the fullest extent possible every day.

Now that you know how to find motivation in challenging situations in life and inspire yourself to keep pursuing your life's goals and dreams, next let us dive into nots and bolts of personal development and discover a life-long student within you. This and much more is discussed in great length in the next chapter.

Chapter 6 - Life-Long Student Never Stops Learning – How To's of Personal Development and Leadership

An Unspoken Requirement of Knowledge Seeking – Building extreme determination to succeed in life no matter what

Nature of 'false commitments'

Some way we often make false commitments to learn something new each day, and we tell ourselves and others that we are committed to that goal no matter what else may come up in front of us. However, how long does our commitment to learn and invest into our personal and professional growth lasts? In most cases not long at all. We try for few days, we seek different tools and resources that we can draw new information and knowledge from, but then reality kicks in when we realize that instead of reading or listening to books, listening to new personal development courses through many digital channels available online today, we can just watch a tv series instead that contributes zero benefit to our knowledge and growth, play video games, because, they allow our mind to escape reality into imaginary world where we can be whomever we choose to be without a need to learn, even if it is just temporary. Next thing you know, our goals and commitments that we have made to ourselves are long forgotten and have been traded in for the temporary distractions of life. Then we realize another thing that it is difficult to get back to the same learning-focused mindset that we once had. I am certainly not saying that starting over is impossible, but it is difficult, especially when we have a history of not following through on our commitments.

What happens when we choose to ignore the unspoken but very real requirement to learn and grow ourselves every day?

Ignoring the obvious – education and 'care-free' learning

What typically happens when we choose to ignore the obvious? Let us say that we choose to continue our education and go to college. Everything is great at first, we meet new people, get our books, move into our dorm, find where the library is, go to our first few lectures, and then, short time thereafter we realize that we have freedom to spend our time however we wish and, because, it's much easier and more fun to simply play and do nothing without engaging our mental resources where long hours of studying are not required, we give up on our own commitment to learn and grow and lose years of precious personal and professional development opportunity. Then when we finally realize that we cannot get that time back, unfortunately same opportunities of care-free learning may no longer be available to us. Do you really want to be in such situation early in life? I do not think so.

Personal development and career growth. How the two relate?

Similar thing happens when we join a workforce. In our resumes or during job interviews we say that we are hungry to learn and enjoy learning new things to continuously grow and develop ourselves. Then, we get hired and begin working. First few weeks, maybe even months everything is going well, we are learning our role and various responsibilities, and then reality of hard work, determination, persistence, and continuous learning requirement kicks in. This is where status quo is no longer acceptable, where we are expected to seek knowledge, learn new skills, enhance existing strengths, and work on addressing our weaknesses. If you have a mindset of "I'll take it easy and wait for opportunities to find me," how long do you think that your adherence to the 'always-learning requirement' would last? Maybe few days, maybe a week, and then we realize that continuous learning and commitment to our growth requires strong discipline to keep going and not giving up no matter how hard it may get. It goes without saying that expectation of desirable career growth and achievement of great or even significant enough accomplishments are highly unlikely if not impossible.

Takeaways

Continuous learning, strong desire for seeking and acquiring knowledge, and extreme commitment to our personal growth and development are all required ingredients for long-term success and happiness. Also, remember that by listening more than you speak, you will learn more every time, it is basic communication essentials that we tend to often ignore.

Speak Less Listen More – Basic Communication Essentials That We Tend to Often Ignore

What is in it for THEM

Have you ever noticed yourself taking so much time speaking that even you forget what the original thought or question was? Or, because you speak so much, since you like to hear to hear your own voice, that you lose the attention of the person or a group with whom you are sharing the information? No one cares what you say or about your opinions unless it solves or addresses some type of question or problem for them. Unless this is the case, you may have listeners nodding their heads, but nothing is being heard, and they most definitely not paying any attention to you or to what you are sharing, can cannot wait to get out of that conversation and/or meeting. So, when you find yourself in such situation, try this, stop talking and see what happens. To give you a sneak peek, what you will notice happening is that people will all the sudden begin sharing their thoughts and ideas, and/or being asking questions.

Dialogue, Not Monologue

So, what is the purpose of the productive conversation and/or meeting? Typically, the main purpose is to learn or to relay new and important information, not for you to speak for 90% of the time, without allowing other people to ask questions or express concerns. You want to have a dialogue, not a monologue. If the purpose of the meeting or conversation not to brainstorm, then you should ask yourself – do you need to have a meeting or conversation after all. Why waste someone else's time if you do not intend to listen to them and hear that they have to say.

How to have an effective conversation

The basics of an effective communication is simple – speak less, listen more. Allow another party to share their thoughts, ideas, opinions freely and without interruptions from you. Listen more and take notes, whether mental or on paper. Show another person that you care and are paying attention. At the end of conversation, feel free to ask follow-up questions based on notes that you have taken, and ask for clarification points as needed. As tempting as it may be sometimes to interject you point of view while someone is speaking, do not. Wait until they are done before sharing your point(s) of view. If people with whom you are speaking feel that they are being heard, they, in turn, will listen and pay attention whenever it is your turn to speak. It is amazing how this works, and all we should do is stop talking and just listen.

Believe it or not but you do not know it all. Therefore, to keep learning and developing personally and professionally, we must remember about the importance of silence when it is appropriate, while giving your undivided attention to people around you versus letting your ego to control the conversation. Speaking of listening and learning, you can find time to listen to one or more books per month using Audible service by Amazon. So, no more excuses.

Five Things I Love About Audible by Amazon

If you have heard of Amazon, which I hope you did, then you must have heard about Amazon's platform for audiobook and Audible Originals titles to listen through application called Audible. After installing Audible app on your mobile devise or tablet and enrolling in a paid subscription plan, you are good to go, and can begin exploring massive library of Amazon audio books and Audible Originals titles for your enjoyment.

Here are 5 reasons why I love Audible.

1. It is an affordable way to immerse yourself into thousands of books to choose from Amazon. With enrollment in Audible paid service, you receive 1 purchase credit each month with which you can purchase a new audiobook that you are interested in reading. Whether it is fiction, non-fiction, business, personal development, you can easily find it in Audible store.
2. Great looking and easy to use Audible app. It is extremely easy to navigate and use Audible app and begin creating your own audiobook library.
3. Offline Listening. If you travel as of as I do, or commute to work every day for long periods of time, you may run into spotty cell reception. With Audible you can download your favorite book on your mobile device and listen to it in offline mode without a need of a cell signal reception. This can be especially convenient when traveling by plane where WIFI may not be available or is too expensive. With Audible, time commuting passes by very quickly with benefit of learning something new by listening to an awesome book.
4. Ability to share your accomplishments and progress of the books that you have completed with your friends and other Audible listeners. You may also share your feedback about each book you have read.
5. Audible provides an ability to learn and grow at a time and place that is the most convenient for you. So, no more excuses of not having time or ability to read an interesting new book each month

So, what are you waiting for, go and check out Audible by Amazon, and you will be asking yourself – why I did not know or have not tried this awesome service sooner?

Learning and personal development does not stop with reading books either, one must be able to read and easily recognize when perception that you indet to give of yourself and of your true and genuine character to others. So, how can one correct negative or incorrect perception?

Perception Management Techniques. How to Correct Negative or Incorrect Perception

What is perception?

Perception is essentially how one sees, thinks, or understands another person or situation from their own point of view based on interaction with or observation of a specific person or situation.

Why perception is such an important part of a leadership and personal development?

Have you ever met someone for the very first time and after speaking with that person as well as observing how he or she acts around you and other people, you had created your own personality and behavior profile of this person in your mind? That is exactly how perception is created, whether it is accurate or inaccurate.

The reason why it is so important to make sure other people have accurate perception of you is, because, you want for your actual personality traits to be known and understood, as well as your true intentions to be considered when important business or promotional decisions are being made and based on facts versus inaccurate perception that other people may have about you. Additionally, incorrect perception creates tension and sometimes negativity, which may lead to negative effect and reduction in overall productivity of a business.

Why do we do it? Why do we create potentially incorrect perception of someone based on our observations versus simply speaking with a person in question and asking questions to learn more about them and to address our perception concerns?

In most situations we are simply afraid or uncomfortable in approaching another person whether it is our colleague or business leader with no specific reason at all. Instead, many people choose to fall back on their original perception as their reality, whether it is accurate or not. That is how incorrect perception of you or someone else is created.

Now let us look at perception of you in the eyes of others (ex. Your colleagues, clients, business partners, etc.). How would you feel if someone had a negative or incorrect perception of you? I am sure that it would not be an incredibly good or positive feeling to have.

I have been there and know that it is uncomfortable to be viewed from incorrect perception, especially if you are unaware of the misperception and unable to address it right away.

How does one learn about and addresses incorrect perception of himself or herself and what is Perception Management?

Steps that one may take to learn about his or her perception:

Ask for open and honest feedback about you from your colleagues, business leaders, employees during the business meetings and/or individual meeting sessions

Be open to and willing to receive direct and constructive feedback during these sessions. It is one of the most important steps in successful feedback uncovering.

Do not interrupt or try to address incorrect perception with the person speaking during the meeting

Encourage additional and detailed feedback

Take notes of the information that is being shared with you

Conduct regular feedback sessions to encourage continuous feedback for you

This could be a quick 15-30 min sessions held once per month, or whatever time frequency works best in your situation

When you are meeting with your business leader, employee, or colleague for the very first time, you may discuss your preferred communication and leadership styles, and at the same time encourage an open feedback from the person you are speaking with to be shared with you in the future

What are the ways to an effective perception management?

Focus on the feedback received versus your ego

Do not react negatively to the constructive feedback shared with you by others when it comes to incorrect perception

Be open and willing to receive negative feedback

Ask for clarification or examples for an additional clarity and to make sure you are focusing on addressing the perception shared with you versus the one you thought that you have heard

Do not interrupt another person while they are sharing their perception with you, instead take good and detailed notes

After you had received the feedback from an individual or a group, then address incorrect perception with them by sharing your true intentions or specific behavior(s) observed

Thank the person or group for sharing their valuable feedback with you and encourage open feedback going forward

Set up regular feedback sessions with your group or individually to show your commitment to an open communication

Always be mindful of the perception of yourself that you may be giving out to others to ensure that perception shared is the perception that is intended to be shared

Act on addressing incorrect perception after it was shared with you and explain to the individual or a group who shared the feedback on how you are planning to address specific perception behavior observed

Ask others for help in addressing and overcoming your areas of opportunity

Before you take a particular action, think about how your action can be perceived by the person or group who is a recipient of such action or information

Do not assume that everyone receives the correct perception of you and the one you intend to give. Ask for feedback.

Smile more often, regardless how overwhelm or busy you may be

Spend some time interacting with you employees daily. It does not have to be long, just few minutes per day.

Be available for questions and feedback. Keep your office door open, when at all possible.

Leave your personal problems or worries at home, do not bring them with you to your place of business

Lead by example. Do not ask your employees to do something, unless you are willing to do it yourself, when needed.

What if you are not comfortable to speak in public? What just a thought of presenting and speaking in front of other people gives you chills? Not to worry. In the next section I will cover some ways that can help you to overcome the fear of public speaking.

How to Overcome the Fear of Public Speaking

Let me start of by saying that I was extremely afraid of public speaking several years ago. Partially, this was due to me not being fluent in English language at that time and not being able to explain myself clearly in front of an audience, regardless of its size.

Then in college I enrolled into a public speaking class, which put me outside of my comfort zone. I did not have a choice of being afraid or present in front of the class, since I had to receive a good grade to earn necessary credits for the class. Therefore, I had to learn to put my fear of public speaking behind me and to move forward.

How did I manage to overcome my fear of public speaking, and transitioned from being afraid to enjoying presenting and speaking in front of audiences of any size?

Step 1: Practice and more practice!

I am sure that you have heard a saying that 'practice make it perfect.' Same with public speaking, the more you practice the easier it gets.

Before you present in front of an audience, practice your speech in front of a mirror several times. Yes, I know that it will be awkward, but do it. You will notice how many times you will stumble, forget words, even when no one is watching or listening to you.

It is all about practicing your craft until you are no longer making mistakes, do not stumble, and sound confident.

Step 2: Begin increasing the size of the audience gradually!

Start off with a mirror, then ask your close friend or family member to be your audience. People that you know and trust will be honest with you and share any improvements or adjustments that you need to make in your presentation. Ask them upfront to share all feedback that they may have after the presentation.

After the feedback is received, incorporate appropriate adjustments before proceeding in increasing the size of your audience.

Once you are ready and had practiced your speech several times with people that you know and trust, then begin expanding the size of your audience to larger groups, if possible. Sometimes all you may have is your immediate audience such as your friends and family members, and that is perfectly ok. Practice until you feel noticeably confident in your delivery. However, if you have ability to expand the size of your audience, then do so. The more feedback you can receive, the more you can practice your speech in front of larger audience, the easier it would be for you when presenting in non-practice environment.

Step 3: Become an expert in the information that you are presenting on!

You should be so knowledgeable in the information that you are presenting on that you can answer any question from an audience and provide highly informative and accurate response with strong confidence.

One way to become a subject matter expert is by conducting very thorough and detailed research, utilizing all sources of information available to you. Make sure to study and understand information derived as part of your research. It is not enough to simply read about a particular subject, you must fully understand what you are reading about so you can teach others.

IF you have conducted extraordinarily strong research, read, and understand all the information gathered during your research and preparation, then you should be able to present this information with confidence and answer any question that may come your way from an audience.

By following ALL three steps discussed here in its entirety, you should have nothing to fear with regards to public speaking.

Here is why:

You have conducted incredibly detailed and thorough research on the subject that you will be presenting on

AND

You are a subject matter on the topic that you are presenting on to the point where you can answer any question that will come your way and be able to teach others

AND

You had practiced and perfected your presentation in front of an audience, starting with just yourself in front of a mirror to family, friends, and people that you know

These are necessary ingredients to help you overcome a fear of public speaking.

Remember, the more you practice, the easier it should become. It will be uncomfortable at first, but each subsequent presentation should and will get easier, until the point when you are looking forward to presenting in front of others and genuinely enjoying the challenge.

What if it is not the fear public speaking but procrastination is what is holding you back from achieving your goals? Let us learn more about procrastination and how to stop unproductive procrastination before it begins impacting your daily life.

How to Stop Procrastinating

Have you procrastinated before? I know I have, many times. Sometimes I procrastinated because I chose to do so, and other times I procrastinated because I was unable to start or complete a particular task not by choice, or at least I thought so. That is why I believe that there are at least two types of procrastination that many of us had practiced or observed before – intentional and unintentional.

What is intentional procrastination?

Intentional procrastination is the most obvious type and the most visible. We can generally tell when someone is procrastinating, because they choose to do so, and it is usually due to lack of desire to complete a particular talk or assignment (ex. not completing homework due to taking on another activity such as playing video games or spending time outside). In this situation, we choose not to do our homework because we have made a conscious decision to play video games or go outside, in hopes of completing assignments given at a later time. We all know how the rest of the story goes, we play video games until it is way too late and go to bed to get few hours of sleep before it is time to get up and get ready for the next day. Homework usually does not get completed and, in turn, we get in trouble at school/university with our teacher/professor, or even worse, we fail a test, which results in a poor grade. I know that these examples are centered around schoolwork, however, these examples could also be applied anywhere else – work, business, etc.

This is one of the obvious examples of intentional procrastination, where we make a choice not to do something at this time, and instead put it on the backburner.

What is unintentional procrastination?

Unintentional procrastination is when even though you may have a desire to complete a particular task now, but due to specific circumstances unable to or unwilling to do so.

Example of unintentional procrastination could be a desire to publish a blog post or podcast episode, however, due to lack of internet or PC or both, you are unable to do so right away, and having to delay publishing until the next day, or until you have what needed to accomplish this task. Many would label this as lack of resources with present desire. However, could you find a way to publish a blog or podcast even though you may not have all resources or tools needed? I think so. Everything boils down to having strong enough desire and willingness to act despite minor roadblocks. If you do not have the tools needed, perhaps you know someone who does, and you can reach out to them for assistance. If you are traveling on business, and do not have internet or fast enough WIFI in your room, there's always internet available in the hotel lobby that you should be able to use. There are ways to accomplish a task, you just must want it bad enough.

Is procrastination always bad?

Not necessarily. Sometimes procrastination could lead to greater discoveries or more complete results. I am not saying that procrastination should be utilized on the regular basis, but occasionally, if used correctly, could be a way to complete a specific goal while delivering a complete product. Why is that? Sometimes 'strategic procrastination' allows more time to complete a particular research without worrying about getting it done as soon as possible, which may be incomplete, or lack needed context. Instead, appropriate amount of time is spent on a specific task to ensure it is 100% complete to your satisfaction and all necessary requirements are met. When writing a blog, podcast, book, etc., 'strategic procrastination' allows for more time to think about the topic, complete several practice drafts, until it is perfect and is ready to be published.

There is a fine distinction between 'strategic procrastination' and intentional procrastination, even though they appear to have a lot of similarity. With 'strategic procrastination' even though you are placing completion date on pause, you continue to conduct research, idea generation, and brainstorming during the 'pause phase.' Where is with intentional procrastination, you are engaged in other activities not related to a task given or goal. Example: goal is to complete writing a book, but instead, you are watching TV.

How do you stop intentional and unintentional procrastination?

Create a list of all tasks/items that you need to complete if there is more than one

Prioritize your tasks based on level of importance and/or their due dates.

If you only have one task that you must complete, then prioritize it against other activities that you WANT to do at that specific moment

List possible outcomes/issues for each task if it was to be placed on hold delaying its completion time

When you only have one task that you need to complete and you have it prioritized with other non-important activities that you want to do, then ask yourself if your wants will still be there the next day and if they could wait, allowing you to complete the task you must complete today.

In most cases you will find that other less important things can wait

Think about and visualize in your mind how you would feel once you have completed what is needed to be done, and all you must do is do the things that you want without specific deadlines to worry about, and you can simply enjoy that time.

I am sure that you would feel a sense of relief, and will begin working on completing required items/tasks/goals in front of you to get to the point of completion as soon as possible

Focus your attention and energy o the item(s) at the top of your list and work until you have reached the bottom of your list

Take adequate break time between each task to refresh your mind

Ask yourself how lack of completion of each task could impact you personally, now and in the future, and how it can impact others that depend on you

If completion of a particular task requires a quiet environment then find a place where you will not have any distractions to get the job done (ex. library, your home office, etc.)

When needed, reach out for help, if you are unable to complete a task by yourself. There is nothing working with asking for help

With intentional procrastination, ask yourself how important it is for that that a specific goal or task gets completed as soon as possible vs. waiting longer.

If it is important to you, then you will find time, energy, tools, and resources to get it done

Do not create excuses for your lack of desire of getting something done

Nobody wants to hear excuses, especially if it is your boss or teacher/professor. They are looking for solutions, not excuses

If necessary, break down one task/goal into smaller, easier to digest sub-tasks/goals to make it easier to follow and complete a longer or larger task

Think about your lifetime goal and how you are planning on achieving it. Always keep this at the top of your mind

Just DO IT, do not procrastinate!

By procrastinating all you are doing is creating a backlog of things to do, which will have to be completed by you regardless, so why wait.

Do it now, do it today. Remember, do not look for excuses, look for solutions in everything you do

Procrastination leads to frustration and stress

Do not create unnecessary stress for yourself and others by putting your goals on the backburner.

In addition to overcoming procrastination, one must always be aware of self-image and how he or she is being perceived, to ensure that perception you are giving is the one you intend to give.

Do You Really Know Your Reality? How Are You Being Perceived and What is Your Image

Many of us would say that we know ourselves better than anyone else. We think that we know how we communicate with others, what our preferred communication style is, whether we are direct or indirect, and we also think that we know how we are perceived by people around us. However, what we think we know and what is real usually are vastly different realities.

We often are so ignorant about our reality that all we know is what we think, and do not have any desire to ask others for honest feedback about us. How do others see us based on the way we communicate, our body language, our manors, gestures, and physical appearance?

Are we being viewed the way we feel we are, or are we viewed completely different from our reality? If you really have an opportunity and courage to step outside of your comfort zone, overcome your personal ego, and seek feedback from people other than your immediate family members, for example your colleagues, you will most likely hear their reality, the way you are being perceived, and their perception will be very much different from the reality that you have created for yourself in your mind.

You may want to be viewed as someone who is caring, someone who values relationships and genuinely cares for others, however, if what is visible to others does not reflect how you really feel through your actions, emotions, the tone of your voice, or even your smile, how can we expect for people to see the other side of us? We need to let others in, to get to know us for who we really are vs. the person on the outside - our image, which is created over many years and shaped by our culture, our family, people with whom we interact on the daily basis, and, of course, the environment around us.

It is easy to say than done

You are probably thinking, well Alex, aren't we supposed to be tough, independent, confident and in many cases direct to move forward in life and in our careers? The short answer is yes. It is often necessary to be tough, determined, direct, and persistent to keep moving forward in life and our careers. However, what we should remember that that is that is not the requirement to live by all the time. There are many times when we need to be warm, engaging, welcoming, and caring to build extremely valuable relationships with others, which can be even more important to them and you as well.

Business side vs. Personal Side

It is not an easy task to uncover and display your true personality to others, especially if they are the people whom you never met before. It is hard work, which requires self-discovery, bravery to ask for honest feedback, and even more importantly, being open to receive constructive and sometimes harsh feedback from others. However, it is with that honest and direct feedback is when you learn the most about yourself and able to focus on the areas of your personality and perception that you need to work on improving.

Who cares about perception?

You may not care about others' perception of you, but they certainly care how your actions, your behavior affects them. This is even more important if these are the people with whom you work or do business. If you are direct by nature and if you treat everyone else if a direct manner, when the only thing you care for is making sure that your deadlines and expectations are met, but the people that you work with are in desperate need for some genuine acknowledgement of their efforts, and for someone to tell and show them that their boss cares about them, how long do you think that they will tolerate such environment if their needs are not met? Do you think that they will want to try harder to deliver good results and encourage others? I do not think so.

What can you do to recognize when it is time to change?

First, take some time to really listen to what your peers and people with whom you interact are trying to tell you? Listen to their comments, feedback, suggestions, wants and needs. As leaders, we often miss important pieces of critical information, simply because we do not know how to listen. We hear what other people are telling us, but we are not really listening to them. Information goes in and out. Next time someone is speaking and sharing something with you at work or outside of work, put everything that you are doing at that moment, and yes, that includes your phone, and listen to them without interrupting.

Second, be open to and willing to change how you interact with others and flex your communication style when appropriate. Remember to be flexible to match your audience. Your direct approach may not work for someone who prefers more softer communication approach, just like someone who prefers to receive directions in a direct manner, may be less receptive when you are trying to sugar coat things.

Third, encourage and seek feedback from others. Where else will you receive raw and unfiltered truth than from the people you work with when they are presented with an opportunity to be open and honest with you. To make a comfortable and safe environment for people to share, you need to set the foundation and explain the reasons why their honest feedback is important to you and them. If you know how your employees wants and needs are and how they prefer to be communicated with, then you can adjust your communication style to match theirs and deliver the information where it can be received by them and you.

Lastly, remember that you interact and work with people who have feelings, opinions, and desires. Therefore, be human, show that you care about others, and not just with your words but more importantly with your actions. Do not expect immediate changes in people's behaviors and their interactions with you right off the bet, it takes time, for them to see that you stand behind your words and back your words with your actions. Be human first, and boss second.

So, do you have the level of concentration that it takes to tackle any challenges on your path, whether it is rebuilding or maintaining the perception you intend to give and/or going after your carefully planned and written down goals and dreams that you are pursuing in life? If you are still working on developing concentration, next section of this chapter will provide additional resources that you may use to develop or strengthen your concentration, which can also be used to help you change your existing habits or establish new ones over time.

Developing Concentration Using Various 'Triggers and Rewards' Created by Us or By the Environment That We Live In

Lack of concentration and real-life distractions around us

Lack of concentration when learning about a particular subject or listening to a speaker on the stage could often have a negative outcome in terms of information absorption and retention. It is also extremely easy to lose concentration when various distractions are present, such as: people talking, loud noises, etc. So, how do you stay focused with various distractions being present around you?

Can concentration and focus be improved?

Sure, it may sound much easier said than done, however, concentration can be improved even if you find it difficult to remain focused on one thing for longer than few seconds or minutes. It all boils down to developing a new habit to stay focused and concentrated or re-writing an existing one already created in your brain long time ago.

Habit creation through 'triggers and rewards'

The process of habit creation or habit change through 'triggers and rewards,' reviewed in this article, is explained in an interesting book written by Charles Duhigg called "The Power of Habit: Why we do what we do in life and business." One of the techniques explained in his book in detail is using 'triggers and rewards' to help establish new habit and record it in your brain to be used in the future. So, before I go into application of this technique to help improve concentration, let us quickly review what is trigger and reward when it comes to habit creation.

'Triggers'

Trigger essentially can be anything that triggers an action in your brain. For example, trigger can be an alarm going off in the morning, which triggers an action to get out of your bed, or toothbrush sitting on top of your bathroom sink counter, triggering an action to brush your teeth. Triggers can be visual, like in the example with the toothbrush – seeing the toothbrush triggers an action to act, or audible – such as in the example with alarm clock, where hearing a familiar sound triggers an action.

'Rewards'

Reward is exactly what you think it is - recciving a reward of any kind after the expected action has been taken and completed. This could be going out to a nice dinner after successfully completing an important project, drinking a delicious protein shake after finishing a workout session. Essentially, a reward is what you want and/or receive upon completion of a specific task or activity.

How do triggers and rewards help in creating new habits or overwrite existing ones?

For us to know, or for our brain to know that we need to take action of any kind, we need to come in contact with a trigger and activate a specific action. When we get into our car, seat belt indicator and/or sound indicator are telling us to put our seatbelt on, this triggers us to physically take a seatbelt and buckle it in. If there were no visual and/or sound indicators informing us to buckle, would we still do so every time we get inside of our car? Hopefully, we still would, however, the likelihood of us forgetting without any reminder is relatively high. That is why triggers are important to trigger actions in our brain.

Without rewards our desire to take an action is much lower, if at all present. For example, when studying for an exam, you expect to make a particularly good grade after taking a test. Your reward in this example is high mark for the test score, that what you want and expect. When everything goes as expected and high mark is received, you are much more likely to study hard again for the next test to feel great after scoring high and proudly presenting your score to others. Rewards are different for everyone. What motivates one person to act may not be viewed as motivational by someone else. That is why when developing a new habit, you should find something that motivates you to go through with task at hand.

How can 'trigger and reward technique' help to improve concentration and focus long-term?

Now that we have reviewed what is considered to be a 'trigger and reward' and why they are important in helping to develop new habits, transferring this technique to help improve concentration and focus should be an amazingly simple task. All you need is to determine what your trigger and reward is going to be or to create new.

Little later I will share few examples of triggers and rewards that work for me to help me stay concentrated and focus when needed. Once again, triggers and rewards that work for me may not work for you, that is why you should experiment and find what works for you. More importantly, the reward selected must be realistic, available, and motivational to have a strong desire to take action and do so repeatedly long-term, until the habit becomes something that you do without thinking.

Here are some examples of 'triggers and rewards,' that are unique to me, to concentrate and focus.

Writing: 10am on Saturdays – trigger is to go to the library to spend time to write and putting my thoughts on paper. Reward – is to go home at 5pm and spend time with my family. There are few hours that I must write, due to working full time M-F. Library allows me to focus in quiet environment and concentrate on my work.

Training/Development: When I enter conference room or auditorium to attend training or personal development material, my obvious trigger is entering the designated room/space and seeing a presenter. This trigger prompts me to take out my notebook and being taking notes. My rewards are: information received during the session which will help me to learn and expand my knowledge base, and notebook full of notes to refer to and share with other when appropriate.

Now you just need to find new or recognize existing triggers which can serve as reminder to act on concentrating and focusing and assign appropriate reward(s) to motivate you and follow through with task at hand.

Now that you know a way to help develop and/or strengthen concertation and establish new or overwrite existing habits, next let us review the topic of establishing and utilizing appropriate level of assertiveness, when situation at hand calls for it.

How to Become More Assertive – "Recognize and Recommend" Approach

Can anyone become more assertive when the situation calls for it? I think so. What happens most of the time is us failing to recognize that we need to turn it up a notch and show some assertiveness. Instead, we continue to act without making any adjustments to our approach and then wondering why we are not being taken as seriously as we would like.

Unleashing the confidence inside

Not everyone is naturally assertive. Some of us are much more soft-spoken and prefer softer approach to any conversation, even though somewhere deep inside we are ready to unleash that confident and assertive persona that we have been keeping closely guarded to be liked and accepted by others regardless of situation that we may be in.

Taking the time to think and recognize

Do most people have the necessary level of assertiveness within them and can use it when situation call for it? Sure. However, in most cases we fail to recognize the time when we need to be more assertive, because we forget to take time that we need and recognize that thigs are not going the way we expect them to, we are afraid to ask questions not wanting to appear rude or too direct, even though the other person may be waiting for us to step it up and display some confidence and assertiveness. Unfortunately, we tend to focus on what others may think of us, how they may perceive us, therefore, we keep our extensive knowledge and expertise to ourselves, thereby missing on some major opportunities in business and in life. So, it is important not to get consumed by others' thoughts and opinions and when appropriate voice our own views and concerns.

It is not what you say but how you say it.

What is also important to remember, that it is not what you say, but how you say it. Instead of telling someone what to do and how to do it, position it in the way of recommendation, inviting everyone to share their ideas, while tying in their ideas to your recommendation. People want and often expect to be part of the decision-making process, so let them. At the end of the day, you would want to be included in the decision-making process and asked for your input as well, right?

Collaboration is the key to a productive negotiation

Collaboration is a critical part of any productive negotiation. What is important to remember is taking the necessary time to recognize where you are in the conversation and not being afraid to share your recommendations when it is the most appropriate. This is even more critical for business leaders and managers, as people who work with them often depend on their opinions and decisions to move the business forward. By being more assertive and by sharing your views and ideas, should help you to see others think of your recommendations and create a more effective constructive argument and help them see and understand your point of view. Do not be afraid to speak up when opportunity calls for it.

Just like we never should stop learning if our desire and goal is to continue growing and developing personally and professionally throughout our life, similarly we should understand the concept of building a strong foundation on which we can build the future that we seek. As you know, a solid and strong foundation is a required to build a house. Same concept is applicable to building the foundation for our future. This and many other topics are covered in length in the next chapter of this book.

Chapter 7 – Creating Strong Foundation and Inviting Opportunities into Our Lives

Change Foundation, Change Your Future

Think of foundation as massive roots of a tree, where everything above the ground, what you see, is your present and future, and everything below the ground – the roots – is what you are doing to create your present and future. So, how do you create the future and life that you want for yourself? As T. Harv Eker said: "If you want to change the fruit, you have to change the roots. If you want to change the visible, you have to change the invisible first."

Our focus is often wrong

Often, we tend to focus on the fruit, or what we see above the ground, good or bad. Some are completely satisfied with what they see on the 'tree', they have a job that pays the bills and maybe there is something even left over for little bit of fun with friends and family. And that is ok, if you are satisfied with this type of lifestyle. However, I am guessing, because you are reading or listening to this, you are not satisfied with where you are today and want something more, something better. Would not be nice to do and have what you really want, not living paycheck to paycheck, have significant amount of money saved in your savings account, have plenty of money saved for fun and leisure – vacations, shopping, entertainment, etc.

Perhaps, but then you realize that you have extremely strict budget, enough to cover your monthly obligations, food, and gas for your car to take you to and from your full-time job, maybe even a part-time job on the weekends. So, that is what you forget about fun activities, postpone your few days of vacation or staycation, turn on the tv and stay at home, sitting on your couch without any action, until it is time for you to go back to work. Another worry that person in this situation may have is that hopefully nothing else takes place which may require them to spend money, such as car breaking down, that you must repair, otherwise you will not be able to get to work, and other unexpected expenses for which you did not plan for and do not have money saved up in your 'rainy day' account. Then what do you do? Whom do you blame for lack of money and/or time? I can tell you what I used to do, I used to blame everything and everyone around me, but never myself or lack of effort on my part.

Focusing on your 'roots,' your foundation

I say used to, because, I have learned, and now clearly understand while sharing with others, what it is not the fruit or visible that person should focus their energy and attention on, but instead, the focus should go towards the 'root', your foundation, the part of you that nobody can see or know except for you. Only you can know and see the foundation that you are building. Only you can see how deep and strong your 'roots' are. You can take away from your existing foundation by making decisions that do not contribute any value but take value away – spending more than you make, blaming others for your failures, stop trying after facing a roadblock, spreading negativity, complaining how bad everything is in your life, etc.

However, you can also add to your foundation, grow your 'roots', make your foundation stronger and begin building it to create happier and more successful future for yourself and others around you.

How do you focus on your foundation, the invisible, to create the life that you really want?

Stop complaining and telling everyone around you how bad everything is, all this does is attract more negative energy to you

Trust in yourself and what you can achieve by conducting self-analysis regularly and practice daily self-motivating mantras. Repeat motivational mantras out loud daily wherever it is most convenient for you, but do it, do not skip it.

Have a winning attitude at work, at home, or wherever you may be. Focus on the positive in every situation. Positive energy is contagious and will take you far.

If you decide to start something, whether it is your own business, create another stream of income, going for the position that you want in your company, whatever it may be for you, just do it. Do not wait for a better time, as there will never be a better time than NOW! You may not have everything you may need now to start, then start with what you have. The key here is to start and get moving.

You are the one who creates your foundation and your future, and you determine how strong your foundation or 'roots' will be and what it's going to look like. If you want to change your present, then you need to change your invisible, your 'roots', to see a result that you wish to see.

So, if you ask me if money can grow on trees, I will tell you that it depends on the 'roots' below the ground, your foundation, and what kind of 'ingredients' are being added to help 'roots' grow. How hard are you willing to work to change and improve your foundation?

Strong foundation is a fist step in setting yourself up for future success. But how do you get there? How do you stay focused and on track to reach your goals? Next section of this chapter covers effective knowledge application and easy-to-follow goal setting techniques to help you stay on and keep moving forward towards achieving your goals in life.

From Theory into Practice. Effective Knowledge Application and Easy-To-Follow Goal Setting Techniques

The question that many people ask themselves when it comes to leadership and personal development in general is: How do I apply what I learn through various resources, regarding leadership theory into practice in the real life? That is a valid and good question to ask, because there is so much of good information available to us online, information and lessons we receive in various personal development conferences and workshops, and information we receive from the people that we work with every day. Therefore, the question of application and results obtainment is always present.

This appears as an incredibly challenging question; however, it is amazingly simple to answer. The information that we retain will remain only a theory unless you make a conscious decision and effort to use the information that you had learned immediately following a particular training, webinar, or conference that you had attended.

Many people would probably say: "Well, I am using the information that I had learned, but I do not see any results." The question here is: Are you really using and applying what you had learned daily, at work, in your business, or at home? Most people say that they do, but they only take good and detailed notes during training or conference, feel deeply passionate and driven at that moment, maybe even a day after, however, then the notebook and desire get lost somewhere and the time invested in your personal development, which you will never get back, goes to waste including the money that you may have paid for it.

How do you make sure that information received, and leadership theories shared with you by other business leaders do not go to waste? All you need to do is use it, and I really mean it, use what you learn, apply theories in real life and see how it becomes applicable in your specific situation. Not every theory may be applicable in your situation, but that is why you need to test it. Do not stop if the first time you try something new it does not bring the immediate results as you were expecting. Honestly, you will most likely not see the results you are hoping for after just the first or even second try. That is why you must apply it daily, be deeply committed to reaching a specific goal that you have set, and do not stop until you have achieved it. Many people stop halfway, and that is why they never see the expected results.

All best practices, leadership exercises and suggestions were tested by the people who are teaching them, and they have achieved great results after hard work and daily application and practice. Do not give up, keep going, and you will get there.

Another important part of successful application of your knowledge received through seminars, workshops, conferences, and other types of training is establishing personal goals and following through on the goals that you have set. Without clear and attainable goals, it is extremely difficult and almost impossible to retain and apply information learned. Goals help you to stay on track and serve as a guide in your journey to success however you may view success in your personal and professional life.

It is important that set goals are realistic and attainable. You can and should create multiple incremental goals, almost as a system of check points along the way towards your bigger goal. When you set smaller incremental goals and achieve them, you will stay motivated, positive, and determined by celebrating small victories. On the other hand, when you set unrealistic or large goals that are difficult to attain, you will most likely be less motivated and determined when you realize how complex your goal is and how far you are from reaching it. Extremely hard and unrealistic goals are also one of the reasons as to why many people give up on their goals and lifetime dreams.

Important to remember that regardless of the goal(s) complexity you will encounter obstacles along the way, even when you are setting smaller and attainable goals. Therefore, do not get discouraged when you are faced with an obstacle. Look at each obstacle as a challenge and an opportunity to learn. Most of the time it is how we look at each problem or obstacle that determines successful outcome from failure. When you are positive, determined, and goal-focused, you will find a way to overcome any obstacle on your path and will inspire and encourage others.

Emotional connection to the core reason of your goal or dream will help you to re-focus when you are faced with an obstacle. Whenever you are faced with one, here's simple technique to re-focus yourself on your goal(s).

Close your eyes and in your mind ask yourself the following questions:

Why have you set a particular goal?

How have you felt when you were establishing that goal?

How will you feel when you finally accomplish your goal?

Why is reaching this goal important to you or your family?

It is important to visually go back to that time when you were establishing a particular goal and be in that moment. Then transfer your feeling and your answers on paper so you can review them whenever you are faced with a same obstacle in the future.

Having an emotional connection with your goal will help you to stay motivated and goal driven.

Lastly, goals must be written and reviewed regularly, preferably daily. Without written goals, you have no way of checking your progress and do not have a way to keep yourself accountable. Seek assistance from your family and people that you trust who will be able to understand and support you on your journey, as well as keep you accountable when you are faced with an obstacle or when you are getting away from your commitments.

In summary, apply and practice daily what you learn, work hard on improving your skills, establish and set clear and realistic goals, and follow through on the goals that you have set. Do not get discouraged when you are faced with an obstacle on your path of self-improvement. Know that every obstacle is simply a challenge that can be resolved with strong belief in yourself, your strengths, and your knowledge. Maintain strong desire and drive to achieve any goal that you have set for yourself, and be persistence regardless how challenging the obstacle may be. Believe that you can achieve it and you will.

Having strong foundation is important, knowing where you are going in terms of setting goals and detailed plan of achieving them is also important, however, if your mindset is not set to focus on actions that can help you to grow personally and professionally, reaching your goals would be challenging or even impossible. So, how do we set our mind to focus on success and growth? So, let us explore this and other questions around the topic of mindset in the next section of this chapter.

'Minimum-Wage' Mindset

'Minimum-wage mindset' results in 'minimum-wage results'

I want to start with a quote by T. Harv Eker: "Rich people have their money work hard for them. Poor people work hard for their money." You may of course argue that this is not the case, but how many wealthy and successful people have you seen or know who think as someone who is earning just enough to get by?

Minimum-wage mindset

So, how does someone with a 'minimum-wage mindset' thinks, or what is a 'minimum-wage mindset?' Often this is someone who still lives in their past, they live with fixed beliefs of the past and with what they were conditioned to think and believe in since they were little kids. Now, I am not saying here that to become rich and successful you need to give up and forget everything that you had learned as a child from your parents, teachers, peers. Many of our character attributes learned early in life are valuable and important to remember, such as respect, courtesy, empathy, punctuality, etc. What I am saying though is that we need to learn to change and adapt to the time we live in today, while keeping our unique character values and beliefs.

Often what is holding us back limiting our ability to advance in life, and in turn reaching our full potential, is that we tend to get stuck in the past, refusing to change, adapt, and recognize that time had passed, people had changed, and expectations to reach success had changed.

Business environment that we live in today changes daily and requires flexibility, willingness to learn, and demands extremely strong work ethic. You cannot go to work with a mindset that I need to punch in, work my 8 – 9 hours, and punch out, while still expecting to be successful and reaching a lifestyle where you can have everything that you want whenever you want.

Punch in, Punch out mentality

Sure, you can absolutely work your regular 9-5 job, get your 40 hours per week, and have just enough money in your back account to pay your monthly obligations, and then have just few dollars left, if that, until the next paycheck, which is still who weeks away, while all you have is $5 in your account. So, what do you do? You begin looking for a second or even third job to take care of your family and their wants and needs. In this case forget about taking long vacation, since you must work and cannot be away for more than two-three days at most, which are typically your regular days off, during which you have errands to run and paying bills. If this is the lifestyle you desire and comfortable with, then this post may not be for you, unless you are looking for a way to improve your current situation and achieve something bigger in life. If you are currently in the paycheck to paycheck, working two to three jobs situation, I want to let you know that I know how it feels because I have been there and understand the feeling as if you virtually live at work without seeing your family for several days. The good thing is you do not have to remain in such situation. You can change your present if you have extreme desire to do so and strongly believe in yourself.

To being changing your present and begin creating the life that you want, you need to understand the mindset of someone who sees the world as a while canvas, where dream life can be created, where anything is possible.

Growth and Success Mindset, where minimum wage is unacceptable

This person may start working a minimum wage job, however, he or she will be immediately looking for opportunities and ways to improve their financial and professional wellbeing, and not by obtaining another job or secondary job, but by growing within existing role to keep moving forward. So many times, people begin a new job and once minimum required skills have been learned, they lose interest, desire, and drive to keep moving forward and continue growing themselves and business while acquiring new skills outside of what is required. How can you expect to change your present if you are standing still?

Success-Focused Mindset

People who are successful in life have worked extremely hard every day to reach to the top of their game. They have invested a lot of personal time towards their personal and professional development through formal and self-education, with tools and resources that were available to them at that time, not making excuses that it is difficult, impossible, or that they do not know where to start.

Act now or wait for the 'right moment'

Successful people seek every opportunity to grow their knowledge and take advantage of what they can do today versus waiting for the right time to come. It is just like with New Year's resolutions, many people commit to lose weight, go to school, make more money, on December 31st, but then January 1st comes, and nothing happens, simply because something else came up and commitment made earlier was placed to the side. Very few people press 'resume' on the goals that they have set and instead wait for the right time to come, or next year.

Why do we wait for the New Year to begin improving our life? It is all in your mind. If you have an extraordinarily strong desire to change your present for the better, then there should be no reason to wait for a specific date, that time is now.

Successful people hold on to their commitments no matter what. What is the easiest way to lose trust of another person? It is not following through on your promises. It works the same way in business and in life in general. When you set a goal, then do everything you can to reach it, and do not stop until it has been reached. Do not make promises that you cannot deliver on.

Learning from mistakes

Successful people learn from their mistakes, make necessary improvements, and try again without repeating the same mistake twice. As Steven Denn said: "You can never make the same mistake twice because the second time you make it it's not mistake, it's a choice." So, do not let temporary failures or mistakes stop you, learn from them and try again. Many successful and famous people failed multiple times before reaching success.

If you really want something in life, if you want to change your present and create a life of your dreams, then you should really consider understanding your mindset and see if it aligns with your goals. 'Minimum-wage mindset' will not create a millionaire lifestyle.

Just like we should learn from our mistakes, make adjustments, improvements, and try again until we reach the outcome that we are seeking, another way to learn is through the use of questions, seeking to know and understand before acting. How can one learn through the use of questions? This and other questions are covered next.

Learning Through Asking Questions

We all have different learning styles and preferences. Some learn by simply reading the material and visually memorizing everything they read and see. Others learn best by doing the task versus reading about in the books. And then there are some who use a combination of visual memorization, asking questions and hands on. For me personally, I have an awfully bad visual memory, I can read something and few minutes later I would forget what I have just read, so I most definitely do not have a good visual memory.

If you are among the lucky few who has an exceptional photographic memory, what you read about here would be simply an icing on the cake for you. However, if you are like me, someone who does not share the benefit of great photo memory, you will hopefully walk away with some tools and tricks to remember more, retain information better, and, in general be more equipped for the reality of our business lives.

Learning through repetition

To retain information that I receive through reading books, attending training courses and workshops, I use repetition when reviewing the content acquired through notes and other materials available (books, audio, visual images). So, yes, this approach often requires re-reading written materials multiple times. For example, if I want to remember a particular content from the book that I have read or listened to, I would re-read or re-listen a specific chapter multiple times until the information is engrained in my brain. Often, the audio book that I may be listening has such an interesting content and I am unable to capture that content on paper, I would re-listen the entire book over and over until it is forever in my brain.

I know some of you are probably thinking that it would take me an exceedingly long period of time and multiple repetitions before the information learned is forever stored in my head, and you will be correct by thinking this way. That is why I would typically be the last person leaving a test taking room or training, because I may still be reviewing the information in my mind.

Learning through highlighting and search of takeaways

Another way that helps me to retain information learned is by highlighting key phrases and takeaways as I go through the content. You are probably thinking, "well I highlight what seems to be an important information as I study," but the question here is - are you taking that information which you have highlighted and transferring it to your notebook to re-read later until it is engrained in your brain? I do. What many of us do is highlighting key information and moving on to something new, thinking that just because we highlighted the information it will be remembered by our brain. However, unless you have a particularly good photographic/visual memory, even though you had highlighted few important takeaways, that information would typically be quickly forgotten without reviewing it again and again.

Learning by asking questions

In addition to re-reading information multiple times, highlighting key takeaways during study phase and taking notes, I also learn by asking questions. So, if there is something that I am initially unfamiliar with and do not yet have a deep level of understanding, I would find someone who does, and ask questions until all questions are answered in my head. The person who you seek to ask questions could be your colleague, teacher, parent, or your business leader who has experience in a field in question.

What is holding us back?

What happens a lot though, many people are hesitant to ask any questions, because they are afraid or do not want to appear less knowledgeable in front of others. Therefore, even though they do not have a good understanding of a subject or business process, they prefer to rely on their limited understanding of the process whether it is accurate or not, in turn often making mistakes which are hard to fix. Who cares what other people may think of you? Why does that matter? It should not. One simple question to someone who may be more experienced in a specific area, could often resolve any misunderstanding or unanswered questions.

Not so surprising personal development insight

Most people enjoy when they are being approached by someone else seeking their input and guidance, and often are happy to share their knowledge with others. So, remember this next time you have a question that you need help answering. There is only one rule when it comes to asking questions, that is not asking the same question more than once, but other than that ask away. As Nora Roberts said: "If you don't ask, the answer is always no."

Asking the right questions and being a subject matter expert in what you are discussing, teaching, or coaching is important. Similarly, understanding the difference between pro-active vs. re-active approaches when it comes to managing a business, career, as well as personal daily schedule is also an important component of being effective in everything that we do.

Pro-Active vs. Re-Active Approach in Business and in Life

I am sure you have heard about pro-active and re-active approaches at work, in your place of business, or somewhere else outside of business walls. This type of conversation would typically come up when discussing almost late to late projects – re-active, or advanced planning and strategy – pro-active. Why understanding the difference between two approaches matters and how this knowledge can be used in daily business and personal life applications?

Re-Active Approach to problem solving and life situations

Re-active approach could also be associated with procrastination. Since, I believe, we all know what procrastination is, understanding re-active approach in business and life should be rather simple. The way I view re-active approach is when projects or tasks are assigned by business leader(s) to an individual to complete by specific deadline, while meeting certain quality standards expected by the company, however, despite all these expectations and requirements the person responsible for completion of these tasks fails to understand, plan, and begin acting on the task at hand until it is near or right at deadline.

What happens as result of practicing re-active approach and procrastination?

What typically happens when someone chooses to procrastinate and follow more re-active, delayed approach, is sacrifice in quality, since you have little or no time to effectively plan, brainstorm, organize and execute on a plan, which in turn causes for the project or task to be completed close or even past deadline. Low quality and/or missed deadlines create unhappy leadership team and negative impact on person's professional reputation. Who wants to be this person, I would guess not many people would want to be in such situation, as it does not provide any benefit to a person's growth and career development?

What is an example of re-active approach in personal life outside of business environment?

Consider taking your family on a trip to Disney World for the very first time. Many first timers to Disney World know that such trip with family and kids requires a lot of pre-planning and organization several months in advance. However, very few people and families whose to follow recommendations of others and begin planning when it is almost time to leave for the trip, if planning at all, not reviewing all available resources online and offline with many different recommendations to save money and create once a lifetime experience for the parents and children alike. As a result, many things such as renting a stroller for smaller kids, food passes, park passes, lodgings, transportation, becomes a headache when family arrives at Disney Worlds, and instead of enjoying the time with kids, parents spend countless hours and large amount of money tending to what is needed vs. relaxing, which usually results in frustration and less than exceptional Disney experience. That is an example of re-active approach to planning. Is this the experience that you want?

Pro-Active approach and its application in business and personal life

Pro-active approach is, of course, the opposite of re-active. This approach in business and personal life outside of business walls encompasses acting on tasks and projects at hand immediately, creating plan and timeline for project's completion in advance of the deadline set, making sure that all expectations and requirements are met ahead of time, and keeping business leaders in the know about projects progress without being reminded to do so. With pro-active approach to timelines and problem discovery and solution can be uncovered much quicker and with higher quality, due to project owner having adequate amount of time to engage many different resources for their assistance and valuable feedback. As a result, with pro-active approach business leaders know exactly where business is going and timelines when previously set milestones will be reached. Thus, everyone is happy and satisfied with results. Same Disney planning exampled shared earlier can be used for explaining a real-life application of the pro-active approach, all that you need to do is look at that same example from a different angle, when all recommended planning and preparation steps were completed several months in advance vs. waiting until the last minute.

Why am I sharing these two approaches? How does understanding of each one can help someone in improving personally and professionally?

The reason why understanding the difference and application of these two different approaches is important is, because, depending on which approach we choose and/or prefer usually results in the outcome typical for each one. So, if our preferred approach is more re-active to everything we do, then we should expect to remain where we are today with extremely limited movement forward to where we desire to be. Do we want to procrastinate and have a vacation filled with frustration, or do we want to have a great time with our family filled with joy and happiness? The choice is ours to make, and the way we choose to live our personal and professional life is also ours.

Typically, when we favor re-active approach to problem solving, we tend to find ways to explain reasons for our lack of inaction, in other words, we tend to create excuse, which is exactly what we do when we fail to follow through on our promises and our goals. If we hope to accomplish our goals and dreams in life, then we should stop creating excuses for our own lack of action.

Stop Creating Excuses for Not Following Through on Your Plans and Promises

What was said cannot be undone

I have always been a firm believer that once a person says something and/or makes a commitment to do something that, what was said cannot be undone, and one must follow through. Perhaps, time might have changed what is expected a little, as I feel that expectations behind commitments are little looser now than few years ago, but nonetheless it is still something that absolutely exists and is expected. It is like making a wedding vows, once you said it, you cannot change your mind the next day, because you have made a commitment to yourself and another person you love. So, why should the sense of commitment and responsibility be any different or less valued when one makes a promise to themselves and others to follow through on a particular plan or task? It should not be. Regardless of the nature of the promise or commitment made, I feel that once word is given it cannot be undone or taken back. That is why it is critical that we spend necessary amount of time thinking through the situation, analyzing pros and cons, understanding risks and commitment required, before verbalizing or putting your acceptance on paper agreeing to take on a particular task or challenge, whether it is personal goal or professional agreement.

Consequences of broken commitments

There are several negative consequences that exist when one breaks his or her promise and chooses to no follow through.

One – any previously established trust that you may have built over long period of time, will be typically diminished, and replaced with caution. Now, whenever someone who broke trust makes any other future commitments, he or she would be approached with caution and low level of trust. Therefore, it may be challenging for a person in this situation to expect the same level of trust and autonomy in decision making from others when it comes to important projects and assignments.

Two – personal and professional reputation may suffer in the eyes of business partners or even family members and friends. When you are known as someone who does not keep his or her promises and commitments, the likelihood of someone coming to you for an advice when it comes to planning, goal setting, and organization, would typically be relatively low.

Three – One will likely be perceived by others as someone who creates an 'empty noise' – talks a lot, promises many things, however, when it comes time to deliver on promises made, that person is nowhere to be found. I think at some point in our lives we all have dealt with this type of individual in the place or business of somewhere else.

These are just three of many negative consequences that come with lack of follow through on commitments made by an individual. I am sure if we keep going and list all possible outcomes, the list could be rather extensive.

What does this have to do with personal commitments that we make to ourselves vs. other people?

Commitments made to ourselves are as important as those made to others. I often hear and see people making big promises to begin working and taking action to accomplish personal goals, whether it is fitness, self-education, goal planning, getting rid of bad habits, be more pro-active and stop procrastination, starting their own business to do what they say they love, but no actionable steps is being taken to do what was committed to and promised. For example, in reference to personal development and leadership, if someone is telling me that they want to become a better leader in their business, or begin investing more time and energy into their self-education every day by means of reading more, utilizing information available in leadership and personal development books and e-books, podcasts, blogs, I would typically wait and see if a person actually follows through on what he or she said they are going to do. In many cases what happens is, we take a first step, being learning, reading, and this would typically last for few days, maybe even a week, and then we get tired, lose interest, desire to keep powering through occasional challenges, and then we stop.

What happens after we choose to stop and not follow through on our own commitments?

As soon as we decide to stop and put our commitments to the side, that is when excuses come in. We begin generating various excuses as to why we were "unable" to follow through. Most of the excuses would typically have no direct correlation to the actual problem – failure to keep their word and not follow through on promise given. Please do not get me wrong, there are situations that may sometimes actually keep us from completing what we have set out and committed to do, however, the frequency of such situations taking place is small. In most cases, it is our own decision to stop, to give up, showing no desire to try, is what causes us to limit our personal and professional growth.

Please remember, we can either help ourselves to keep moving forwards towards desired outcomes or hold ourselves back creating many different reasons why we are not where we want to be.

Over time, I have heard many people say that they want to be successful, they want to have the ideal lifestyle pictured in their mind, and run their own business, however, they were either too afraid to start something new on their own or claimed not having time to start and run their business while working full time with a mountain of bills and other responsibilities to take care of. So, in the next chapter of this book my goal is to challenge excuses or perceived limits mentioned earlier and show you that one can start and run an online business part-time, while still working full time.

Chapter 8 – Starting and Running a Part-Time Online Business While Working Full Time

How to Start and Run Your Own Online Business While Working Full-Time - Create the Life That You Want with Limited Time Available by Structuring Your Week for Ultimate Efficiency

Many of us find ourselves in challenging and difficult situations that sometimes seem impossible to get out of. Whether it is a lack of money, not being able to take vacations and spend time with your family, purchasing the car that you always wanted, or even going out and having a nice dinner with your wife or husband. When we find ourselves in these situations, what are we doing to address them to reach to what we really want in life? Some may say that "I am working hard 60+ hours every week to bring money home," or "I take every overtime opportunity that may be offered to me by my employer to increase my paycheck by few dollars." So, you probably thinking, how did I come up with such statements? Well, they all came from me and my own experiences, something that I did when I had difficult time in providing for my family and putting food on our table. Everything that I am sharing with you came from my own experience at some point of my life, therefore, I know how you feel if you are going through similar challenges and asking yourself similar questions.

What have I done to change my life and stop asking questions mentioned earlier?

I changed my mindset, I changed how I think and see any challenges on my path and changed how I respond to each challenge. Most importantly, I have decided to follow my passion and start my own business while working a full-time job.

My passion is leadership and personal development. Helping other people just like you and me to realize their full potential by sharing my knowledge and experiences, both personal and professional, is what encourages and fulfills my goal in life – helping and serving others through coaching, motivating, and mentoring. There are so many people all over the world who want to reach their highest potential in life, improve and expand their leadership skills, improve their own and their family's lifestyle, or simply be happy with life. But they simply do not know the way or currently may not see a way to have access to information desired, to grow and develop personally and professionally. There are many reasons why some of us may not see a way to invest in our own development and our future. Lack of money or time tend to be two biggest obstacles for many individuals. I faced remarkably similar challenges throughout my life. Some other reasons why many of us stop trying to reach our dreams are: lack of needed resources or tools, fear of failure, fear of taking risks. These are not all the reasons that sometimes stop us from moving forward, you may be facing some other reason that is specific to you or your situation. I had same fears and obstacles that I had to face earlier in my life and continue to face today. However, neither one of these challenges worth giving up on your passion in life and stop trying, therefore, I did not stop or gave up on my passion.

You and only you are capable in changing the direction of your life and designing your new future. Do not let you fears, or obstacles dictate your actions. Your mind will do everything it can to protect you from various dangers and risks, that is its purpose. That is why you should look at each situation from big picture perspective, considering all the calculated risks, before taking action towards your goal. If you stop and give up on your passion, it becomes a habit, habit that is difficult to break. Keep in mind I did not say impossible, because anything is possible if you really, really, want it.

If you want a better life, make more money, do what you absolutely love, then you must change what you are doing today. By changing I do not mean quitting your job or take another major step which may impact your life negatively. In many cases you can still have a full-time job, which provides you with security that you need to start your own business part-time, and begin you journey towards the life that you want. You do, however, would need to change how you think, how you respond to challenges that you face every day, how much time and energy you invest in your own development. It will be difficult at first, especially if you have difficulty in finding any spare time now, but it should get easier with time and practice. There are many automation tools available online to help you run your business while working full time.

Create a life that you always dreamed of, and this starts with you, analyzing your current situation, to understand where you are and where you want to go, and then creating a detailed plan of how you are going to get there – incremental goal setting. Start small, learn as you go, continue growing yourself as a leader, and invest in your personal development every day. Visit www.heartandmindofaleader.com and allow me to help you on your journey with free access to leadership and personal development content available through blog posts and podcast episodes. New content is added weekly, so you always have new and relevant information available to you.

In the next section of this chapter, I will share how you can structure your week/month for ultimate efficiency and effectiveness to simply get things done.

Running an online business while working full time. How to structure your week for ultimate efficiency.

I am sure that many of you who are reading this book are working full time job and are looking for ways to grow your passive income, or to start a new passive income stream. I was in exactly same situation few months ago. I was searching for a way to start my own business online, following my passion in the field of leadership and personal development, while working full time and continuing developing personally and professionally. Sounds like a difficult task to accomplish, right? Well, the truth is - yes, it is difficult at first, especially at the beginning stages, first few weeks, and months. However, it is an achievable task if you genuinely want to build a successful online business, and if you are extremely passionate about your goal or dream in life, in the niche you are interested in getting into. The structure that I am about to share with you is designed for people who are extremely passionate about helping others through their work, by sharing their lifetime passion represented in their business and everything they do every day.

My weekly business structure is designed for ultimate efficiency, and is fueled by your strong desire to succeed, while doing what you love. Additionally, my structure is designed for individuals who are working full time jobs and have extremely limited time remaining at the end of the day. It does not matter whether you have two days off during the week of on the weekend. What is required is strong will and desire to follow your dream every day.

You are probably thinking why I keep repeating what is required, and keep reiterating strong will, desire, passion, drive to success and goal of helping others? The reason why these items or ingredients are important and critical, because, without them many people their pursuit of their goals or lifetime dreams after just few weeks of hard work, on top of your 40+ hours per week at your full-time job. So, if you are still interested, which I hope you are, let me share my weekly structure that I use to run my online business while working full time.

My weekly online business operations structure

Reserve one of your days off, for me it is Saturday, to focus on writing, typing, recording your blog posts and podcast episodes.

If you have an office at home where you can spend 4-5 hours without any interruptions, then you would not even need to leave your house

In my situation, I do not have a home office, therefore, I make a weekly trip to a library where it is nice and quiet and focus on spending 4-5 hours writing the content for my website. I also have two young children, which make it difficult to focus and gather your thoughts while they are playing.

In most libraries you should be able to find study rooms where you can write behind a closed door in complete silence

Use these 4-5 hours that you must write or type, not spending this time browsing internet on your phone or laptop. I prefer to write using notebook and pen or pencil versus typing on my laptop. I find it easier to reflect all my thoughts when I have pen in my hand and paper to write on, not the laptop keyboard. However, if you prefer to type while you are thinking and you can do so comfortably, then you can save yourself about 30-45 minutes, since you would not have to type everything you just wrote, like I do.

Once I am done writing, I head back home and begin adding the content that I just wrote to my website. I use Weebly (Weebly.com) as my website building tool and hosting service. What I like about Weebly is its ease of use and drag-and-drop website building and editing functionality. This helps me to save a lot of time, since I do not have to write any codes, but simply adding the content desired and schedule it to publish.

Currently, I publish all my blog posts every Monday morning. Once the content is added to my website builder, I schedule it to publish at the time and day that I want, all automated and simple.

Podcasts I record while kids are asleep or playing with my wife outside, and schedule to publish them the same way I do for blog posts

Keep in mind that if I need to run some errands or go watch a movie, I can absolutely do so, if I have completed and scheduled both blog post and podcast to publish.

I use my other day off, for me it is Sunday, to add content to my social media posting/scheduling tool – Buffer (Buffer.com). Buffer allows me to add content that I want to publish throughout the week on various social media platforms and publish the content at the specific time and day of the week automatically.

The process of adding the content to Buffer takes me approximately 2-3 hours each week

I take another 1-2 hours on Sunday to add my content to other platforms and services I use to publish my podcasts (ex. Stitcher.com, Libsyn.com, Podbean.com iTunes, and Google Play Music)

Rest of the day on Sunday I spend with my family and kids. I also dedicate any available time I have each evening to spend with them as well

This weekly process enables me to work full time, while running my online business during the two days off that I have during the week. It is not easy, and very demanding process and schedule, that is why if you are missing passion and desire to reach your lifetime goal and dream, while doing what it takes to get there, you will find difficult to follow through and stick to the plan.

Passion, strong desire to succeed, and helping others, are your essential ingredients to fuel your progress towards success and dream fulfillment.

Time Management and Prioritization. Finding What Works for You and the Business

Delivering results within required timeframe and before set deadlines without sacrificing quality is what we are expected to know and be able to do, whether we are working at our own business or for someone else. So, how do you deliver by set deadlines and with highest quality possible?

Are time management techniques and ways to prioritize your work approach change for every business or are they the same regardless of where you go?

Overall, time management is a skill that must be learned and perfected over time; however, one approach does not always meet business requirements of every business. It is important to remember that even if you have developed particularly good and strong skills to manage time and prioritize your work, matching and aligning what you know to each individual business requirements is what is often expected by business leaders. Each business is different; therefore, your approach should change accordingly versus thinking that 'one size fits all' approach is a way to go.

One constant is prioritization

Prioritizing your work, projects, initiatives, or even ideas is one constant skill that remains unchanged regardless of where you may be. To be the best in what you do and the most effective, you should be prioritizing your tasks based on urgency and level of importance, sometimes level of complexity and time.

Often, we may find ourselves with many projects on our plate and noticeably short period of time to get them all completed. Therefore, the first thing that you should always think about is prioritize each task based on level of importance and due dates. Once you have all tasks in their respective order with dates assigned, then it is the time to analyze and see if deadlines set by your business leader can be achieved with ease or if some negotiation is needed to extend the deadline or if specific tasks can be delegated to someone else, to ensure that deadlines are met.

Communication and transparency are the key to an effective project management and completion

Most business leaders would appreciate if you stopped by their office and make them aware that deadlines that they have set for you to complete a particular project may not be achieved without sacrificing quality, because of xyz. Therefore, asking for help or to see if perhaps the completion deadline is flexible and can be extended is almost always a good idea. What many business leaders do not like is for someone to wait until the last minute before informing them that more time is needed when the deadline is right around the corner and it is too late to make any adjustments. So, keep your business leader s in the loop throughout the life of the project by setting periodic check points to review progress, share updates, as well as to review any potential delays and challenges. Most of the time even the most challenging situations can be solved if appropriate stakeholders are informed and are given an opportunity to help early in the game.

Time Management Process is a Variable

Time management, however, is a variable that should be carefully designed with business requirements and company culture in mind.

Some companies expect you to be at work from start to the end of your scheduled work shift, with no flexibility, and to have all the work completed before you can go home for the day. Typically, retail establishments require you either stock shelves with products, hang all the clothes scattered around the store and put out new items, if it is a clothing store, count the money, balance the register, clean the store, and only then go home. However, in the environment where you have some flexibility and choice when you can complete your work, if deadlines are being met, you are given an opportunity to organize what you do and when you do it at the time and place that is most convenient to you. Therefore, it is important to understand, respect, and support each individual business model and culture, and to find a way to fit your organizational methods that most effective ways to complete work at hand that would work for the business while providing you with the flexibility and freedom of choice you seek

Speaking of freedom of choice, if your goal is to live the life on your own terms, doing what you love, while materializing the lifestyle you always wanted, and invest into your personal and professional growth and development, is to start something of your own – opening your own business, going after an opportunity to find yourself in a busy world of today.

Starting a Business – An Opportunity to Find Yourself in a Busy World of Today

Fear of taking risks and uncertainty

Many people talk about how bad they need and want to start their own business, however, very few do start one. How often do you hear from your friends or family members how bad they want to start something of their own, be their own boss, create their own schedule, and make more money? I would say often. But why aren't they taking the necessary steps to start something, something they care and passionate about? The answer in most cases is fear and uncertainty. People do not know what they should expect once they choose to take a first step toward becoming self-employed, becoming an entrepreneur. They do not know if their business will turn out to be a successful one or the one that would fail. We are afraid to take risks because of the unknown. We do not want to fail and experience disappointment and discouragement, we are comfortable remaining in the same place where we are now, even though we know that remaining in the same position will not change our present or make it better. We are unhappy where we are, yet we choose to remain there because we are afraid to try. Why? Isn't it worth to at least try and see what happens? What do you have to lose? If you fail, you will be right where you are today anyways.

Some other reasons why many people choose to remain where they are: not enough time, no money, and existing obligations. These may look like valid reasons not to pursue your dream of starting your own business, however, these are simply the excuses that we create in our minds to justify our lack of action.

Creating excuses as-a-way to procrastinate

Let us take a closer look at first excuse - "lack of time." Some would say that they cannot start their own business because they are working full time and do not have time for anything else. But is that really the case? No one is telling you to quit your job to have more time in the day to dedicate to your business. One can still have and run their own business while working a full-time job. This also takes care of another excuse of having "existing obligations" to worry about, such as: paying bills, put food on family's table, paying mortgage, etc. If you can manage working full time job, thereby continuing to bring in the money you need to take care of your obligations, at least until your business is off the ground and starts to bring in profit and dedicating few minutes or hours each day to run your own business part time, then you can begin following your dream, doing what you are interested in and love. Is it possible to work full time and run your own business part time? Absolutely. All it takes is the desire to try and dedication to keep going when it is difficult and when you are tired. This takes care of two out of three excuses mentioned earlier. So, what about "not having the money or resources" excuse?

No money and/or resources excuse

Many people use this excuse all the time and continue to live the life they say that they want to change. When it comes to this excuse it is important to remember that you do not have to start big, have a lot of money for a startup capital, have all the best tools or equipment. You can start with what you have today and do what you can today. What I am saying here is that you can start your own business with very minimal or no resources utilizing basic tools available to us. There is a lot of free resources available online that we all have access to, all you need is an internet connection and few minutes of your time. If you do not have an internet at home, then go to the library. Once your business gets going and you start making money, then you may begin investing more in marketing, and enhance existing tools and products. Time will never be right, therefore, there is no reason to keep waiting. Our mind's main function is to keep us safe. So, if you want to change where you are today, then you need to begin listening to your heart as well to understand what you genuinely want, not just what your mind is suggesting that you do. As T.

Harv Eker said: "Lack of money is not a problem it is merely a symptom of what is going on inside of you."

Starting your own business as powerful personal development tool

Starting your own business can be an enormously powerful tool in personal development and growth. The process of starting something new, taking a risk and stepping into the unknown can be one of the best ways to face and overcome your fears. It may be challenging process at first, however, typically anything that is easy to reach or achieve is not worth pursuing as you are not learning when things are easy, you learn when things are challenging and difficult. Once you learn how to overcome your own fears and remove roadblocks on your path, you will gain a sense of power and courage, while obtaining knowledge and experience. Facing difficulties and engaging in the process of solution-finding can be a great way to uncover and understand your own opportunity areas and develop your strengths. Of course, when it comes to starting your own business, it is the choice that only you can make. So, you need to ask yourself what you want and if you are ready to pursue that what you want today.

If you love writing, sharing your experiences and knowledge with others both in written and verbal form then, you may want to consider launching your own blog and podcast online. Next, I will share some steps that you can take to start your own blog and/or podcast online, based on my own trial and error experience. Perhaps, what I share with you could help you to avoid some of the mistakes I made starting out. If blogging or podcasting is not your thing, that is ok, find what works for you, what you love to do and passionate about, and go after it.

How to start your own blog and podcast online - based on my own trial and error experience

Completing the first step – Confirming your own commitment to your passion

I will start by saying that before you embark on a journey of entrepreneurship launching your own website, blog, and podcast, please make sure that this is something that you really want and ready to commit to long-term. There is nothing worse than spending many hours or day of your precious time to launch a blog, to only abandon the idea few days, weeks, or months later. You will not receive your time and resources back, so unless you are serious and determined towards starting something of your own, you may want to look another venture to where you will invest your time. However, I am going to assume here that you are serious, committed, and passionate about starting your own blog and podcast, thereby, ready to take on the challenge.

Finding a hosting and website building solution

When I was launching the heartandmindofaleader.com I had no idea where to start, all I had was an idea how I want for my site to look like and content that I want to share with the world. However, I had no idea about best hosting solutions available, best website builders that do not require any technical or coding knowledge to manage, and site that would be easy to update and maintain. So, I began my online research of various website hosting providers, and there is a lot of them out there, therefore, it took me several days to pinpoint two providers that I was going to test. First provider was Bluehost (bluehost.com), and second was Weebly (weebly.com). I started with Bluehost, it had many positive reviews from other bloggers and recommendations, so I registered, paid fees, and proceeded to designing my site. Bluehost is using WordPress site builder tools which are supposedly amazingly simple and easy to use and update. However, after few hours of playing around with the site, trying to figure out how everything works in Bluehost and WordPress, I found it to be confusing and not as easy as everyone was describing the experience. Maybe it was just my lack of technical knowledge at the time that was the reason for my confusion and challenges I experienced with Bluehost, I do not know, but I decided to leave Bluehost and give Weebly a try. This was the best decision I have made when launching my own site.

Weebly.com – Easy to Use and Manage Website Building and Hosting Solution

Weebly is a website building tool that I currently use to build, host, and manage the heartandmindofaleader.com, and I would not want it any other way. This is one of the easiest and great looking website building tools that I had come across thus far. Weekly uses simple drag and drop website building structure, which makes building and designing experience fun, versus being challenging, difficult, and frustrating. My blog was up and running in a matter of few minutes after completing registration. As I had mentioned earlier, I do not know much about coding, therefore, when I can simply drag the item that I want to add to my website, whether it is an image, video, audio file, or other media element, that is what I call easy, simple, and convenient. So, if you are looking for a hosting solution and website builder for your blog and podcast give Weebly a try. I think you will really like.

Starting you own podcast

Unlike blog, podcast requires additional tools and resources in addition to hosting and builder tools mentioned earlier. You need a way to record and publish your podcast to other podcasting platforms for maximum exposure and to each listener outside of just your own site. Very few people use their laptop or desktop computer to listen to podcasts, instead, most people listen to podcasts on the go using their mobile device or tablet. Therefore, you should consider providing people access to your podcast show through different podcasting platforms, such as: Stitcher (stitcher.com), Libsyn (Libsyn.com), Podbean (Podbean.com), Google Play Music, and/or Apple iTunes.

Podcasting Recording Process

I begin my recording process using one of the audio recording tools called Total Recorder (Totalrecorder.com). You can use that one that works for you, but that is the one I found to be extremely easy to use to record my podcast episodes. I use Total Recorder when I am at home and able to use my home pc for the recording. Whenever I travel, I use standard audio recording apps already installed on my phone, then transfer the file to the podcast management platform I use and recommend – Libsyn.com. Libsyn.com is a quite easy to use, as you can see, I am all about making things easy, to manage and share your recorded audio episodes with your future or current listeners. You can easily connect your site to Libsyn.com with your unique RSS feed link, which can be obtained during the set-up process and being podcasting. Once your episode is published in Libsyn.com, you can schedule for it to go live immediately or at the specific day and time, then you can customize it however you like in Weebly (if you use Weebly as your site builder), add images, look, and feel that you want before publishing the episode on your own website. Remember, your recorded audio file must be in the MP3 format to be published in Libsyn.com and many other podcasting platforms. If your recorded file is not already in MP3, there are many programs that you can find online to convert the file into MP3 format. Also, you would want to invest in a good microphone to record your shows. I use Blue Yeti USB microphone, and absolutely love it. Sound Quality does matter.

Here's couple other resources that you may consider when creating your own website, blog, and/or podcast.

Five Things I Like About Buffer.com Service

For those that do not know what Buffer.com is, it is a social media post automation tool that can be used to share your wonderfully written and compelling posts on multiple social media platforms at one time. Therefore, if you are like me, someone who is engaged on multiple social media platforms at once, then you will absolutely find Buffer to be your best friend, helper, and the big-time saver, so that you can go back to writing inspiring content and let Buffer do the posting work for you.

What do I like about Buffer.com?

1. Simplicity of use. Whether you are using Buffer on your desktop or your mobile phone, Buffer site/app allows you to create, manager, and track the progress of your posts via simple, clean, and easy to follow interface
2. Scheduling of posts. With Buffer you can easily select times of the day you want Buffer to publish your pre-set posts and select which days of the week to publish on. Do you want to publish one post per day or several, it is your call.
3. Connect multiple social media accounts to your Buffer profile. With Buffer you may connect accounts such as: Facebook, Twitter, Google+, Instagram, Pinterest, and LinkedIn.
4. Ability to repost previously scheduled posts with a click of a button. Like a particular post you had published before. You can easily republish that post on one or all connected social media profiles.
5. Adding images and/or links to your posts. Want to make your post stand out, no problem. You can easily add your favorite images and/or links to your posts in Buffer. It is a great way to help your audience to find your website, podcast, or blog.

I hope you find this article and points shared helpful in running your business online more efficiently and effectively.

Five Things I Like About Weebly.com Site Builder and Hosting Platform

Whether you are brand new to website design like me or an expert, powerful website builder – Weebly is a great tool to consider. After researching multiple website builders when I was getting ready to launch my first website, I have chosen to go with Weebly as my website builder and hosting platform for the following reasons:

1. Simple, drag & drop site builder. When I was thinking about building a website, I had no idea where to begin or how would I go about managing, updating, or hosting it. Weebly answered my needs and questions with easy to user drag & drop website creator and

editor, where you do not need to be a developer or know HTML to create and edit content or look and feel of your site. All you need to do is select an element that you want to add, such as 'text block', from the menu of different elements, drag it to where you want for that text to appear on a page, and just press 'publish'. It is that easy.

2. Adding multiple web pages to your site with ease. Want to add more pages to your already great looking site, just go to the pages menu and click a button to add a new page. This page can be a new blog page or standard website page, it is your call. You can just as easily delete pages if it no longer serves a need or purpose of your business's mission or goal.
3. Great tool to create your first blog or podcast online. With Weebly's simple drag & drop design and great selection of different web page elements that can be added, you can quickly create great looking blog or podcast pages in minutes. Weebly makes it easy to upload audio and video files right to your website, include key notes and takeaways, great looking images, and share it with your audience online.
4. Tracking of website performance. You can easily track your website performance right on your Weebly dashboard (desktop or mobile app). Want to see how many unique visitors came to your site each week, or how many page views your site received, this information can be easily found right in your Weebly dashboard. If you have a store on your Weebly site, you can also see how many sales you have had at any time.
5. Themes and Apps. There are many themes for you to choose from to help you make your new or existing site look great. Tired of an existing theme? Want to try something new? No problem. Just go to these selections, pick the one you like and apply it to your site. It is that simple. You can also explore different free and paid apps available in Weebly Apps section. Perhaps you want to add a new site builder element, or site tracking and management utility, with Weebly it is easy to do. Simply visit Apps section in your Weebly editor and explore.

I hope you find this site building and hosting solution as easy and fun to use as I did and still do today.

In Conclusion…

The goal of this chapter was to give you some ideas, tools, and tips to help launch your first or next website, start your own business online, launch your podcast show, or begin blogging. Best of luck to you in your entrepreneurial journey!

Whether you are running your own business or work for another company, you are partnering with, leading, and/or managing other people. Will you be a leader that everyone wants to follow?

Chapter 9 – Leadership, Empowerment, and People Development

Your Title Does Not Define Your Limits – Nothing that is worth achieving comes easy

Whether you are just starting your professional career in a corporate world, or if you have several years of experience working in a corporate structure just know that whatever your current title or position may be, it does not set a limit on your professional growth, ambition, and what you can bring to the table at the end of the day

Career Growth and Personal Development Obstacles

I know you may say that because of your current title or role your reach is somewhat limited or that you do not have necessary tools and resources that can only be obtained at a certain level along the corporate ladder. However, even though you may not have all tools and resources immediately available to you right this minute, what you do have is your drive, determination, persistence, and desire to improve, both personally and professionally, growing yourself every day one lesson and one experience at a time, until success you are seeking is within your reach, and no, it does not have to take 10+ years to reach it.

Sounds easier than done?

I know that this sounds easier than done, and it is true, nothing worth achieving comes easy and requires personal commitment and extreme desire to reach that one thing you are seeking – higher or better position within a company, better lifestyle, etc. I know people who have started their corporate journeys at the very beginning of that high and long corporate ladder and have achieved great success in their professional careers in few short years, sometimes even months. It has been proven time and time again that it can be done, regardless of where you may have started or where along the journey you may be today. So, what skills that one must have, and how should those skills be used to move to the next step in your professional career journey?

1. I had mentioned extreme persistence earlier as one of the required skills that one must have to keep moving forward. Why is persistence particularly important? Because persistence is like a fuel in a car, it is what allows you to keep going, driving forward every day. We face various challenges daily at work and at home and some of those challenges or roadblocks can be exceedingly difficult to overcome if you do not have the fuel that helps you to focus on the goal or end-result you want to achieve, that is where extreme persistence and desire to win comes into play. There have been many times in

my life where from initial assessment and perception situation or opportunities seemed unrealistic and way out of my reach. However, because of my natural strong persistent character, I was able to find ways and detours to keep moving forward towards that what I wanted despite what everyone was saying or thinking, and despite initial barriers, or at least that is what they seemed to be originally. So, without strong persistence it would be difficult to overcome obstacles, challenges, and internal limiting thoughts encountered in life and your professional careers. If it were not for my persistence, I still would not speak English, finish school, and achieve success, based on my personal interpretation of success, in my professional career.

2. Energy. Why is energy important, and how can it relate to your personal and professional growth? Well, high levels of personal energy lead to high levels of performance and results. Low energy, well, you get the point. You need high inner energy to perform at your maximum capacity, and that is where great things happen. You energize yourself to perform, and you energize those around you to perform and help you reaching your business goals. Nobody wants to be around someone who is constantly complaining about how tired they are or how difficult something may be, because it drains your energy, points your mind in the wrong direction. So, always keep your personal energy high, energize others, and keep moving forward. Remember, everything in life is energy. So, if you want higher levels of success or for better opportunities to present themselves, you need to put out and maintain high levels of personal inner energy.

3. Strong belief in yourself and your own abilities. Why is this important? If you do not believe that you can accomplish something, you are right, you cannot and nothing or no one would be able to help you to change that. However, if you believe in yourself and know that you can and will achieve that what you set your mind on, you can and will achieve it. Now, do not get discouraged if something does not happen immediately or as quickly as you would have liked. Just know that if you believe that it can be achieved and that you can get there, then you will eventually get there. Remember, no one except you know exactly what you are capable of. So, if someone tells you that you cannot achieve something because of x, y, or z, go ahead and prove them wrong by becoming ridiculously successful at whatever they said you cannot do.

4. Desire and willingness to learn. Listen, you cannot be successful in whatever you are doing unless you are willing to put in time and effort in learning about whatever it may be. So, if you are starting a new entry level job with a goal of reaching the top of the corporate ladder or eventually starting your own business, you must, and I repeat, you must become the subject matter expert in whatever you are doing, and not just in your immediate role or position with specific title assigned to it, but well outside of your immediate role, and in the positions two or three levels above you. It does not matter where you are now, what matters is where you want to go. So, if you want to move from beginner entry level role into a higher-level executive position within the company, then you must think and act as if you are in that role already. Some come into a role thinking that all I need to do is just do my job and focus on my immediate responsibilities that were outlined in the job description or explained during initial new hire training, and I

will achieve the position and lifestyle I am seeking. However, it does not work that way. By following and just doing bare minimum results. You have got to think big picture, always look for opportunities to learn, expand your knowledge, experience, skill set, and think from a position that you have in mind, not from the position where you are now. What that means is seeking and accepting new and more challenging opportunities, take on complex and challenging projects, and always look for ways to help to move your company forward. It is ok that you may not know how to do everything that a particular task or project requires, say yes, and then learn, ask questions, and learn again. This is how you grow personally, professionally, and in your existing role, while setting yourself up for success and future that is just around the corner. Are you ready to take your career to the next level? If so, what you waiting for? Go and get it. You know you can, and you will, but also remember about the importance of work and family balance and why it is important.

Work and Family Balance – Why is It Important to Have Balance

I am sure this is not the first time you hear about the importance of work and family balance. Personally, it is a lot easier said than done. When at work, we have a multitude of projects, various assignments, emails, and other duties that we are responsible for as leaders. We, of course, do not want to fall behind and potentially miss deadlines set for us or by us. Therefore, we spend long hours at work or our business until the work is done, so that we are not shuffling work from today to another day. Sounds familiar?

Salary vs. Hourly

When you are on salary, especially if you are managing your own business, team, or department, you are not limited by 8-hour workday. Therefore, you essentially have the freedom to create your own hours and schedule, with main objective in mind – complete the work, project(s), or other important tasks that must be completed daily, weekly, and monthly. Sometimes, when you can complete all your work early, you are generally able to go home sooner. However, you may also spend 12+ hours in the office, when you are overwhelmed with work or have a large project that you are working on with tight deadlines.

What we tend to forget as leaders, is to have a healthy balance between work and family. We often spend more time at our place of business and less time with our family and children. I will be the first one to admit that it is one of my biggest opportunity areas to this day. I tend to find myself with several projects and various reports that I am working on at any given time, and simply cannot leave the work that I can do today for the next day to work on, therefore, I will usually stay I the office until the work is done. Usually, tomorrow brings new projects and tasks that would simply add more to my project management queue. I am sure there are many leaders that find themselves in a similar situation daily. When I would go to one of my previous bosses and ask if I can go home, he would always tell me: "If you can say that you have completed 100% of all of your work today, and you can put your stamp of approval on it, then you yes, you may go home." What that thought me was not to transfer my workload to the next day, but to complete what is on my to do list the same day without changing due dates.

How to create more balance between your terribly busy work life and to spend more time with your family and friends?

What I found that works for me is to commit in taking at least 2-3 days off each month and dedicate those days to my family only, not work. Sometimes it may require to not checking your work emails, of course, in this instance you would want to make sure that you have someone in your business that will be your back up while you are out of the office and have your out of the office reply set accordingly. This way, you would not have to worry about potentially missing or not responding to an escalated situation when it arises and needs an immediate attention. Same goes for taking vacation(s) during the year. If you company or your business offers paid vacation time, then it is a good idea to take some time off during the year and visit the places that you always wanted to visit. Being able to take several days off will require good amount of planning on your part to ensure that you have enough of vacation time available, your work is complete, and there are no outstanding projects that are pending. Everyone has their own preferences for where they want to spend their perfect vacation. If your idea of a perfect vacation is to go to the beach, taking road trip and travel across the United States, or maybe it is staying in the comfort of your own home and read books, whatever it may be for you, use that time for yourself and your family versus thinking about work. Believe it or not, but when you come back from vacation, you work will be there waiting on you.

Advantages of taking time off

When you occasionally take time off throughout the month and vacation or who during the year, you will stay refreshed, energized, full or new ideas, and ready to tackle whatever task may be in front of you. Good luck to you, and remember, you are the creator of a perfect work and family life balance, so keep it nicely always balanced.

In addition to creation of work-life balance, you are also responsible for creating the professional image at work or in your place of business where you are viewed as an expert at what you do and can be counted for help and guidance when situation calls for it. Are you a subject matter expert at what you do or specialize? Are you seeking opportunities to expand and enhance your skill set and continue adding to your list of professional strengths, or do you feel a sense of entitlement and are expecting for opportunities to find you?

Tenure and Sense of Entitlement vs. Focusing on the Importance of Being the Best at What You Do or Specialize

Often, we wonder why we may not receive the promotion or the project that we thought we will receive and get disappointed when we do not and wonder why. "I know I had it, why not me?" are the questions that we ask in our mind or sometimes out loud. You might have put in several years working for a particular company; however, your specific situation and/or position seems to remain unchanged. Why is that?

Sense of entitlement

What may be happening here is feeling sense of entitlement. In your mind, you expect to receive that next available promotion, new position, or new exciting project, simply because you have been working for a particular company for many years and in some instance much longer than someone who recently took over a new role that you were after. Feeling of entitlement could lead us the wrong path where we begin pointing blame on someone or something else, instead of focusing on our own opportunities to address. Remember, it is never another person or situation that is preventing you from succeeding, it is you and your opportunities that you need to uncover and address.

Facing your own insecurities

Playing a blame game has never gotten anyone to a positive outcome, all it does is places your own insecurities out in the open versus addressing them. Come up with a game plan and act on it despite roadblocks encountered along the way.

Tenure does not guarantee success

Please do not get me wrong here, having tenure is a good thing, but long tenure is not a guarantee of your success. Instead, it is an important piece of your foundation.

What you do matters

Instead of focusing on tenure, focus on:

What do you do for a business?

What value do you bring in while working there?

What problems are you helping to solve?

What solutions are you presenting to address specific challenges that team, department, or company may be facing?

These are important questions to ask yourself any time you are thinking about taking the next step in your career.

So, if you are in sales, are you the best salesperson in your company, and if so, why? What value do you bring in with your awesome sales skills? If you are not the best salesperson in your business, then ask yourself why would hiring manager choose you for a role that you want. At the end of the day most companies are in business of making money by helping to solve specific problems for their customers. So, when you look at yourself from this perspective, what value do you bring to your company to help fulfill its mission? If you are unable to answer this question, then this may be your opportunity to seek constructive feedback to ensure that you understand where you are today and where you are going. Then, align your actions and energy to match your and business goals and expectations.

Another critical component of any business is marketing, and there are many ways that business choose to market their products and services – website, print, social media, etc. However, one way to find out how your business is doing is to ask your customers. Word of mouth is an immensely powerful way advertising. Your customer will tell you and others that they know what they think about you and your business, and if they would recommend your business to their friends and family. So, unhappy customer is most certainly a negative marketing for your business.

Unhappy Customer = Negative Marketing for Your Business

How was your experience? – The power of negative feedback

We as consumers of everyday products and services come to expect for our experience with a particular product or service that we purchase to be exceptional, and there is no middle ground. We will either be extremely satisfied or extremely dissatisfied. As a result, almost all businesses have a main goal – to provide its customers with great customer experience and product satisfaction. Most of the marketing created by businesses have some reference to 'customer experience' as a main attribute and focus point. However, does every company lives up to their commitment to provide exceptional customer experience and goes out of their way to ensure that each customer's need and expectation is met? Quick answer is no, but the significant progress to improve customer satisfaction has been made overall over the period of last few years. The opportunity to close the gap of where customer leaves unhappy or dissatisfied, and in some instances terribly upset, is still present and should be taken very seriously by businesses that are not living up to their customers' expectations.

What are the consequences of poor customer review or experience for a business?

I strongly believe that regardless how much money is spent to create beautiful and engaging marketing collateral, if the consumer leaves your business dissatisfied or upset, their power of negative feedback via word of mouth or via digital and social media platforms will have a significant, and in some instances detrimental negative effect on the business in question and their business image.

When we, as consumers, are unhappy with a service or product we encounter, we immediately share our negative experience with everyone we know verbally or by sharing it on social media platforms. Additionally, if we receive a survey from a company to share our experience, we most certainly will complete the survey, regardless of where we may be or how long the process may take. Why? Because we, as consumers, want for our opinions to be heard in hopes of improving the experience in the future. Also, the likelihood of us returning to the business where we have received poor customer experience is extremely low, since there are so many other options available offering the same or similar products and/or services. This is especially true in the restaurant and hospitality industries. Thus, the consumer takes their business somewhere else, and business which they have left loses long-term and loyal customer. So, does it make sense for any business to make sure that all their customers receive an exceptional experience, where anything less is unacceptable? Of course, it does, if that business expects to remain successful and continue to grow.

What can a business do to ensure that their customers are satisfied with their products and services, and to continue to live up to customers' expectations?

Ensure that company staff in all levels of the organization is fully trained in products and services offered by the company

Ensure that all business staff receives extensive customer service training, regardless of prior experience

All business employees should know and understand company's vision and mission statements. More importantly, understand what is in it for them, and how they can contribute to company's overall success

All employees should understand, buy in, and live company's culture every day. If an employee does not know, understand, and own their part in company's success and direction, they may become disengaged and uninterested, which may result in them providing less than great customer service to their customers

Company conducts regular customer satisfaction surveys, and act on satisfaction survey feedback, especially if any of the feedback is less than great. How do you know what your customers are saying about your business without giving them an opportunity to share feedback? You do not. And it is equally critical to act on the feedback provided, otherwise there is no value in those surveys. For example, if customer recommends a change to a process, procedure, or product, business should take each recommendation seriously and explore process/product for improvements.

Have presence on all major social media platforms, such as: Facebook, Twitter, Instagram, Pinterest, Tumblr, and LinkedIn. Customer should have an ability to visit company's social media pages to leave feedback, follow latest business updates, and to stay actively engaged in the life of the business.

Have adequate customer support personnel available to answer customers' calls, questions, and inquiries during optimum business hours build around their customers' needs and availability, including weekends.

These are just some steps of many that any business can take to improve their customer satisfaction, retain their existing and loyal customers, and, of course, acquire new.

At the end of the day, what matters to a customer is for businesses to recognize and respect what the customer wants and expects when purchasing and utilizing products and services sold or offered by the business every day, not just some days, while committing to provide an exceptional customer service. Why would a loyal consumer leave any business, if their wants, needs, and expectations are being consistently met? They would not, and instead they will remain a customer who recommends the business, products, or services to everyone they know. Do not underestimate the power of unhappy customer and the negative business marketing. What about your employees and their development and involvement in life of a business? Do they feel empowered?

Empowerment Through Involvement

Many people say, I am included, that "I learn the best by doing." Information learned during training, seminar or conference is great, but unless it is applied in practice in the real life, there is little to no value in it. Therefore, hands-on experience is one of the best ways to learn and apply what you had learned.

Some of the best training sessions I had attended included group hands-on projects and assignments, where group had to brainstorm, create a plan, and present to a larger audience in a set period of time. This is great opportunity to share your thoughts and opinions with the rest of the group, collaborate, and present the best overall solution. It is an actual hands-on exercise that helps for the information to stick in your head versus just on paper.

It is not going to be perfect the first time around

When you transition from theory to practice, do not expect to be perfect from the start, there is going to be some trial and error, there will be roadblocks and mistakes made, but this initial period will pass. It is like in sales or first time receiving or making a call to/from a prospective customer, you are nervous because of the unknown. You may have all the information, training, and tool needed to do a job, but until you do it, make few calls, only then everything will start to come together – learning by doing takes over. After a period of time, you are no longer afraid and feel extremely comfortable, maybe even ready to teach others.

Developing teams and leaders through empowerment

How are the most successful teams built?

There are so many ways in use today by managers and leaders alike to build and grow a team, however, the most successful team which creates and develops successful leaders, is the one that is empowered.

What is the empowered team?

It is the team that can function and deliver strong results with or without a business leader present. It is the team which relies on each other's expertise and support to perform. It is the team that is empowered to make necessary business decisions without having to wait for an approval or direction from a business leader, if all business policies and processes are being adhered to as required. Often, critical opportunities are missed by a business simply because teams are unable to function on their own while leader is unavailable, to approve or authorize even the basic step in the performance process. Team members could have acted, but they did not because they are not empowered to make such decisions without prior approval.

Empowered teams create empowered leaders

When team operates as one unit, when team is encouraged to make tough calls, incorporate out of the box thinking and innovate, great leaders emerge from such team. Empowerment encourages thinking, risk taking, leadership, and innovation. Naturally, leaders which strong determination, persistence, trust or their peers, and charisma, will begin leading other team members towards a common goal without official title.

Why not every team in every business creates empowered teams?

Some business leaders are simply afraid to let go and to allow team members to make important decisions, instead requiring their approval for each new task or process. Some business leaders do not invest enough of their time to grow and develop new leaders which already exist in each team and are waiting for an opportunity to be discovered and mentored. This type of leadership typically creates disengaged employees and potential future leaders with a lot of potential choose to leave the business and seek opportunities for growth elsewhere.

Benefits of empowering through involvement

Lower turnover, reduction in hiring costs

Greater job satisfaction

Happier employees – happier customers

Improvement in customer service metrics and customer retention

Great leaders and employees are developed and retained long-term

Stronger sense of involvement, trust, transparency, and dedication to company's vision among employees

So, with all these benefits in mind why not create and foster teams that are empowered and involved in decision making process in every business? There is no good reason for not doing so. As Benjamin Franklin said: "Tell me and I forget. Teach me and I remember. Involve me and I learn."

So, how can a business leader help identify and develop potential in his or her employees? Are your employees motivated by a paycheck they receive or are they motivated by opportunities to learn and grow that are available in the place of business?

Identifying and Developing Potential in Others - Do You Really Care or Are You in for an Easy Ride

Are you motivated by a paycheck or opportunity to learn and grow?

Typically, a seasoned leader or manager can quickly if not immediately tell during an interview or when leading a new team if someone is there to find a career and grow with a business, or if he or she is there for a paycheck and paycheck only.

This could be determined through asking questions that are open-ended vs. yes and no, encouraging a person to speak freely and openly. Of course, each manager knows what specifically they are looking for in someone's answers, and if a person they are speaking with a good fit for the position, team, and their business.

Why are you wearing shorts and a t-shirt?

It is even more important to observe how a person answers each question, their tone, use of body language, and, of course, their dress code. If someone comes to the interview dressed as if they just left a gym or finished running errands and decided to stop by, how committed do you think they are to the job they are applying for? Do they really treat this opportunity as something special and important for their future growth and success, as well as success of the business, or do they simply need a job, probably second or third in the last twelve months?

Steps of talent discover and development – Why create a false reality?

So, bringing the right people on board is the first particularly important step. The next step is to uncover and begin building a career path with employees who are deeply committed to their own success and future, not just within business walls but also outside, on their own time. Many people will tell you that they are interested in their own personal development, interested in achieving their personal goals and dreams, and are ready to immerse themselves into learning. However, next thing you know, they leave work and learning stops. Then as a leader, you are asking yourself a question – why create a false reality, why pretend to be someone you are not? It is important to remember, that no one can or wants to make someone want to learn and grow personally and professionally, there is no reason for a leader to waste their time if a person is not interested in taking the next step in their personal development and career path.

Success only comes to those who are ready to receive it

If you are not ready to invest your time and energy into your own development, no one can help you or do it for you. Therefore, there is no need to pretend to want something more in life or in your career if you are not willing or ready to put in the work, and not just for a day, week, month, or year, the lifestyle would need to change for the rest of your life. Sounds like a strong commitment. It is, to change where you are and get closer to where you want to be, current mindset and habits must change.

Unlocking the potential – characteristic of someone who is ready to learn and take their career to the next level

This is where great leaders come in, leaders that can uncover and develop talented and committed individuals, while helping them to find the path to follow to achieve their goals and eventually live the life they always wanted to live. These individuals that want more than what is being provided, they are willing to go an extra mile to not only reach, but to exceed performance expectations that they are presented with. These individuals create their own performance benchmarks and work hard to achieve them. They are always ready for more challenging tasks and projects, because, they are excited by the challenge, and they are not afraid to ask questions for better understanding, or to ask for help when it is needed. These individuals are always looking for opportunities to help improve the business, and pro-actively bring their ideas and solutions to the business leaders. Lastly, they are not afraid to speak up and share their thoughts and opinions when appropriate or when asked.

With these characteristics in mind, it is quite easy to uncover and recognize individuals who are ready to learn regardless the size of your team or business, all you must do is to keep your eyes and ears open, and keep an open door, open communication policy in your place of business. Once you have established trust with your employees, people who are willing to and are ready to take their development to the next level will naturally gravitate towards you.

What to do once you have discovered an individual who is ready to learn and comes to you for guidance and help?

Next and important step is to sit down and have an open and constructive discovery conversation with an employee, to know and understand their goals and aspirations in their professional career and in life.

Once leader understand employee is wants, needs, and goals, he or she should develop an incredibly detailed and challenging plan of development together with an employee. At the end of the day, it is an employee who owns their growth and development, where a leader serves as a guide and mentor, as well as someone who holds an employee accountable to their goas that they have set to accomplish. This plan should be a live document, and must be reviewed and updated regularly, checking off completed goals, and setting new. The progress never stops, neither does learning. However, you cannot do everything by yourself, regardless of your skills and expertise, to see your business and employees grow, the business leader must be able to work with and through others.

Executive Leadership – Working with and Through Others

At the beginning of our professional careers – using knowledge power to get in

As most of us start our professional careers, typically after completing many years of school, we only have one thing and that is our knowledge that we have acquired over the years of schooling. We have various theories that we have learned but have not tested them yet in the real life outside of books, projects, and exams. We are hungry for challenge, new life in the real-world of career seeking, earning income, and getting into the environment where we can begin using all that knowledge from books and our teachers. So, this is when we begin using our knowledge power, while starting our journey in the new career and new company. We cannot offer anything yet to our employer, except for our knowledge, which we are eager to put to the test.

Transitioning knowledge power into Experience Power – using knowledge to acquire experience

After working for few years in one or multiple companies, utilizing our knowledge and building experience, we increase our professional portfolio and grow our resume with each work experience we encounter. Over the years we learn different positions within the company we work in, anything from entry level to executive level. Years add up and so is our professional experience which we actively use to get into better, higher paid positions. Of course, as we grow professionally, we grow the amount of experience we have in a particular field or line of work. If we are committed to constantly learning new things, and ways to improve personally and professionally every day, we not only acquiring more experience, but we also uncover and grow our strengths while addressing our opportunities or weaknesses. When we invest time and resources in our personal development, we are investing in our growth and future opportunities that do become available to us over time. Initial knowledge will only get so far before experience begins to play a larger role as new opportunities present themselves to us. In most cases you are heavily relying on your knowledge and experience to get things done. Yes, you may engage your team and may even delegate few tasks, however, you mostly rely on yourself, because, you know you can do a specific task in most cases better than others. This way of working and managing will only get you far enough in your professional career before you must rely on others to help you accomplish tasks at hand and to be able to work smarter, more effectively, and efficiently. You must realize that doing everything on your own is an overly complex and ineffective practice, therefore, you need to engage the rest of your experienced team to get this done.

Executive Leadership – getting things done with and through others

Executive leader has many responsibilities and high expectations for the work to be completed on time and for it to be done correctly with highest quality possible. Therefore, executive leader trusts and works through his or her highly experienced team members by delegating if not all then most of the day-to-day tasks and projects to them, while focusing his or her time and energy on high level strategy items to keep moving the company and business forward. By trying to do everything on your own, all your time and energy will be focused on daily issuers, problems, tasks, while strategic and important tasks and initiatives would go nowhere, thereby, negatively effecting the business and its growth. So, to be a successful leader remember to trust your team, and giving them an opportunity to learn, make mistakes, overcome obstacles, and help you in driving the business forward. Focus your time and energy where it is needed the most, that includes developing and growing your people, and empower your team to take on tasks where they have experience in, giving them an opportunity to do what they know best. Do not try to do everything yourself. I am not saying that you cannot do everything on your own if you really wanted to, because you can., but it is not the practice that good leader should be engaging in to continue to learn and grow, while helping his or her team to do the same.

Do you believe that feedback given by a business leader or manager is received the same way by every employee, or do you think that each employee receives and understands feedback differently? If you think it is the latter, you are correct. Let us review this topic in more detail in the next section.

Constructive and Deconstructive Feedback – Sharing the Feedback That Matters

What is the difference between constructive and deconstructive feedback?

What we hear most often when referring to receiving feedback is constructive feedback, whether it comes from our parents, relatives, friends, or our boss at work. Constructive feedback is intended to highlight opportunity areas that we may have that we need to work on to improve personally and/or improve our professional performance to advance in our careers. Failure to act on the constructive feedback received typically results in lack of progress in our professional and/or personal life, which in turn yields a greater job dissatisfaction due to lack of progress or advancement, or lack of pay level desired. It works the same way in our life outside of professional arena. For example, if someone is recommending you exercise more, eat healthier or stop stoking, and you choose to ignore their recommendation and feedback despite them explaining all the positive outcomes of taking recommended actions, the results you should expect to see are negative. Lack of action equals to lack of result. So, constructive feedback is important for us to receive and act on to continue to grow personally and professionally.

What is deconstructive feedback? Is it needed and why does it exist?

Deconstructive feedback is the complete, opposite of constructive. Meaning, when someone is sharing a deconstructive feedback with you, it is not intended to help you improve or get better at something, it is to discourage you from trying, pointing all the things that you are doing wrong or why you cannot succeed, and not sharing any ways to help you to overcome any opportunity areas that you may have. So, does the deconstructive feedback help you in any way? Of course not, all it does is discourage you from finding a way to improve and learn and keeping you where you are without taking any action. Sometimes, we may receive deconstructive feedback from other people without them even realizing that the feedback that they are sharing is not helping us in any way and, instead, discouraging us from trying to work harder and more effectively. Just like with constructive feedback, deconstructive feedback could be received in non-professional setting. For example, when someone you know is telling you that you should think about eating healthier, but do not share any ways or tips how you can do so, the feedback you receive does not help you, and instead all it does is demotivates you even more to look for a healthier food items. Therefore, deconstructive feedback serves no purpose unless it is combined with constructive feedback element, helping you and showing you how a specific behaviors or opportunities can be improved by you.

Remember, when sharing any feedback with another person at home or at work, make sure that the feedback you are sharing is constructive in nature and is designed to help the person receiving feedback to improve or get better at something, not demotivate, and discourage them.

Think about what you want to share, write it out if needed, and make sure that message you are about to share brings value to another person with each interaction.

Now, it is one thing to share feedback or relay information one-on-one, but what about sharing feedback and relaying important information to the group of people? When sharing information with a group, especially if it is a large group, one important thing that leader must remember and master is keeping your audience always engaged, regardless how long your presentation may be. So, do you keep a group of people engaged and listening to information you are sharing? This and other important questions are discussed in greater detail next, so keep on reading.

Group Presentation Tips – Ways to Present with Confidence and Keeping Your Audience Engaged

Steps to an effective presentation

To give an effective group presentation two things must happen, one – the presenter must be comfortable to speak in front of a group, regardless of its size, and two – the presenter must keep their audience engaged and interested throughout the entire presentation.

I am not including the obvious steps that one must take prior to the presentation, such as: conducting detailed research about the topic to be presented on, creating presentation outline or agenda, and ensure that all necessary room arrangements are completed, such as: location, presentation materials, audio and visual technology, and room temperature. All these steps are must before any presentation and can be completed by almost any moderately experienced presenter. However, feeling comfortable and relaxed during presentation, even with the top-level executives present vs. feeling nervous and scared, as well as being able to keep your audience engaged, is a step that must be mastered if we want to take our presentation and our message to the next level.

How to feel more comfortable and relaxed during presentation?

Many speakers, even more experienced, still feel nervous whenever they need to step onto the state or in the conference room to present. They have done their preparation, they know the content and what they want to discuss and share with listeners/attendees, however, for some reason fear and nervousness comes to play whenever it is a go time. Why is that the case? A lot of times the presentation that we give can determine our future growth or advancement within the company or implementation of the initiative we are presenting on. Therefore, we are so afraid that we may make a mistake that will destroy any opportunities we may be going after. Even though we have spent countless hours studying and preparing our presentation, we still feel that we may have missed something.

You can never know everything, and that OK

Here is a thing, we can never know everything. There is always going to be something that we do not know, regardless of all the research and study completed, and that is completely normal. In most situations and presentations, we should know and be ready to answer most questions coming our way from the audience, if we have done necessary amount of research and preparation beforehand. If there is a one-off question that you do not know, you should be comfortable to take that question offline for further research and provide the answer at the later time. It is better to do that than pretending that you know the answer and make something up, it is rather obvious when a person does not know the answer and is trying to create something out of thin air. Do not be that person. Instead, take down the question, and ask the person asking it if you can come back to them with the answer after the meeting, as you need to investigate it further. Knowing this process and expectations, speaker/presenter should feel more comfortable going into the presentation.

You are speaking to people, not robots

When you are presenting in front of others, remember that they are people, just like you are, regardless of different titles they might have achieved within the company or outside of your immediate business. Therefore, please know that if you are observed as extremely nervous and scared, your audience will quickly recognize it and will use it to see how well you present under pressure and will typically test your level of understanding of the topic presented to the smallest detail. In this case, the perception that your audience may receive is if you did not prepare enough or know much about the topic you are presenting on, and that is why you are nervous. So, take it easy, relax, you know the subject or topic inside and out, assuming you did you necessary preparation beforehand, you've lived it for some time, there's nothing that you could be asked that you don't already know the answer to, and even if there is something you might have missed during the research, you can take the question offline and come back with an answer later in the presentation or after the meeting. With all these things in mind, there should be no reason for anyone to be nervous or scared to step in a room full of people and present with ease and confidence.

How do you keep your audience engaged throughout the entire presentation?

Best way you can do that is by going into the presentation not with a plan to speak for most of the presentation, but with an objective to create a conversation vs. monologue. Nobody wants to sit in a room for 1+ hours just to listen for someone to speak the entire time. If you take most of the presentation to yourself, people will quickly disconnect from the presentation and disconnect from you as a presenter. However, if listeners feel that they are part of the presentation where they are encouraged to share their opinions and feedback, they would be much more connected to you and the content.

It is never about you, and always about the listener…

One way you can keep your audience engaged is by pausing regularly and checking for understanding, while welcoming input and ideas from all attendees. Remember, it is never about you, and all about the listener. Think about this when you are building your presentation. You may have created an exceptionally beautiful presentation deck with advanced graphics, images and other content, this deck may be 50+ slides long, and you may think that It is great, but ask yourself if your audience would feel the same. Considering your indented audience, do you feel that they would be interested watching you present slides full of detailed content for 1+ hours and still be engaged? In most cases these types of presentations end with "Do you have any questions?" and there's silence in the room, or the answer is "No," because, everyone is checked out and ready to get out the room to go about their business. Therefore, remember to build your presentation around your intended audience to create engagement, allowing multiple opportunities to ask questions and provide input, and create a dialogue. You should be a facilitator of the conversation where your audience does most of the talking, not the other way around. Focus on telling the story vs. reading the information off the slide, people can read on their own. Discuss key points and takeaways, inviting feedback and input from others.

These few points should help you to enhance your presentation and turn it into a productive and engaging two-way conversation, where audience chooses to be part of it vs. being required to attend. Additionally, you will receive effective and constructive feedback you are seeking to move project or idea forward.

Being an effective and engaging communicator is important, but leadership and team development does stop with group presentations and feedback sharing. The topic of team development and leadership is interesting and broad, especially if you are passionate about building high-performing teams with engaged and dedicated to their own and business's success employees. Next chapter of this book is focused on this very topic – Team Development and Leadership.

Chapter 10 – Team Development and Leadership

We Are in This Together No Matter the Position or the Title – Working together as one highly efficient and effective team

It is an awesome feeling and sight when a group of people work together as one team to accomplish a common goal, task, or project. Why? Because each person in a group knows their specific responsibility and are highly skill in what they do. Therefore, when they work in a team, everything runs like clock-work – efficient, effective, and on time. Nobody is thinking about what other members of the same team are doing, they just worry about their own task/project at hand and give their undivided attention and energy towards that one thing. Also, when a specific task has been completed, they move on to another project without waiting until someone comes to them to tell them what to do, they just do it.

One of the examples of an awesome teamwork that I have observed recently is a construction crew working on building a new house. Crew arrives early in the morning while most people steel asleep and begin setting up their work area, bring required materials, begin mixing concrete to lay bricks later, creating a functional place to work throughout the day. Then each individual person of the crew begins to work on their own project in the overall main objective or goal of building a house. They bring materials tools and materials that they need for work and begin. One person may be working on preparing the concrete throughout the day and deliver it to other crew members who need it. Another person may be laying bricks, and that is what they do all day until the job is done. The best part is, project manager who is overseeing the entire project and serves as point of contact for all questions that may arise from the builder, supplier, or person whose house is being built, he does not stand there, doing nothing and micromanaging, instead, he rolls up his sleeves and begins to do his part in helping the crew with construction work. Therefore, when you look at the work of an effective construction crew you see highly efficient, focused, and supporting team that works together to accomplish the main goal, regardless of their individual positions or titles.

If every team can work together just like in the example with construction crew shared earlier, we would see time spent on completion of a particular assignment or project reduce significantly, and as we all know that time is money. Therefore, if we can complete a project in less time delivering the same high-quality work, then we would be able to save time and money, and as result complete more projects, make more sales, and create more revenue for our business.

Unfortunately, very often instead of focusing on our own work and do it to the best of our ability because we are the subject matter experts in a particular line of work, instead we tend to focus our attention on others and monitor as well as often criticize their work even though we may have limited knowledge or understanding of a task at hand. Therefore, what happens in this situation the one who is being monitored or micromanaged tends to constantly worry about what they are doing and how they are doing it, even though they are the subject matter experts in their line of work, but because they are constantly being corrected, they being to second-guess themselves. When this happens productivity drops, time is wasted, and project's completion time is therefore extended, often missing originally set deadlines. Why not allow a subject matter expert to do their work without interruptions and constant control? Why not focus on your own tasks that need to be completed, tasks in which you are a subject matter expert? Why not have confidence in your team members, help them, not criticize them, and work together as one effective and efficient team? Wouldn't you agree that working together is much more fun and enjoyable vs. working alone? It is challenging to build an effective, high-performing, and collaborative team without an important skill of diplomacy. Why with diplomacy being so important in an effective dialogue it is not being used as often as it needs to be in important conversations and negotiations? This and other questions are what is coming up next.

Diplomacy – Being in control of the dialogue while compromising, actively listening, and showing respect to those with whom we interact

If someone asked me – "What is the most important skill in any productive and effective dialogue?" without any hesitation I would say "Diplomacy." So, why is diplomacy is so important for an effective dialogue and why it is not being used as often as it needs to be in important conversations and negotiations that many of us participate in on the regular basis.

Unfortunately, there is not one good answer to this question, however, one thing that stands out to me what I am thinking about diplomacy is people's desire to be right to satisfy our own egos and feel good even if conversation takes a negative/unproductive turn. We want to be and feel right even when we are wrong. Why? Because the illusion of being right helps to boost our ego and allows us to feel good about ourselves and our actions. But what we often forget to consider is how other people feel about our words and our actions. We miss a critical part of the bigger picture, and that is that dialogue can never be effective without mutual respect, understanding, and often compromise.

Compromise is an especially important component of any diplomatic negotiation. Without compromise and genuine respect for another party in the dialogue, it is your opinion vs. someone else's where both sides walk away from conversation with high boosted ego but in disagreement. So, what exactly are we accomplishing by being right at the expense of another person's defeat, walking away from conversation with feeling of bitterness? We accomplish absolutely nothing in such situation, all we are doing is damaging our relationship with another person or group. So, the issue remains unresolved and once positive relationship is now damaged. Does anyone win in such situation? Of course, the answer is 'no.'

Therefore, being diplomatic, by listening vs. arguing, being respectful of another person's or group's point of view and perspective, be willing to compromise, considering all sides of the dialogue is important in having a positive, effective, and mutually beneficial conversation, dialogue, and overall engagement. Remember, these points next time you engage in any conversation. Remember to be diplomatic vs. allowing your ego to only focus on your own thoughts and opinions.

So, how can one develop and lead a self-managed and highly effective team? Keep on reading to find out.

How to Develop and Lead a Self-Managed Teams

Wouldn't it be nice if you can go on a long vacation somewhere overseas and not worry about your business? Be able to turn off your cell phone and not having to check your emails every few minutes?

It is possible to reach this point of self-managed team and business. Will it take a lot of work on your part initially? Of course, it would, but putting in necessary amount of effort would absolutely worth every minute that you had invested in developing your team.

Sometimes business leaders make a mistake thinking that just because someone has been in the specific line of work for an exceptionally long time and has a lot of experience, that he or she does not need any additional development, coaching, and guidance. This is far away from the truth. To build a self-managed team and business, you, as their leader, need to invest into individual coaching and mentoring of every single employee, while focusing on their goals and dreams in life.

People will only care about your business as much as you care about them and their future. Your employees need to see and understand your overall vision, where business is heading, why a certain path is chosen by you, and what role are they playing in the process.

Your employees, business partners, team leaders, are all an important part, if not crucial part, of your business success and are drivers of your vision. Without your team members, regardless of the team's size, you do not have a business.

Therefore, it is critical to invest in your team members' development by building on top of their already existing strengths and experience, while uncovering and correcting their opportunity areas. Regardless how much experience someone may have, they are always looking for ways to learn more and for someone to show them the way. They are looking for a leader and mentor who is genuinely interested and dedicated in their personal development and growth. When you are able to explain your vision to your team, explain the 'why' behind it, clearly identify their individual roles in the process or reaching company's goals and performance objectives, feel that they are part of the business versus just working there, understand the value that they contribute, and see how their and your actions are getting them closer to their life-time dreams, you have created a dedicated and self-managed team and business.

Put yourself in your team members' shoes. How would you feel when you come to work and do not feel valued or appreciated, and how do you feel when you are? I know that if feels hundred times better when you feel valued, respected, and appreciated for what you do. Apply the same type of analysis when you are building, developing, and leading your team.

What are some of the steps that you may take to build a self-managed team and business?

Learn about your team members, their likes, hobbies, families, etc. It feels great when your colleague knows the names of your kids and their ages, and/or knows about your favorite hobby.

Spend several minutes each day interacting with your team. If you sit in your office the entire day and do not spend any time with your team, how do you think they feel about your level of engagement and interest in their needs and wants? Remember, perception management is an important for a leader.

Meet with each team member individually and learn about their career goals and life-time dreams, while sharing more information about you and your goals and dreams.

Create a goal worksheet outlining steps that your team members can take with your guidance, coaching, and support, to get closer to reaching their personal goals and dreams.

Create a follow up system, weekly or monthly, where you meet and review your team members' progress on their personal development journey

Be available for feedback and questions when your team members need you.

Act on the feedback that is shared with you, and if unable to act on the specific suggestions provided right away, be sure that your team members understand that their feedback is valuable as well as understand as to why action may not be taken right away, if at all. Perhaps, there's resourcing limitations, policies, or business needs.

Be as transparent as you can be, to build trust and engagement

Empower your leaders and encourage pro-active and big picture thinking

Support your team, even when they make mistakes, while helping them to learn from mistakes made and grow personally and professionally.

When your team members come to you with questions and need direction, before answering the question, ask your team members how would have answered the question. Look for big picture thinking considering all possible outcomes, both positive and negative

Encourage your team leaders to come to you with solution(s) ready when presenting a problem

When you as a leader must make important decisions, be sure to explain the 'why' behind those decisions, for your team to understand your reasoning and factors considered

Ask your team members for their feedback and suggestions when working on projects

Effectively delegate tasks and projects to your team leaders versus handling it all yourself. Effective delegation is an important part of leadership development. Make sure to check in periodically to monitor the progress of the project assigned and to offer an opportunity to ask questions to ensure complete understanding

Establish a process of issue escalation when you are not around (ex. long vacation or business travel). Make sure that you team members know, understand, and follow proper issue escalation path, especially for urgent matters.

Engage with your team members daily and show the non-business side of you. People not only should feel comfortable coming to you with their questions and concerns, but also to simply talk about life, joke and laugh together.

Best of luck to you in building and leading a successful, happy, engaged, and self-managed team and business. You deserve taking a vacation and focus your energy on your family and friends. Remember, your team, people that work with you, are your business.

As Tim Fargo said: "People respond well to managers who stop being bosses and start being leaders. They go the extra mile if they genuinely believe that your success is their success and vice versa."

Team leadership and development does not happen without leader having to conduct many difficult conversations with his or her employees. So, what should a leader to prepare and conduct an effective conversation with employees of the business regardless conversation's complexity? Let us explore this and other questions in the next section.

How to Have a Difficult Conversation. Steps to Prepare and Conduct an Effective Conversation, Regardless of Its Complexity

Have you ever had to have a difficult conversation with someone you either knew or worked with? I have, and I will tell you it was not an easy task at first. I was extremely nervous, unprepared to receive push back and objections, and was not sure how to respond. I think that I was even more nervous than then person whom I was addressing. Therefore, do not feel bad if you were in the same situation previously, and do not think that because of such experience you are a bad leader, because you are not. Since my first experience of having a difficult conversation, I have had many more difficult conversations, and I will tell you that even today I still feel nervous when I must have such conversation.

Ability to have an effective difficult conversation is a skill that you can learn and develop with practice.

Difficult conversations are often necessary to address and correct someone's behavior as well as relay critical and important information, something that he or she may not be open to at that time or agree to. However, the conversation still needs to take place, and you are the one who may be required to deliver it.

What are some examples of difficult conversations?

One example is providing constructive feedback to one of your employees or peers, when you know that he or she is not usually open to such feedback. Therefore, is it your responsibility as a leader to determine the best way to have a constructive and often direct conversation with an employee or peer while inspiring him or her to act and move forward, versus remaining where they are or, even worse, going backwards. I will discuss ways to have an effective conversation while delivering a constructive feedback a little later.

Another example of a difficult conversation is addressing someone's inappropriate behavior in a place of business. As leaders we are the ones who must have behavior-addressing conversations, which can be rather challenging at times. The main reason why this type of conversation can be challenging is because you often do not know how another person may react when negative feedback is presented to them. The person to whom you are speaking with may be incredibly positive and open to your feedback and coaching, or he or she may be extremely negative and non-receptive. Therefore, there are several unknowns in the preparation of having a difficult conversation with someone else.

There are, of course, many more examples of difficult conversations that you as a leader may run into, however, my goal is not to list every possible example, but to share some ways that you may use to prepare yourself for difficult conversations, and to ensure that these interactions are productive and encourage action.

I do not know a single person who enjoys having difficult conversations where constructive and often negative feedback must be presented to another person to encourage action and/or correct wrong behavior. Of course, we all enjoy having positive conversations where we share some good news with another individual or praising them for an excellent work that they have done. We usually go into these types of conversations without any preparation or any anxiety, because we know that the person will be happy to hear good news, there will not be any push back or disagreement, and the person will leave on an incredibly positive note looking forward to meeting with you again. I wish that all our conversations were positive, where we only discussed something good, however, that is not always the case. This is a good thing that we, as leaders, often must have difficult conversations, because, if all conversations were of a positive nature, we would never learn how to overcome our fears of facing another person and presenting negative/constructive feedback to them, and helping people to improve, while addressing their weaknesses and opportunity areas. Additionally, difficult conversations help us, as leaders, to enhance our strengths, overcome various obstacles, and as result we become more confident and respected leaders.

What steps can you take to turn negative difficult conversation into productive and action-oriented with a positive focus? How can you go from feeling nervous and unprepared to confident and knowledgeable by following few simple steps?

I am glad that you asked, because I am happy to share some of the ways that I use to help me overcome the challenge of difficult conversations and converting them into conversations that you lead with confidence and people focus.

Steps to prepare and conduct an effective conversation, regardless of its complexity

Conduct detailed research regarding the topic of conversation that you are going to address

Make sure that your conversation is based on facts and not assumptions

Create a conversation track by writing down your conversation plan on paper, listing all important parts of the conversation from Intro to Conclusion and Takeaways

Review your conversation plan several times and make necessary corrections/adjustments to your talk track

Practice your conversation out loud by reading through it. You may do it in-front of a mirror to observe your body language

Schedule adequate amount of time for your conversation, incorporating time for questions and answers

Prepare answers to anticipated questions/objections that you may receive from the person with whom you will be speaking, to be prepared and not caught off guard

You should know what questions are likely to come up from the research that you have conducted previously

Lack of confidence is a result of poor planning and research

Be prepared to present factual information when asked by another party

If you do not have facts to back your comments your credibility and knowledge will be tested and questioned. This will also result in damage to your confidence and reputation

At the beginning of the conversation explain the reason for a meeting, to address the first question in the person's mind

When sharing constructive feedback, make sure that you are facing the person with whom you are speaking with

Always maintain eye contact while speaking

Looking to the side or somewhere else, other than the person in-front of you, will make them question your confidence and comfort level

Focus on and present information while addressing specific situation, performance, or behavior

Pause several times during the conversation, to allow another person to ask questions and check for understanding

Answer all questions/objections with confidence, while providing specific examples gathered during your initial research prior to the conversation

Do not argue or attempt to talk over another person. Pause and allow him or her to voice their opinions before responding

Do not be nervous. Remember, it is another person, just like you, sitting in-front of you who needs your feedback and help

Recap your conversation at the end, and once again ask for questions. Attempt to answer all questions if you can. If you need to do additional research to answer some questions, then inform the person with whom you are speaking that you will need to conduct additional research to answer their question(s).

Be honest and transparent. If you do not know the answer, do not make it up. Instead, conduct additional research if needed

Close the conversation with takeaways while recognizing something positive that the person with whom you are speaking has contributed or displayed previously

Reinforce the person's ability to correct specific situation, behavior, or performance

The steps that I have shared with you are the steps that I use when I need to have a difficult conversation with another person. Following these steps helps me to structure my conversation, maintain my confidence, display a deep level of knowledge of the specific situation, and relate my sincere care and desire to help to the person with whom I am speaking with.

You cannot always control how the person will react to the information/coaching presented after the conversation, but you can control how you interact and present yourself during and after the conversation.

Be the confident leader that you are, and lead by example always.

The Importance of Constructive Feedback

How many times in your professional career or in school have you received constructive feedback from one of your peers, professors, or business leaders?

Based on my personal experience I have received direct constructive feedback many times, too many to count. Constructive feedback/criticism is usually given to help the person who is receiving the feedback to improve or change a specific behavior or practice, realize own opportunity areas, and address them. If you are not receiving regular feedback from your business leader about your performance and personal development regularly, then you should reach out for feedback. You as a leader should own your own development versus waiting until someone comes to you.

Why is constructive feedback important for personal and professional development?

Feedback helps uncover opportunity areas and enables you to focus on addressing those opportunity areas to continue developing and growing as a leader. We often tend to overlook or sometimes even ignore our own opportunity areas, partially because of our own ego, and partially because we hope that our opportunity areas will somehow take care of themselves. Well, the truth is, it does not work this way. To overcome your opportunity areas or leadership struggles, you need to uncover them first, and then create a plan of action to address them. That is why receiving and being open to a constructive feedback/criticism is extremely important to grow personally and professionally.

Sometimes you must overcome your own ego before you can be open to constructive feedback/criticism shared with you by other people. We often feel that we know and see everything, however, it is far from being true. Yes, we know a lot if not all about our own personality, our goals, and our strengths, but we often fail to understand how some of our actions, words that we use, or our emotions effect other people around us. Therefore, it is important to ask for constructive feedback/criticism from your peers, business leaders, teachers, and family members regularly.

Some of the steps that you may take to receive constructive feedback that you need on the regular basis are:

If you have someone who you report to in the company that you work for, such as your business leaders, see if you can set up regular feedback session with your leader. This feedback session could be weekly, bi-weekly, or monthly, and can take anywhere from 15 mins to 1 hour. The length of the session will depend on your leader's availability in their busy schedule. These sessions should be utilized to ask and encourage constructive feedback/criticism from your business leader about your performance, perception, and your professional development. Remember, for these sessions to be effective, you need to be open to receiving constructive feedback/criticism, which sometimes may be direct and may test your true willingness to learn and grow.

When regularly scheduled feedback sessions are not an option, you may do a quick check in with your business leader when he or she have few minutes available (5-10 mins.), and ask for constructive feedback during those quick check-ins.

In addition to the options already listed, you may also reach out for feedback to your peers in your business. It is equally important to know and understand feedback received from your peers. Being open to their feedback will help you to establish positive and productive working relationships with them, which should help you in your career in the long run.

What is the one critical part of constructive feedback process?

Of course, it is feedback implementation into action. Simply receiving feedback and being open to it is not going to address your performance or help you in overcoming your opportunity areas. It is feedback implementation and use are what should help to drive your personal and professional growth. An example of this would be learning about many different healthy eating habits and fitness exercises, and then continuing to follow unhealthy eating habits and do not exercise. Therefore, it is important to follow through on the feedback provided to you to see the expected results.

Remember, your goal is to be awesome every day, not some day. You are awesome!

Additional key points and takeaways:

Create a follow up process after sharing constructive feedback to check if the information share was retained and is being used

Encourage open feedback and ways that people can share their concerns and ask questions

If not, all questions were answered during the original conversation, be sure to conduct necessary research and provide your responses to the person with whom you spoke previously, as you had promised

Even after you become more confident and comfortable with having difficult conversations, continue to use the conversation planner every time. By doing so, you we retain the structure and consistency needed

Continue to practice delivering constructive feedback, even when you are not delivering one. Practice makes it perfect.

In addition to practicing delivering constructive feedback to your employees, you should also remember that if your goal is to build and lead an effective and high-performing team, having your team's trust in you as their leader and the direction in which you are taking the business is critical. Without your team's trust in you, it will be challenging for you to accomplish anything, let alone becoming a high-performing team with team members who support and promote your business's goals and objectives.

Team Building and Trust. How to Become a Team-Centric Leader

Team building is a remarkably interesting and challenging task. If you had previously managed a group of people, regardless of its size you know what I mean. Of course, managing 2-3 people vs. a group of 40-50 people has its differences, however, the main concept of successful team building is always the same – establishing and fostering team trust.

You can be very experienced manager, who has managed many different teams over the years, however, the main question you should ask yourself – did I simply managed the team(s) and delivered expected performance results and/or revenue, or was I developer of people and teams?

There are many different managing/leadership styles and each stale or approach is unique and different. Some people respond very well to managers who are direct and only focused on meeting and sometimes exceeding performance goals and objectives. Their goal is to come to work and do exactly what is expected of them and nothing more, then clock out and go home and do the same the next day. However, most people are looking for something more, they are looking and wanting to grow and develop professionally and personally, enhance their strengths, and overcome their opportunity areas.

How do you start in people development? What are your first steps?

The very first thing that you should start with is learning about each individual person on your team or teams, learning about their likes, dislikes, hobbies, family, career goals, and their unique personal and professional desires or wishes.

Do not expect for people to share their personal and professional desires or wishes the very first or second time you meet with them. It takes time to build trust with each person before they choose to open up to you and share their personal goals.

Trust is an important ingredient in successful team building. Without trust people will never share their true goals and wishes in life or career with you as their leader. Without trust you will receive a standard job-related response (ex. earn more money, get promoted, etc.), so trust is important in team development.

How do you establish trust?

One of the ways to establish trust is to follow-through on your promises every single time. If you know that you will be unable to deliver on what you about to promise, then do not promise it. Lack of follow through is one way to destroy any trust that you might have already established with your team.

Another way to establish trust is to be transparent when sharing relevant information with your team. If your followers feel that you are hiding something from them, they will not trust you. Be personable, people like to talk to people who are honest and personable. Bring your team along with your story, tell them about your past career struggles, obstacles that you had to overcome to succeed, tell them about yourself. For people to relate to you and your story, they need to know about you. I have seen many situations where others will turn away from their goals and dreams because they simply do not believe that they can accomplish them and reach their ultimate life-time dream(s). Therefore, if you have an impactful personal story that you can share with your followers, where you had to overcome many obstacles to reach your goal(s) or the leadership position that you may be in, they will relate their obstacles and their story to yours and see that it can be done. Once you have established trust with every member of your team, only then you can proceed with sharing your vision and team's mission statement. If you skip the step that I have outlined above—by helping your team related to your story and establish their trust in you as their leader—they may not be open or willing to support your vision and where you intend on taking them as a team.

Do not get discouraged if you are unable to obtain everyone is buy in initially. All that means is that you need to continue to work harder in establishing trust with every person on your team and continue uncovering personal goals and objectives with individuals who are not yet ready to support and promote your vision. It is not their fault, they are just not ready to follow you and may need more time learning about you as their leader and you leading them by example, as well as showing your team that you are genuinely interested in their development and growth personally and professionally.

Every person is unique and deserves individual attention. Then need to trust you first before they can share their thoughts and opinions openly with you as their leader. Therefore, it is important that you keep the open channel of communication with every person that you lead. Only then people will come to you and share their concerns and feelings and give you an opportunity to address them to regain or obtain their trust.

Once you have a team that trusts you 100%, support your goals and vision, then you are ready to share your expectations to achieve specific targets or performance goals and establish clear deadlines. But do not forget to bring your team along and explain what is in it for them and what are risks if performance goals and objectives are not met. If people trust you and support you, they will work harder to meet expectations and objectives set for the team.

Key takeaways:

Trust your team

Listen to their feedback and suggestions

Follow-through on your promises

Meet with your team regularly to create an avenue for them to share their thoughts, feelings, and concerns.

Your team members are your supporters and drivers of your vision. Therefore, be the type of leader whom they are willing to follow, and you will lead your business to success. Without your team you do not have a business!

Remember feedback is a conversation and it should never be a monologue where you as a leader give feedback to your employees without encouraging an open dialogue. If you want to learn how your employees feel and how your business is doing, you should listen more and speak less. Therefore, employee feedback and engagement are important for a leader and the business.

The Importance of Employee Engagement and Feedback

The reason why employee engagement is important to any organization, regardless of its size, is because it determines in which direction the organization will go. This could be the direction of success and growth, or the direction of eventual failure. It is important to develop and foster engaged workforce, where employees want to come to work every day, constantly searching for opportunities to learn and grow themselves and others, share ideas for improvement, and are open in sharing feedback.

Businesses with engaged employees are constantly changing and are looking for opportunities to improve existing processes and procedures. Leaders of businesses with highly engaged employees are focused on improving customer experience every day and on creating value for their customers. By customers I do not only mean external customers, but also internal customers – its employees. Everything begins with creating a comfortable, trusting, transparent, and caring environment to work in. In such environment employee is always welcomed and encouraged, business leaders, regardless of their titles, work alongside with frontline employees who are first to interact and assist external customers.

Most valuable and critical feedback comes directly from your customers. They will be the first group of people who will point out opportunity areas of any business, recognize company's strengths and weaknesses, and share valuable feedback for process improvements needed. Your frontline employees are your valuable link or bridge between your external customers and your business. Therefore, it is in your best interest as a business leader to create an atmosphere where your employees are encouraged and recognized for sharing their valuable feedback with business leaders, whether the feedback shared is positive or negative. They should not feel that they should only share positive feedback, but negative and constructive feedback as well, since most of business inefficiencies come from customers recognizing an opportunity for improvement.

How do you create an environment with high employee engagement?

Make sure to create and uphold an 'open door' policy for your employees. In the business where leaders support an 'open door policy,' employees are much more likely to come in and share the feedback versus when your office door is always closed. I completely understand that there will be exceptions during the day where your office door needs to be closed for conference calls and other important meetings, however, outside of those exceptions your door should remain open

When employee comes to you to share their feedback, put everything that you were doing on pause and give your undivided attention to your employee

If you promise something to your employees, be sure to always follow through. Otherwise, lack of follow through may affect employees' trust in your words

Seek and encourage employee participation in team meetings and other company events. During such events ask employees to share their ideas and best practices to help their peers and external customers

Always take your employees' feedback seriously and do not discount anything that is being said as unimportant. Remember, feedback your internal employees are sharing with you not only comes from them, but also your external customers

Know your employees, their likes, hobbies, family, and their goals and dreams. It is important to know and understand what is important to them and what they are looking to accomplish in career and life

Be as transparent as you can be and keep your employees in the know about upcoming changes within the business and explain the 'why' behind any major changes. Your employees should be able to answer one important question behind any change – "What's in it for me?"

Engage your team in various projects that you may be working on, because, at the end of the day everything you do is for your internal and external customers

Smile when you interact with your employees because smile goes a long way

Be yourself with others. Do not pretend to be someone who you are not. Your employees may not immediately tell you, but they know when you are not your real you

Trust your team. They will make mistakes, but who does not. It is your responsibility, as their leader, to show them the correct path, and support them along the way

At this point you should have good understanding what is an engaged team and how to create an engaging employee environment. Look for every opportunity to create and foster an environment where your employees are happy, have full confidence and trust in your leadership, and know the direction of your business. As Zig Ziglar once said: "You don't build a business you build people and then people build the business."

As you have seen me mentioning several time in this book that leader never stops learning, please remember that learning does not stop in books and online blog posts, always seek opportunities to learn from people how have already achieved success in life and are ready to share their experiences with you.

The Importance of Studying Successful People and Never-Stop-Learning Mentality

What is a 'never stop learning' mentality and why is it important for leadership development?

Never stop learning mentality is having an extraordinarily strong desire and determination to constantly seeking more knowledge in various areas of interest and passion through formal education and training, as well as through self-learning. One must always be hungry for more information and knowledge, regardless of education level achieved, position or title in the company, or the amount of wealth accumulated. As I have mentioned in my prior modules, podcasts, and e-books, leader never stops learning. Even the most successful leaders, who have already achieved great success and wealth, continue to read, research, and enhance their knowledge, to be the subject matter experts in their respected fields of business or line of work.

I have seen many people stop growing their knowledge bank after completing school or after attending few business seminars and conferences, because they felt that everything that they need to know, they already knew. However, as we all know, business industry, technology, leadership strategies, team management techniques, and virtually everything around us continues to change every day. Therefore, what we have learned few years, months, or even days ago, may no longer be applicable or relevant at a present time. That is exactly the reason why one must continue to learn utilizing various channels, to stay current in ever-changing business environment.

Social media and online environment have significantly changed in the last several years and continue to change daily. If you are looking to start your own business, you can do everything from registering the business name to the website building and marketing all online, without leaving the comfort of your own home. Could you have done the same 20-30 years ago, probably not. Therefore, continuous education and knowledge building is a must for a leader, regardless of leader's current level of knowledge or experience.

There are so many great tools and resources available to us through physical books and online materials, but unfortunately, in many cases available resources remain under-utilized. Reading books is an exceptionally good start in personal development. Online materials available on the author's website or blog is another great development resource, especially if you enjoy their work and want to follow their future work. Many companies, entrepreneurs, authors, have free and paid resources available on their business websites for anyone who wishes to learn more. So, why not utilize all resources and information available to us, and continue to expand our knowledge?

Do not stop learning and seeking for more information, regardless of where you may be in your personal development or your level of experience. If there is a strong will to learn and grow personally and professionally, you will find a way to the information and knowledge that you are seeking. If you are seeking additional information to help with improving your understanding of interview process and enhancing your interviewing skills while having fun in the process, then I hope you find the next chapter helpful.

Chapter 11 - Interview Tips & Resources for Beginners and Experts Alike

How to Enjoy, Have Fun, and Do Well in Job Interviews? – Overcoming the fear of job interviews

Experiencing the fear of interviewing

Whether you have participated in one or multiple interviews thus far, you may still experience the feeling of fear before or during interview. Can this sense of fear experienced by interviewee be justified or explained pointing to a specific trigger or an event? Usually, the answer is 'yes', however, in most situations, there are no significant factors that I was able to determine in many years of participating in or conducting interviews on both sides of the table as interviewee and interviewer. So, let us talk about some factors or triggers that can be a source of fear before and during an interview

Factors and Triggers before and during an interview

One of those reasons is obvious – lack of preparation and research conducted about the company and position that one may be interviewing for. Now, there is not much that I can say here, except that one needs to spend some time doing in-depth research about an industry, company, and position that he or she is applying to in advance of an actual interview. If you are not prepared, then you should not expect much in the outcome of the interview. Typically, interviewer can tell after 1-2 questions if someone has invested time preparing for an interview vs. someone who has not, and yes, when going to interviews unprepared at the fault of your own, it is normal to experience fear, the fear of the unknown. In this situation all that one is worrying about is not to be asked a question that he or she does not know the answer to.

Other not-so-obvious reasons of experiencing fear of interviews and ways to overcome them

Another reason why someone may experience fear before or during an interview is not having experience, education, and/or knowledge of the specific industry and/or position of choice. Person who finds themselves in such situation is worried about their feature, asking themselves if they are ready and able to do the job. So, once again, the fear of unknown takes over. One way to help avoid being in such situation is to conduct a detailed research, asking other people who may have experience in the industry and conducting self-discovery exercise where you reflect on your own experience, education, training, and the position that you are applying for. If you feel that you have what it takes to be successful in the specific industry and company you are considering, then you can proceed with confidence and comfort towards the interview phase of job seeking experience. If you still feel uncomfortable, then perhaps you may need to spend more time exploring alternate opportunities.

So, if the reasons that typically result in fear of interviews do not apply to me, should I still be nervous?

Nervous, sure, but not fearful of being interviewed. Being nervous before any major event, this includes interviews, is normal, and if you are not nervous then you are lying to yourself. However, if you are well prepared for an interview, done all necessary research, possess experience and/or knowledge required for the position you are applying for, then there should be no reason to experience fear before or during an interview. Instead, one should feel comfortable, prepared, and confident throughout the entire process. Treat each interview as a competition. See how well you can do and enjoy, yes, I said enjoy every interview that you may participate in throughout your professional career.

Every day and every interaction are an interview

At the end of the day, remember, we are being interviewed daily, whether it is when we meet someone new, interact with others while waiting in line at the grocery store, airport, hotel, or whenever interacting with other people, which is pretty much every day and everywhere. We are constantly being asked questions, and we provide answers. So, how does formal interview process any different, outside of having to adhere to a business professional dress code? It is not different, however, many of make it different in our own mind before we even walk into an interview room or pick up a phone. So, stop convincing yourself that interviewing is scary, uncomfortable, and fear-creating process, because it is not. We create that fear in our mind, and we have the power to remove fearful thoughts as soon as they enter our mind. Have fun, showcase your talents, and enjoy interviewing while seeking your new dream future and career.

Avoiding Interviewer's Block

If you ever looked for a job, you had most likely gone through at least one if not more job interviews. To most people job interview is the experience that they are not comfortable talking about unless the experience was positive and resulted in them receiving a job offer. However, in most cases people interviews as difficult, uncomfortable, and scary experience. Why is that the case? Why many of us view interviews a frightening experience and not something to look forward to? Should not interview experience be fun and interesting while maintaining its level of necessary complexity and challenge? You are probably thinking – How is that possible? How can interview experience be possibly fun? Well, based on my personal experience and having to go through many interviews myself as well as conducting them, I believe that interviews can be interesting, challenging, and fun. However, for us to begin viewing interviews in a such way, we must take necessary, and I would go even further to say required steps to prepare, to create an experience that we would enjoy vs. run away from.

What steps we can and should strongly consider taking to prepare for an effective job interview?

Step 1 – Do your research about the company for which you are interviewing. What is important to the company in question and why it matters?

How can anyone expect to do well on the job interview if they do not have a good understanding about the company? This should be the very first item on your research To Do List. Easiest way to conduct your research is online, and typically the best place to start is which company's website.

Things that you should be looking for are:

- Company's mission
- Vision
- Goals and Objectives
- Product and Services
- Financial objectives and historical business performance
- Future business aspirations
- Social responsibility goals and contributions

This is certainly not an all-inclusive list of things to look for and have a good understanding of company's operations, but it is a good basic foundation of the business before proceeding to the next step in the interview preparation process.

Step 2 – Answering an important question – What is in It for Them? In other words, why should they hire you vs. many other candidates for the same role?

This is not just about your personal qualities, skills, abilities, or previous experience, it is about you helping to solve a particular problem that this company may be looking to solve or finding a way to improve or enhance an existing business process which focus on operational efficiency, innovation, and revenue. Of course, you would not know business goals and objectives unless you do a very thorough research outlined in step 1. Therefore, it is important to come with some ideas and specific proposals to show interviewer that you have done your research of their business and have ideas and/or recommendations on how to help the business to achieve specific goals and objectives. To go even further, it is good to have an idea of what you may do in the first 30 to 90 days to help moving the business forward, if hired, while always keeping in mind things that are important to a business and how you can help.

Step 3 – Knowing enough about the company to ask good questions during and after the interview.

If/when you come to an interview and do not have at least 2-3 good questions to ask interviewer at the end of the interview, this could be a signal to the interviewer that you are unprepared, or that you are not really interested in their business. I do not mean a typical question such as: "When should I expect to hear from you?" or "What is the next step in the interview process?", I mean specific question related to company's goals, objectives, new initiatives, or products and/or services. This is your opportunity to create engagement and learn more about the business from a representative of the company. You may not have an opportunity to ask more than 1-2 questions or interviewer may not give you an opportunity to ask any questions, but it is always good to come prepared.

Step 4 – Pay close attention to the questions you are being asked during an interview.

Do not think about the question you may be asked next, instead be present, listen carefully, do not interrupt interviewer, understand the question before responding. Some of us can be so nervous during an interview that instead of focusing on a person in persons in front of us and questions that are being asked, we are thinking more about what question may be coming next, missing entire interview experience, and allowing our mind to wonder somewhere else vs. being focused on the present and on the questions asked. You always want to be present in the conversation and add value to the interaction and dialogue vs. being an 'answering machine.' How many of us like to speak to an 'answering machine?' I would guess, not many. Right?

Step 5 – It is good to have at least one good example for each of your answers.

We may have provided the answer to the immediate question asked, but do we really know what we are talking about? That may be the question that interviewer is thinking about in their mind after receiving an answer to their initial question. Wouldn't you feel more comfortable and confident with the answer received if that answer were followed up with a quick and concise example, perhaps from your own personal example or an example of someone you may know? I would. Now, you may not always be able to provide an example or sharing an example may not be appropriate after a specific question & answer, this is where observing interviewer's non-verbal language becomes important. For example, are they leaning in towards you, possibly wanting to know more or leaning back on their chair likely displaying satisfaction with the answer received? Do you observe a questioning facial expression of the interviewer after providing your answer, or is interviewer nodding in agreement and understanding? These are just some of the non-verbal cues that we want to pay attention to during an interview, and that is why it is important to pay close attention to the person in front of you and their verbal and non-verbal cues, as highlighted in step 4.

Step 6 – Dress for success and arrive to your interview early.

You never know what surprises you may run into on your way to an interview, such as: traffic, car troubles, etc., or parking difficulties upon arriving. You do not want to be late to your interview, that is why it is good to give yourself plenty of time for "what if" situations you may encounter.

Dress code is an important part of an interview process. Even if someone told you that it is acceptable to show up to an interview wearing casual clothes, it is best to be safe than sorry and take it to the next level and wear business casual at a minimum. If the expectation is business casual, I would take it to the next level and wear a suit. Why? Because you want to feel comfortable and confident during an interview, knowing that your dress code is not just meeting but exceeding expectations, and you can focus your attention on the questions asked during an interview vs. worrying if wearing shorts was ok.

Understanding and use of six steps discussed earlier is what I believe creates an enjoyable and fun interview experience both for the person being interviewed and the interviewer. When you are prepared and confident in your answers there should be nothing short of enjoyable and interesting interview dialogue for all involved.

In the next chapter I will share some tips that I've find especially useful as a business professional, so hopefully you will too.

Chapter 12 – Useful Tips for Business Professionals

Business Travel Tips for Beginners – How not to lose your carryon

I am sure you are probably thinking: "How is it possible to lose your carryon?" Well, guess what, it is possible, because I have done it, even though I though the same – that it is not possible to lose your carryon since it is technically with you when you board the plane. Well, not so fast, as my assumption was totally proven false.

So, how is it possible to lose your carryon?

If you are a frequent business traveler or if you travel frequently in general, you have probably had a connection in a small airport, where large plane is 35 seats or less. If you have gone through such airport you are most likely familiar with a valet bag check process. For those who are not familiar, this is where due to the small size of the plane, even though your carryon gets checked through valet check in process at the gate before your board a plane. Also, it is not an optional process, but mandatory. So, when you thought that your carryon was coming with you on the plane, well, you will be disappointed, because you must leave it at the gate with gate agents and hope that it makes it safely to your destination.

Valet gate check process and 'not so fun' bag search process

How the rest of the valet bag check in process works is, after arriving at your destination, as you are leaving the plane, you pick up your carryon bag at the end of the bridge before you enter the terminal. However, as with any process, there may be situations where things do not go as planned. That is what happened with me one time on my trip to a business meeting in another city. My carryon luggage got valet gate-checked with my name and address written on a small luggage tag. To my big surprise, upon arrival at my destination and getting ready to pick up my bag at the end of the bridge, the only carryon bag that was not there, well, you guessed it, it was mine. Oh, and I forgot to mention that all my business clothes, dress shoes, toiletries, and pretty much all other essentials were in that bag, with business meeting coming up next day. So, after spending few minutes in disbelief and confusion, I begun the process of search of my luggage, which as you have guessed it, was not fun. If you have ever lost your bag with any airline, you know what I mean when I say that it was not 'fun'.

Unplanned expenses when you are not ready for them with very tight deadline

In addition to finding my carryon, I had even bigger dilemma – what do I do about clothes for my upcoming business meeting. Thankfully, I was in a large city in California, where there were plenty of options for stores selling clothes, and they were near my hotel. So, I had to go and purchase one-day worth of business clothes and shoes for my meeting. After my involuntary shopping trip, I was prepared for the next day. Problem solved. The funny thing is, that as soon as I arrived back to my hotel after the meeting the following day, my carryon was found and delivered to the hotel. Unfortunately, this proves the point that even carryon can be lost.

So, how do you prepare for the unexpected? What can you learn from my lesson?

First, make sure to wear one pair of casual business clothes and shoes, appropriate for the meeting in question when flying to the meeting destination. I know it is not the most comfortable trip, but at least you are prepared for the unexpected if your carryon or checked in bags get lost. Additionally, you could avoid having to spend money on buying new clothes at the stores that you may not necessarily like or shop at normally.

Second, make sure that you have a tag with your name, address, and contact information, attached to your bags, so that if your carryon gest lost, once found, you could be contacted.

Lastly, keep a pair of business clothes, dress shoes, and necessities (ex. toothbrush, toiletries, etc.) in your checked in luggage and your carryon. This is in the event it your luggage or carryon gets lost.

In summary…

Following these few simple steps can help you avoid frustration, stress, and spending money on new clothes simply because you need them, not because you want new clothes and/or shoes. In most cases your bag(s) will be found, however, it may be well after the important meeting you had to attend, and it is best to be safe than sorry.

Interested in simplifying your travel and lodging accommodations while traveling? Next section will dive into navigating life with loyalty points.

Points and Status-Centered Lifestyle – Navigating life with loyalty points

What is points and status-centered lifestyle

So, what am I talking about here when I say points and status-centered lifestyle? The answer or explanation is amazingly simple – it is going about our day-to-day activities using loyalty points acquired through various business and financial institutions with whom we do business on the regular basis. If you ever traveled by plane, then you should have seen various promotions and advertisements by different airlines and credit card companies offering x amount of points or miles as promotional opportunity in exchange of you applying and being approved for a specific credit card and/or airline loyalty program such as: AA Advantage, Citi, American Airlines, and many other companies, so when such offer is presented to us, we ask ourselves – Do I need it? Is it worth it? What is in it for me?

Do I need it? Is it worth it? What is in it for me?

These are particularly good and proper questions to ask before taking any action, because you want to make sure that: a). you can afford it, b). make sure whatever is being offered as an incentive for signing up makes sense in your specific situation. Because look at it this way, why would you need x number of airline miles if you never travel by plane, or x number of hotel-related points for being member of hotels loyalty program if last time you stayed in the hotel was 10-15 years ago. However, if you travel all the time by plane, frequently use car rental service, and stay in hotels on the regular basis, then being enrolled in one or multiple loyalty programs available today could absolutely make sense in your situation.

Speaking from my personal example, having TSA Pre-Check and being a member of multiple loyalty programs offered by various airline, hotel, car rental, and credit card companies helped me save great amount of time and money while traveling for business or personal reasons. One of my favorite loyalty programs is American Airlines Advantage program, because, of the benefits such as: ability to move up your boarding group and board the plane faster as you acquire a set number of AA points and achieving a specific status, such as: Silver, Gold, Platinum, etc. The higher your status, the sooner you can board the plane and get to your seat. Speaking of airplane seats, as a Gold member of AA Advantage, you may be able to upgrade your seat assignment when booking your flight. So, sitting in the middle seat of the crowded place may no longer be a requirement, instead, it may be an option. These are just some of the benefits that AA Advantage loyalty program may offer. Oh, almost forgot to mention, probably one of the best benefits of the AA Advantage program, in my opinion, is using points acquired to book flights whether you are traveling domestically or internationally. This option alone could be a huge money saver, especially for someone who travels regularly.

Other loyalty programs that I personally enjoy are the ones offered by major hotel chains, such as: Marriott, Starwood, Hilton, etc. Once enrolled in a specific hotel's loyalty program, you can begin acquiring points for each night you stay at a specific hotel. The more nights you stay, then more points you acquire. As number of points accumulated grows, so as your status within a specific hotel loyalty program. Having a specific status level may offer benefits such as: room upgrades, special perks, late checkout, etc. So, if you travel often and stay in hotels during your travel then being a member of hotel's loyalty program may be something you would want to consider.

Loyalty Program Availability = Customer Retention Strategy

Airline and hotel loyalty programs are only two examples of points and status-based membership programs available today. However, every day there are more businesses and financial institutions that choose to be offering their own unique loyalty programs. This is a way for a specific business to earn your continued business and your long-term loyalty with them. It is a wonderful customer retention strategy for virtually any business. Even most gas stations now offer their own version of loyalty programs. So, every time you pump gas, you can earn points, which can then be redeemed for merchandise online or dollars off your total gas bill. One good example here is Plenti program. I use Plenti card every time at participating gas stations when I pump gas, and often use points collected to reduce my total gas bill. The other cool thing about most loyalty programs is that it is typically free to sign up once you are conducting a business or a customer of a specific business or financial institution.

Why am I writing about loyalty programs and how this topic applicable to personal development, growth, and lifestyle design?

Where I believe this point is applicable is the creation and life in comfort, ease, and style, not to mention the benefits of time and money savings when participation in various loyalty programs available today. This is especially important to be aware of various programs available today with various businesses that we already conducting our business with or are customers of. In this case, why not utilize the benefits that may already be available to us. It sure feels great when you can use airline and hotel points acquired to book your next vacation.

I hope that you found this article post useful, and perhaps you will now consider exploring various loyalty program benefits that may already be available to you today. If there is an opportunity to save money and time while traveling more comfortably, then why not?

In Conclusion

I hope that you have enjoyed reading this book and have found a lot of useful and practical information that you can use immediately in your personal and professional lives. The intent of this book was to share my experience, knowledge, and training that I have acquired and practiced over the last several years and continue to use today.

Just 20 years ago I did not speak English at all and used to think and translate from Ukrainian to English using portable translator. Now, I am not only fluent in Ukrainian and Russian, but also in English language. I have read many great leadership, team, and personal development books, led, and developed several wonderful, strong, and high-performing business teams, wrote over 150 articles/blog posts in the field of leadership and personal development, attended many business workshops, leadership conferences. However, despite all these accomplishments and knowledge acquired thus far, I continue to learn and grow every single day by expanding my knowledge through resources that are available to everyone who seeks knowledge, success, and growth in this interesting, challenging, and often unpredictable business world that is filled with opportunities. I encourage you to stay knowledge-hungry and never ever stop learning.